Joyful Perspective

Joyful Perspective

Patricia Boysen

Copyright © 2007 by Patricia Boysen.

Library of Congress Control Number: 2007906196
ISBN: Hardcover   978-1-4257-9862-8
              Softcover   978-1-4257-9852-9

All rights reserved. No part of this book may be reproduced or transmitted in any form or by any means, electronic or mechanical, including photocopying, recording, or by any information storage and retrieval system, without permission in writing from the copyright owner.

This book was printed in the United States of America.

To order additional copies of this book, contact:
Xlibris Corporation
1-888-795-4274
www.Xlibris.com
Orders@Xlibris.com

42843

CONTENTS

Acknowledgements 13

Stand Still 15
Timing Is Everything 16
Show Up 17
It Is Well 19
Sanctuary 21
Introductions 23
Bargains 25
Just Leaves 27
Troubled 28
Flying Upside Down 30
Why Wait? 31
Beautiful Reflection 33
Overwhelming 35
Dead or Dying 37
Joy in the Morning 38
Don't You Dare 40
Clean Thoughts 41
Faucet Drips 43
For the Glory of God 45
Questions 47
The Gift Box 49
Daddy's Little Girl 50
Going Through It 51
Image 53
Sacrifices 55
Under Satan's Radar 57
Cruel Words 59
Beyond Understanding 61
Vertically Challenged 63
Lost and Found 65
No Worries 67
Positive vs. Negative 69
Law or Love 71

Grateful	73
Handle With Care	74
Gratitude	75
In Everything	76
Overnight Sensation	77
Clothing	78
Five Minutes	80
Amazing Love	82
The Value of Suffering	84
Majestic Skies	86
Shark Bait	88
Get Out of the Way	90
Attitude Is Everything	91
Fear and Trembling	93
Disabled?	95
Attempted Deception	97
Knees or No Knees	99
Empty Spaces	100
Mighty Reference	102
Suffering	103
Precious Gifts	104
Pigs	106
Whatever	108
Anno Domini	109
Emotions	111
Seeking God's Favor	112
The Power of the Cross	114
The Perfect 911	115
Better Than the Job	117
Hurt Feelings	119
Food for Thought	121
A Wider View	123
Filthy	124
Falling Asleep	126
Changes	127
Tax Exempt	128
Written in Heaven	130
Gardening	131
Praising or Cursing	132
Broken or Crushed	133
Perfect Timing	135
Small Matters	137

The Understanding of the Centurion	139
Neighbors	141
Fan the Flames	143
Prayer Changes Things	145
Whitewash	146
Impress Your Children	148
Strengthen Me	150
Shoulder to Shoulder	151
Thank You, Lord	152
Beauty by God	153
Selfish Prayers	155
God First	157
The Only Thing	158
Gentle Victories	159
Prophet	161
Exceeding Great Joy	163
For Such a Time	165
The Most Wonderful Time of the Year	166
Beheaded	167
Mary Had A Baby	169
Feliz Navidad, Maybe	171
Anguish or Freedom	173
Shivering	174
Glory to God	176
Flowing Through	178
Your Own Petard	180
Did I Ask You a Question?	182
Job's Example	183
Do Whatever He Tells You	185
Rabbi, I Want	186
Secret Living	187
Tools of the Trade	189
Important Opinions	190
Treasures	191
Life Lessons	192
Big Mountains	193
Authority	195
Bold Questions	197
Sheep	199
Speaking Heartese	200
Comparisons	202
Stepping Stone	203

Word Bites	205
Patterned Behavior	206
Fearful	207
Joke or No Joke	208
Naming Names	209
Be Yourself	210
Shout or Whisper	211
Famine	212
Healing Power	213
Well Dressed	215
Cheer Up	216
Useless Backpack	217
Citizenship	218
Consumed	220
Blind Faith	222
God's Good Work	224
Plenty	226
Surprise!	228
A Christian FCAT	229
Healing	230
Faithful Friends	231
Jesus Is My Copilot?	233
House Calls	234
Walk Right Through	235
Prizes	236
Deserving	238
One God	240
Casting Aspersions	241
Perspective	243
Golden or Tarnished?	244
Young Shoulders	246
Seasons	248
Building Projects	249
The Lord Speaks	251
When Music Plays	253
Moses's MLM	255
Full or Empty	257
Minas Talents and Gifts	258
Planting Seeds	260
Abba	262
Undesirables	264
Tunnels	265

A Great Chasm	266
A Child's Offering	268
Answer Carefully	270
Watchful Eyes	272
Whose Will Be Done?	274
Get Behind Me	275
Everywhere You Look	276
Someone Else's Plans	278
True Love Words	280
Deals, Deals, Deals	282
Cactus of the Mind	284
"And God's People Said"	286
Out of the Depths	288
Impressions	289
Love You Forever	291
Cross to Bear	292
Presents	294
It's Not Fair	296
Delightful	298
Body Parts	299
Running Away	301
Make and Model	302
Translation Please	303
Satisfaction	305
Careful Listening	306
Near Death	307
No Secrets	309
Treasured Words	311
Feed My Lambs	313
New Sight	315
Light Speed	317
Cost of Worship	319
Blessings	321
A Humble Woman	322
Loving Gestures	324
The Right Food	326
Trust	328
Thief	329
Praise Him Still	331
Jude Doxology	333
J-O-Y	334

DEDICATION

To my husband, Otto, there is no way I could do this or much of anything else without his support and his faith in God and in me. And to Gram for her love of God, life and odd little sayings.

Acknowledgements

I would like to thank my husband, Otto; our children Paul, Joseph, Jeffrey, and Laura; our in-love children Mike, Erin and Michelle; our grandchildren Joey, Faith, Lily, Isabelle, Samuel, and Madelyn for all the love they bring to me. To Mom, Dad, and Brenda, thank you for making me part of our family and sharing Doug, Emily, and Sarah with me. Thank you to Kathy, my sister by birth and most important my sister in Christ. Thank you to Mary and Karen for listening, critiquing, and praying. Thank you to Charlene, who started all of this with me and encourages me every day to keep it going and keep it real.

Most of all, thank you to Jesus Christ, my Lord and Savior, for every blessing and for enabling me to share these words with others.

Stand Still

Be still before the Lord and wait patiently for him; do not fret when men succeed in their ways, when they carry out their wicked schemes. Psalm 37:7

"Don't just do something, stand there." My former pastor, a real take-charge guy, preached a sermon a few years ago called with that very title, "Don't just do something, stand there." It's a very radical thought in these fast-paced, be-your-master days. Very few people that I know would be good at just standing there, and I am one of them. Most of the people I know completely understand why Sarah sent Abraham to Haggar. It is the come on-already feel of our lives. The time's-a-wastin' attitude that if we aren't moving, we're dead. We're not dead, but we are oh so wrong.

Moving is all well and good when prompted by the Holy Spirit, but moving on our own steam can be very detrimental. "I've been praying and praying about this but honestly I don't see a thing happening." The reason might be that while we were praying, we were also running soliciting advice, help, and other options just in case God didn't answer our prayers.

Did it ever occur to you that maybe all of that running is keeping us from seeing the answer? Have you ever lost something? I can almost hear the laughter as people read that line. DUH! Who hasn't, right? Think about how you respond. Panic? Frenzy? "Oh my gosh, where are my keys? I had them, um . . . They were right . . . . I always put them in the same place except when I don't." It goes on and on in our heads as we tear through the house/workplace in search of those keys, shoes, papers, etc. Then exhausted and frustrated, we stand still. Lo and behold, there they are, or the thought comes, that "oh yeah" moment. Maybe if we'd stood still in the first place, the frenzy could have been avoided.

In matters of faith, God cannot get our attention as we are turning over tables to find a solution. We make it far more difficult to see his plan for us while we are frantically pursuing a plan of our own. Don't just do something, stand there. He'll tell you where and how to move, and when he does, it will be right for you.

Timing Is Everything

Is anything too hard for the Lord? I will return to you at the appointed time and Sarah will have a son. Genesis 18:14

In breakfast, as in many things, timing is everything. It's a balancing act really. You want the toast to be ready while the eggs are still hot. I'm sure you understand the concept. In any case this morning for a split second, I realized that I wanted to pause my toaster and was faced with another way in which technology has disrupted the natural flow of life. Our televisions pause, our music and movies can be paused, even our microwave ovens can be paused. There are many places in our lives now where a pause is quite possible. I don't have to give this my attention now; I can pause it and come back later. It's very helpful in most cases, but what is it teaching us? Do we have to really live in the moment if we can pause and come back later?

When we combine that technology with technology that allows us to view movies and television shows whenever we want, call people on a cell phone anytime, anywhere we might begin to feel unlimited. Our sense of control might become disproportionate. We may begin to feel that we have power over even time itself. We do not.

My husband is a very calm, contented man (thank you Lord!), but once in a while, he seems harried. When I ask what's wrong, the answer is almost always the same: "Too much to do, too little time to do it in." I cringe whenever he says it and refrain from correcting the glaring grammar mistake, but a part of me is amused. Even my normally unflappable hubby gets stressed when time crunches him.

How like God we would all feel if just for a day we could really control time. We cannot. Even with all the things we can now pause (and a toaster by the way is not one of them), we have no real control over time. It marches on with no regard to our schedule. Once we realize that time belongs to God and let Him have full control of it, we will encounter less "too much to do and too little time to do it in" seasons. It is amazing what a simple prayer for help in time management can do. Faith can move mountains, even the ones made of minutes.

Show Up

For the grace of God that brings salvation has appeared to all men. It teaches us to say" No" to ungodliness and worldly passions, and to live self-controlled, upright and godly lives in this present age, while we wait for the blessed hope—the glorious appearing of our great God and Savior Jesus Christ, who gave himself for us to redeem us from all wickedness and to purify for himself a people that are his very own, eager to do what is good. Titus 2:11-14

I heard once that Napoleon Bonaparte's battle plan was "show up and see what happens". I don't know if it is a real quote, or if the person was using it to justify their own lack of planning. Whether truth or legend, it isn't much of a plan. If it is true, it didn't work out very well for Napoleon. With a little tweaking it works quite well for those of us yielded to the Holy Spirit.

To simply show up is not enough unless you are showing up without a plan so that the Holy Spirit can lead you. Too often we want to plan out every minute of every day. We want to script each word of difficult conversations. We want a map for every situation that takes us beyond our comfort zone. All of those things are superfluous if we believe that Jesus left his Spirit to guide and protect us.

Most of us aren't comfortable with the inertia of showing up and doing nothing. We are much better with something to do. Where is the trust in that?

If God had said to Abram, "Go three miles North and then turn. Take a left at the third cactus and put your tent there," it would have been very easy. As it was God said to Abram, "Go." And Abram went and took his household with him. He showed up and waited to see what would happen. Great things happened because Abram, soon to become Abraham, demonstrated enormous faith.

It wasn't a once-for-all deal either. There would be other tests of Abraham's faith, the most famous being the requested sacrifice of his son, Isaac. It made no sense to Abraham, but he knew he had to be obedient. He had to show up and see what happened.

The next time you feel God asking you to step up but are unsure of where, show up and see what happens. Alone it's a lousy plan, but with the backing of the Holy Spirit, it is a thing of beauty and amazement.

It Is Well

Dear friends do not be surprised at the painful trial you are suffering as though something strange were happening to you. But rejoice that you participate in the sufferings of Christ so that you may be overjoyed when his glory is revealed. 1 Peter 4:12-13

The old King James translates this verse a little differently. The last part of verse 13 says, "When his glory is revealed ye may be glad also with exceeding joy." We may be glad in the fiery or painful trials, glad. Perhaps like me, when you read that you think, "Oh yeah, the next time I am tested, I'm going to do it well." We plan to hold onto the joy given to us by God. We plan to look to the unknowing eye as if all *is* well when in fact it is not. Then the trial comes and ooops, but *next* time . . .

There is a wonderful old hymn called "It Is Well with My Soul." The words are wonderful, richly full of reliance on God. It is something to aspire to in our own trials. I have always loved it and wondered what trial prompted its creation. One day several years ago after our parish had suffered a sudden and very tragic loss, our music minister sang that hymn. Then he explained it.

It was written by a man, Horatio Spafford, who after suffering financial ruin lost all four of his daughters when the ship in which they were travelling collided with another. He received a telegram from his wife, which read simply, "Saved alone." The Holy Spirit inspired the words to the hymn a few weeks after the accident when the ship in which Spafford was travelling passed by the spot of the accident. Can you imagine it? He is in the spot where all four of his daughters perished, and he feels the power of the Holy Spirit promising him that it is well. Further, he feels the nudge of that same Spirit to write those words which comfort people nearly two hundred years later.

My own life has been assaulted lately. It is nothing like Spafford endured but that faucet drip of one disappointment, crisis, or challenge after the other. A friend asked me the other day how I was handling it. I answered simply, "I'm not." I didn't want her to give me credit for something I wasn't doing. The credit all goes to God, to each member of the Trinity who has met me in all of this. It may be well with my soul because I have realized I can't do a darn thing. All of it I have given to my Father, praying of course. I would have to say this is the closest I've ever come to praying without ceasing. You know what? The circumstances haven't changed, but it is well with my soul.

Rejoice in the Lord always. I will say it again: Rejoice! Philippians 4:4

Sanctuary

Then have them make a sanctuary for me, and I will dwell among them. Exodus 25:8

We sing a song in our church called Sanctuary perhaps you sing it too. Just in case you don't, it says,

> "Lord prepare me to be a sanctuary
> pure and holy
> tried and true."

Prepare me to be a sanctuary. Do you have an altar guild at your church? They are the ladies who make sure that the church is ready for every service. They clean and decorate making sure that God's house, whatever type of building, is in its best shape. They prepare the sanctuary.

I can't help but think that cleaning up a spill or dusting the windows is much easier work than removing sin from a heart that wants so badly to cling to that sin. Think of that last stubborn stain you had to clean. Maybe it was ink on your carpet, or maybe it was chocolate on a really great top. (That one was for my friend Char.) Not only is it hard work to get it out, but you really want to restore the carpet or garment to its original pristine state. That is what we are asking when we sing "prepare me to be a sanctuary."

We don't want God in our messy mess even though we know he doesn't care. He loves us and while he wants what's best for us he is willing to accept us as is. Still we want to clean up, spruce up, to be tried and true. We want to know that when the going gets tough we will stand firm in faith, taking only the actions that are sanctioned by our Father.

Do you think we really know what we are asking? Put yourself in the position of the carpet/garment. Picture the owner just scrubbing away, pouring those chemicals and scrubbing some more. That can't be comfy. When we invite God to make us pure and holy, tried and true, we invite him to clean away, scrub, rub and pour those chemicals. Then he does, and it hurts. That is when we rethink our position. Why is this happening? It hurts, is uncomfortable, is humiliating, etc. Rejoice! At the end of all that discomfort the stain will be gone. We will have grown, changed, and become a better sanctuary.

When the training/cleaning gets a little too hard remember the goal, pure and holy, tried and true. God bless!

Introductions

If my people who are called by my name, will humble themselves and pray and seek my face and turn from their wicked ways, then will I hear from heaven and will forgive their sin and will heal their land. 2 Chronicles 7:14

I know a young man who is on the fast track to self-destruction. His faults all lie in areas that make me crazy. He neglects his children. He's arrogant and self-pitying. He's abusive both physically and verbally. On top of all of that, he likes his illegal substances. His saving grace is that he would be the first one to tell you all of that. He is extremely self-aware, and in the moments when he finds the strength to combat his demons, he is one of the most likeable young men I know. Sadly those moments are getting fewer and farther between.

Although he has been in and out of my prayers since we met for months now concern for him has been quite heavy on my heart. Seeing that gem of goodness, I just want him to bow to the Lord's authority and be the man God created him to be. As I said he is likeable, charismatic. If he were to give his all to God great things could happen. The people he could reach are the type that would never hear a word that came from a preacher.

I was praying for him recently, and it occurred to me that although most of his problems come from a lack of self-esteem, he presents himself as very confident, cocky to be frank. I couldn't help but think that the answer might begin in how he introduces himself. He says his name as if it carries some power, which of course it doesn't. His Father's name on the other hand is all-powerful. I decided to suggest that each time he introduces himself, he add silently, "And my Father loves me very much." It would make him mindful of his true value and temper his need to be omnipotent.

The more I thought about it, I realized that we could all benefit from some private tagline to our own name. Meeting new people can be daunting even to the most confident person. Sometimes we all need a little help. Why not try "hello, I'm Jane Doe" and then silently "a child of God" or "and I'm perfect in my Father's eyes." Knowing who we are in Christ is a huge enabler. We can do things we never dreamed possible if we recognize the power that exists within us through the shed blood of Jesus. The power is always there; we just aren't always smart enough or humble enough to rely on it.

Pray with me that my young friend is able to receive God's love and turn his life around. And the next time you are in a tough situation, remind yourself that your Father thinks you are great.

Bargains

For God so loved the world that he gave his one and only Son that whoever believes in him shall not perish but have everlasting life. For God did not send his Son into the world to condemn it but to save the world through him. John 3:16-17

There are times in almost every life when bargaining with God seems not only appropriate but necessary. "If you will just help me _____ I will _____. I promise." The problem is that even when God answers our prayer in the positive, we often drop our end of the bargain. There are even times when we leave our half up to Him. "If you will, _____ I'll do *anything*." We plead. "Anything you ask, anything." The times are terrifying, the circumstances seemingly insurmountable, so we resort to begging.

It is understandable that a person with little to no relationship with or understanding of God would bargain this way. For a Christian, it is ridiculous. We know better. The best prayer in any and all circumstances is, "Your will be done. Your will not mine." God is not into the barter system, thankfully. If He were, can you imagine that conversation?

From the Father: "Okay let's see, I sent my only dear Son to hang on a Cross and die. What have you got?"

From Jesus: "I spent my life trying to get your attention and then hung on a Cross after being beaten nearly to death. What have you got?"

Our response: "Nothing."

We have nothing. It is idiocy to think that we have something to barter with the sacrifice that was already given for us. When we attempt the bargain, we are offering a crumb in comparison to a never-ending feast. Crazier still sometimes, it seems that God accepts the offer. In that state, we really should be willing to do *anything*. Above and beyond, all that has already been done for us, we are given yet another blessing, one that we bid on, so to speak; but when the bill comes, we don't pay.

Thankfully, grace and blessings flow freely. Our loving Father has no eye toward paybacks. Still we have to remember that one day we will be at the throne, prepared to give him the crowns of glory that He gave to us. That day as we look at His perfection, we will be painfully aware of the times that our word was sawdust instead of gold.

My friend Patty and I say all the time, "You are only as good as your word." How good are the promises we make to God? Next time before we begin the bargaining process, it might be best to make sure we will pay the price.

Just Leaves

> The next day as they were leaving Bethany, Jesus was hungry. Seeing in the distance a fig tree in leaf, he went to find out if it had any fruit. When he reached it he found nothing but leaves, because it was not the season for figs. Then he said to the tree, "May no one ever eat fruit from you again." And his disciples heard him say it.
> Mark 11:12-14

These verses stand alone in Mark. Verse 11 tells us that Jesus is headed to the temple, and verse 15 takes us to the temple to see the tables overturned. In the middle there is this story that we wonder about. Why is it there? Is Jesus angry at the tree?

I don't know, of course, why this is included in the Scripture, but a few things are clear to me. Jesus sees the fig tree, and it has leaves. If there are leaves then there should be figs. It's not the season for figs, but that means it isn't the season for leaves either. Seeing no fruit, Jesus curses the tree. We need to read those verses again. What do they say to us?

They say that all the works all the appearance of piety in the world aren't worth a thing if there's no fruit. Jesus has spent entirely too much time trying to expose the Pharisees to the Pharisees. He wasn't trying to humiliate them he wanted them to see the error of their ways. Over and over he came across people who spoke one way, projected the pious image but were empty and judgmental. Perhaps he had just had enough hypocrisy, and the tree got the wrath of it.

I think it is very important that we periodically examine our own lives. Are we fruitless trees? Do we sprout beautiful leaves but bear no fruit? Are we nothing but noise? Are we empty vessels?

If the answer is yes, then we need to sit with Scripture, listen for the voice of our Lord. Go where He leads us and bear some fruit. It isn't the beauty of the tree or the busyness or the person that matters. It is the result of the activities and the growth that will count when Jesus walks by. Don't let him look at your branches full of leaves only to find them empty of anything worthwhile.

Troubled

Let not your hearts be troubled; you believe in God now believe in me. Jesus said to him, "I am the way, the truth and the life. No one gets to the Father except through me." John 14:1 and 6, NKJV

The NIV translates that same verse John 14:1 as "do not let your hearts be troubled." I suppose there isn't any difference. It means the same thing; we don't need to get anxious or concerned. It is the section of the Gospel of John where Jesus is telling the apostles that he will be moving on. He is explaining that he is headed home to get the house ready for the rest of us.

Can you imagine that scene? "Um, Dad, I went and found those people that you told me about. Well, eventually I'm bringing them all home. That's okay, right? Good, because some of them are more than a little messed up. Some have broken bodies, which I know isn't a problem, but some have broken spirits. Yes, I did tell them not to worry. I told them not to be anxious, to bring all their trouble to me, and I would bring it to you, and you would fix it. The trouble is, Dad, I'm not sure they get it. I think a lot of them want to clean up on their own. Either they don't trust us, or they don't want you to see them all dirty or bruised. Yes, I tried to show them that we don't care what they look like or what they've done before. I told them over and over about the Spirit that would be with them until they get here. They heard me, but I'm not sure they listened or understood. Even my closest friends said they didn't know how to get here."

"Let not your hearts be troubled." Just don't let it happen. "Do not" implies that I have to take action. "Let not" says to me, just lean back into the arms of Jesus and know that all will be well. It sounds simple like the times when well-meaning friends say "don't worry" when they have no clue what you are going through. So how do we do it? The answer is in verse 6.

"Jesus said to him, 'I am the way, the truth and the life.'"

There is no need for us to be troubled; Jesus is the way—not only to the Father but also to peace of mind, body, and soul. Many of us have a harder time being untroubled than troubled. For so many people, trouble is all they've known for so long that they thrive on it. They become, as my son says, "drama mamas." It is hard to leave the familiar, but when the Savior of the world is telling you to do something, it's best to say yes. He *is* the way, the only way. *"Let not your hearts be troubled."*

Flying Upside Down

If you belonged to the world it would love you as its own. As it is, you do not belong to the world but I have chosen you out of the world. This is why the world hates you. John 15:19

This spring my pastor gave a series of sermons on the Beatitudes. At one point during the series, he made an analogy about airplanes. He said that if people who are living according to the worldly standards are flying upright, then as Christians, we are flying upside down, in complete opposition to the norm. We have to dare to be different.

The first thing that came to my mind was not a visual of one upside-down plane in a group of right-side-up planes. It was of John Kennedy Jr. Due to my age and gender, I was quite fond of John and so sad when he died. It was such a big deal, and it is hard to forget the guy was apparently flying upside down. May I say again, he's dead.

I thought about that for a minute as Pastor David was speaking. The image he was going for was great, but when you add John Kennedy to it, the whole thing changes. Or does it? John flew upside down, not a good idea in actual flight, and he died. People have been criticizing the poor man ever since. His actions caused comments and more comments.

I think that is exactly what Pastor David has in mind. We need to fly upside down, die to self, and cause comments. It is more than just avoiding the "near occasion of sin" as I was taught in elementary school. It is getting other people to notice and to wonder why we live the way we live.

Many people want to point fingers and call John Kennedy a bonehead. What fool flies in that weather, doesn't use instruments, etc. They all knew more than he did, even people who have never flown. Be assured many people will want to call you a bonehead too. Think of all that you'll be missing as far as they see it. You will face many comments and criticisms. I think it's worth the price. Anyone can fly right side up and see the world as it wants to be seen and in turn be seen as normal. Flip your plane over. Dare to live a little differently than the rest. The comments may be plentiful but the rewards are eternal.

Why Wait?

Wait for the Lord. Be strong, take heart and wait for the Lord. Psalm 27:14

The creation waits in eager anticipation for the sons of God to be revealed. Romans 8:19

Blessed are all who wait for him. Isaiah 30:18

No one likes to wait. Some people are better at it than others, but no one enjoys it. Sometimes I think it is because we have fear of what might happen to keep us from that for which we are waiting. Other times it's a hurry-up-and-get-it-over-with feeling. Whatever the reasoning behind it, waiting is no fun. It is however a necessary part of life. Or is it?

My sons were watching a documentary on the *Wizard of Oz* the other day. I told them about waiting every spring to see that movie. That led me to tell them a story of my mother and I waiting up until two in the morning to see *Meet Me in St. Louis*. Through it all they nodded politely but with little understanding. My children have grown up with VCRs and DVDs. They have no concept of waiting for the movie. They have little concept of waiting for anything.

My husband and I were discussing that old Beach Boys song "Wouldn't It Be Nice." It's all about the angst of waiting, waiting to be alone together, waiting to be married, waiting it implies, to be sexually active. Kids today don't get that one either. Why wait? Most of the people they hang out with are not waiting. Waiting carries no value, and virginity is quickly becoming as antiquated as telephones with dials.

We teach and preach at them about the benefits of waiting. We try to make a case for waiting but it just doesn't happen very often. They don't have to wait for food due to microwaves and fast-food restaurants. They don't have to wait for photographs due to one-hour processing and digital cameras. Many don't have to wait for phone calls due to cell phones. What do they wait for? What do any of us wait for anymore?

We wait for God. He cannot be rushed. His time is not our time. His agenda is not always the same as ours. Often we have to wait for God. Having been raised in a world devoid of microwaves, VCRs and cell phones I know *how* to wait. I don't like it, but I know how.

Remember the bittersweet tension of waiting for a boy to call? Gone. Remember waiting for your first kiss? Gone. Remember waiting to be married and live in the same home? For the majority, gone. Waiting to find out if it is a boy or girl? Gone. It's so sad. People have no idea what they are missing, that delicious tension of waiting for something wonderful.

I wonder how this next generation, people who have never had to wait can relate to a God who often teaches us in those waiting times. For those of us who grew up waiting, we still want to run ahead and point, "Here, God, it's right here." For those without waiting experience, how do they know enough to stop and wait for that still small voice?

I hate waiting but I am very grateful that I know how. **Wait for the Lord. Be strong take heart and wait for the Lord.**

Beautiful Reflection

> Your beauty should be not come from outward adornment, such as braided hair and the wearing of gold jewelry and fine clothes. Instead it should be that of your inner self, the unfading beauty of a gentle and quiet spirit, which is of great worth in God's sight.
> 1 Peter 3:3-4

There is an old movie about Fanny Brice that stars Barbara Streisand; it tells a great story about beauty. Fanny, like Barbara, was not beautiful in a fashion-magazine way. Some of her features were too big, others not big enough. Fanny's boss wanted her to sing a song called "Beautiful Reflection" while wearing a wedding dress. Fanny, so the story goes, didn't want to do it. She didn't see herself as a beautiful bride type and feared that the audience would laugh. The boss insisted. Rather than get fired, Fanny got creative. As she appeared on stage, wearing a gorgeous wedding gown and singing the words "I am the beautiful reflection of my love's affection," the audience could see that the "bride" was very pregnant. Unheard of in that day, the audience's reaction was first shock and then hysterical laughing. She was indeed a reflection of affection, and we are too.

Like Fanny, some of us may not see ourselves as beautiful, but God sees us that way. He wants the rest of the world to see a beautiful reflection of His affection for us. What would we look like if we lived each day wearing the love and mercy of Christ on our faces? We would be the most gorgeous creatures in the world. Christ's affection for us is much deeper even than a man's love for his precious bride. Our Father loves us enough to send his Son to die for us, and the Son loved us enough to be sent.

Think about the depth of that love for a minute. We are promised that the hairs on our heads are numbered. We are promised that nothing can take us away from that love. We are promised that if we ask for forgiveness, we will get it. And we are told that nothing is more important to God than we are.

In the practical sense God's affection feeds and clothes us. It keeps us safe and warm. It illuminates the right path and tries so hard to steer us away from the wrong ones.

True beauty is not about features or colors. It isn't about noses, eyes, or chins. It is about being the reflection of the love God has for us. All we need to know is how much God loves us, and when that is reflected in our faces, we will be beautiful.

Overwhelming

> When the servant of the man of God got up and out early the next morning, an army with horses and chariots surrounded the city. "Oh my lord, what shall we do?" the servant asked. Don't be afraid," the prophet answered. "Those who are with us are more that those who are with them."
> And Elisha prayed, "O Lord open his eyes so that he may see." Then the Lord opened the servant's eyes, and he looked and saw the hills full of horses and chariots of fire all around Elisha.
> 2 Kings 6:15-17

Elisha is physically blind. He cannot see his servant or his own hand in front of his face for that matter. Yet he can see what God is doing. His physical eyes are old and useless, but his spiritual eyes are in perfect working order. He has no concern when the Arameans come after him because he can *see* what God is doing. He has spent the better part of his life listening and following God's instructions.

His servant is not blessed with the same spiritual sight Elisha enjoys. When he looks, he sees horses and chariots, and he panics as anyone with sense would do. The two of them are armyless, and what we might consider well, seriously outnumbered. But they had one thing the Arameans did not: God's protection. Elisha knew it. He had plenty of experience of God's power in a seemingly desperate situation. In kindness, he asked God to open his servant's eyes. God did, and the servant saw the hills filled with horses and chariots of fire, all there to protect the two of them. The situation was suddenly changed from desperation to certain victory.

Later in the New Testament Paul advises us that *"If God is for us, who can be against us?"* Romans 8:31b. Anyone, I suppose, *can* be against us, but they won't be victorious. Those same legions of angels, horses, chariots, etc., are here for our protection. No matter what situation you are in right now, pray for sight. Pray, "Open my eyes, Lord," that you may see the might way He is protecting you.

Nothing is too big for God. It may seem that the situation you are facing is insurmountable, and for you it may be. Give it to God. Nothing is too much for Him. Remember, *"The one who is in you is greater than the one who is in the world" (1 John 4:4b).*

Dead or Dying

While he was saying this a ruler came and knelt before him and said, "My daughter has just died. But come and put your hand on her and she will live." Matthew 9:18

This is only one of three accounts of the same incident. The story goes on of course; Jesus goes with Jairus to his home, clears everyone out, and raises the little girl from death. The similarities in the three stories outweigh the differences. The man is a ruler and therefore understands authority. The room is full of people, and Jesus clears it out before he does anything. Plus (and this is my favorite similarity) Jesus raises a child from death in a very matter-of-fact, "no big deal, she's just sleeping" way.

All of that considered it is the difference in Matthew's version that stands out to me today. In Mark and Luke, Jairus's daughter is "dying." She's dying but with the healing power of Jesus, she can be whole. Amazing faith on the part of Jairus. Or maybe just desperation. In Matthew's account, she is dead. "My daughter has just died," he says but still asks for Jesus to come and touch her. He believes that Jesus's touch can restore life to his child. He was right. That touch lifted the child not just from her bed but from the grip of death. It's such a huge event. When we list the miracles of Jesus, that one is right up there.

A few verses earlier in Matthew 9:9-13, Jesus calls Matthew to follow him, and Matthew does. Matthew, a tax collector, one of the disreputables as he himself, refers to other tax collectors, leaves it all behind to follow Jesus. He stands up from his deathbed too, only his was not a physical death. It was a spiritual one. Jesus saves him by calling him and saying, "Follow me."

I hope Jairus and his whole family were smart enough to follow Jesus once the little girl was healed. Matthew was smart enough to leave behind his sickness and shame and follow Jesus.

Is Jesus calling you today to be healed of some illness of body or spirit? Say yes. Say thank you and then follow Him.

Joy in the Morning

For his anger lasts only a moment but his favor lasts a lifetime; weeping may remain for a night but joy comes in the morning.
Psalm 30:5

And every day I wake up I breathe another breath of your mercy.
Darrell Evans, "So Good to Me"

Nighttime can be hard. During the day, we are able to focus on God. We can actively make the decisions to turn our thoughts, to dwell on His amazing love and mercy. We can call on our Lord, and He is always there. Nights are different. Sometimes our renegade thoughts are able to take over and even cause nightmares. Even spending our last waking minutes in prayer is sometimes not enough to override the demons that plague our subconscious. I hate that feeling, waking up after a fitful night or waking with a feeling of dread for no apparent reason. The good news is that once we are awake, even a little bit, we can attach once again to our Lord.

The line from Darrell Evan's song says it so well, "And every day I wake up I breathe another breath of your mercy." It doesn't say every day when I wake up, and there is a vast difference, every day, all one word as opposed to every day as in each day, I wake up. He isn't saying every day when I wake up; he is saying that simply waking up each day is evidence of the vast mercy of our Lord and Savior.

We all sin; there is no question in that. Simple or grievous sin is a part of every life, even the very best ones. (See Romans 3:23.) In the Old Testament, sin often resulted in immediate death. Sin equals death. Jesus appearance on this earth didn't change that fact. That is why He had to come and save us. The wages of sin is death Paul says in Romans 6:23. The difference Jesus made is to save us from damnation; from eternal death, we will live because he died. The wages of our sin was his death. So it is truly the mercy of God that allows us sinners to wake every day, and in doing so we breathe in His mercy.

A young friend of mine told me that he is always tired. It doesn't matter how much he sleeps he said because he feels as if he has spent that time crying in his sleep. His life is very difficult right now and most of his misery has been self-inflicted. He doesn't trust in the mercy of God. He doesn't lean on the everlasting arms. Most days he manages to fake a semblance of normal life, but at night the fears in his heart take over, and he falls prey to the enemy. He cries in his sleep. I pray that he will know that God's mercy endures and is for every one. He needs to know what we all need to know. No matter how gray things look at night when we are tired and vulnerable, the Truth is still the Truth. God is still God, and joy comes in the morning.

Don't You Dare

With that then what shall we say in response to this? If God is for us who can be against us? Romans 8:31

Another author made reference to this verse in a way that I found so intriguing. This is one of my favorite verses because so many things conspire to take our joy and peace. So many things work to prove to us that we are wrong and that our God is not mighty. The book I was reading paraphrased the verse this way, "If God is for me who dares to be against me?" Who dares? I love that. What fool would dare to take on the God of the universe? What misguided miscreant would think for a moment that they could defeat God?

Who dares? We do, every day. We dare to think we know better. We dare to try to work out our own salvation and that of everyone we care about. While we understand that we are prayerfully seeking the face of God for answers we sometimes doubt another person's ability to do the same. The good news is we always lose those battles. God is in control.

The only way that fool who dares to challenge the authority of God can win is if we let him. If God is for us, who can be against us? Anyone we are dimwitted enough to trust more than we trust God and anyone to whom we ascribe that power. We must never relinquish the power that God has in our lives to any other person.

Why would anyone dare to go against God? Perhaps they aren't. Perhaps they are just going against us, not seeing God's power in our lives. Let no one question what authority controls your life. Make sure that everyone sees a king's kid when they see you. Then you can walk in the knowledge that if God is for you; no one can dare to be against you.

Clean Thoughts

For out of the overflow of the heart the mouth speaks.
Mathew 12:34b

Working with special-needs children often gives me a new, usually better perspective on life. Their view is very different from mine and is sometimes quite an eye-opener. Every year we have a sing along giving our children a chance to perform for their parents and the rest of the school. There is always a lot of discussion among the adults about the value of the show, the quality of the show, etc. One thing never changes throughout the course of rehearsing and putting on the performances, we learn a lot about our kids.

This year I learned a lesson that reminded me of the above verse from Matthew. Between each planned song, there was supposed to be a CD playing. The CD itself was not important, just some pleasant music to fill the time. Given the ages of the students, a current mix of teenybopper hits was chosen. As the songs played, I sat looking at children with whom my colleagues and I struggle on a daily basis. We strive to take them toward better grammar and more positive speech patterns. I assure you, it is a quite a struggle. We are battling not only intelligence and attention deficits but also environments where lazy speech is the order of the day. Some of our angels cannot even write their own names. Imagine my surprise when every one of them could sing along with at least part of every song on the CD.

One song in particular drew my attention because they were all singing it and obviously liked it very much. The words were sung by a lead singer and then repeated by the group. I listened as my students sang along with most of the other students. It was disturbing. The words were about "shakin' it" and "movin' it." There was no redeeming quality to the song. It was total junk, and yet there were my babies who cannot retain the value of a quarter singing away, every word.

Since that day, I have thought a lot about that incident. It disturbs me that the junk can take such hold when the important, the worthwhile is so easily forgotten, if in fact it was ever learned. I realized that my students aren't much different from some so-called Christians, from real Christians, from me. Have you realized that you can sing every word to some fluff song on the radio but can't recite one line of Scripture without prompting? I may know the plot line to the whole season of some useless TV show, but I can't tell you what certain books in the Bible are about.

The garbage attaches more easily, grabs my attention more quickly, and in that I am no different from my mentally challenged students. Maybe you can relate too.

We need to fill our hearts and minds with thoughts of our Savior and his amazing power.

> **Finally brothers whatever is pure, what is lovely, whatever is admirable—if anything is excellent or praiseworthy—think about such things. Philippians 4:8**

Faucet Drips

> Now the overseer must be above reproach, the husband of but one wife, temperate, self-controlled, respectable, hospitable, able to teach, not given to drunkenness, not violent but gentle, not quarrelsome not a lover of money. He must manage his own family well and see that his children obey him with proper respect. (If anyone does not know how to manage his own family, how can he take care of God's church?) He must not be a recent convert, or he may become conceited and fall under the same judgment as the devil He must also have a good reputation with outsiders so that he will not fall into disgrace and into the devil's trap. 1 Timothy 3:2-7

I've read the account in Scripture of what a church leader should be, and I know that I am not even close. My life much more closely resembles the broken and contrite heart Scriptures. I love my pastor and the one we had before him. They are great men of faith, but they aren't 100 percent the guy in 1 Timothy either. Perhaps where many of us stumble is that perfect-children thing. Remember Paul wasn't married and didn't have kids. This account held me back for a while from pursuing any kind of ministry. I would read it and think I'm hospitable; I'm not a recent convert, but then the obedient children thing and the gentle, well-respected thing would rear their ugly heads. Thankfully you can also flip the pages to read about how much God loves the humble and contrite heart. Even so, there are always new things the enemy can use to prove to us that we are not fit to serve.

Today a lot of ministers have huge miracle stories to tell. I fall short a little there too. I haven't experienced cancer or the loss of a family member. Nor do I have a spouse or child in the military. For all of that I say, "THANK GOD!" So how can I exhibit God's movement in my life? I can bring to the table the miracle of trusting God in the everyday faucet-drip annoyances of life. There is a song called "Trading My Sorrows." I love it. It speaks to trading the junk of life for the love of God. Many of the things he lists in that song I have had to give over. I'm sure you have too. It doesn't take a huge story to make a disciple. It takes discipline.

There is that kooky saying, "When life gives you lemons, make lemonade." Faith says, "Be thankful for the lemons, and God will give you something better." I suppose it is the same sentiment: don't complain, use what you have. It's just that to me, if we see those "lemons" as an opportunity for growth, we'll handle them so much better. We may even enjoy the lemonade.

The last year has brought enormous change into my life and family, not all of it is good, but all of it can work for good. Every day all of us are asked to face things we may not want to face. If your personal life is experiencing a time of peace, all you have to do is watch the news to know that God has not come to vanquish the enemy just yet. We live in a place with a lot of ugliness. So many times we hear people ask, "What can I do?"

We can all live our faith. We can be overseers. We can live as closely as possible to the example set by Jesus. We can not just endure our sorrows but trade them for the joy of the Lord. We all know people who seem to thrive on negativity. Show them the error of their ways by living joyfully. Trade your pain, shame, and weakness for the joy of the Lord. Be pressed but not crushed. When that faucet keeps dripping on your head, trade every annoying drip for joy knowing that God gave you that head and the ability to feel the drip. The enemy hates it when we're joyful. Happiness he can steal, but joy is much harder for him to destroy. When the noise of that dripping faucet gets to be too much, turn up the music of praise in your heart and drown it out.

For the Glory of God

I consider that our present sufferings are not worth comparing with he glory that will be revealed in us. Romans 8:18

It is very rare to see truly amazing acts of bravery. We hear about them a lot especially now that media is so intensive and so easily accessed. It is different to come face-to-face with true, unpretentious bravery. In the past year, have been privileged to stand beside it and to sit behind it at church.

The first instance was when I was called upon to be a prayer partner to an amazing friend of mine who battled with cancer and, praise God, won. I was often awestruck by her behavior. I have met people who do more complaining over paper cuts. It was humbling as well as inspiring to be even a small part of that battle.

Last week in church, I was reminded of my friend's demeanor as I watched an older woman stride up the aisle of our church. Stride, that is, as best as anyone could with one leg and crutches. Oddly it wasn't the fact of the missing leg or the crutches that caught my eye. It was two other facts. One, she wasn't gimping. There seemed to be no hitch in her step at all. She was, if not striding, at least still managing to move with great grace. She walks much more gracefully than I do, and I have both legs. Two, she was alone. There wasn't anyone walking with her, which suggested to me that not only was she walking but she must have driven herself as well. Her entrance, all on its own, was enough to draw my admiration, but I had yet to see the best of her.

There is a portion of our service devoted to singing praise songs. We stand for that portion and there she was, standing with the rest of us. Not too long into the second song, I saw her wobble a bit and worried that perhaps she should be sitting down. Maybe ten seconds later, I realized she was adjusting her balance to her one leg and one of her two crutches. She had freed one hand to lift in praise to God.

My first thought at that sight was about excuses. I've heard them all and used quite a few. "I missed church because my head hurt, neck ached, stomach was upset, I didn't get enough sleep, the baby was up most of the night, etc."

I stood there looking at this woman, this disfigured woman, who by the way must be in her eighties and is stunning, with her hand raised and her face radiant. I said to myself, "That is faith. That is truly a deep love for God."

Last week, I knew she only had one leg because she was wearing pants with one leg pinned up. This week she came in wearing a dress, again alone and again with a smile and nod for everyone she walked past.

I remember as a child hearing the expression "The Lord giveth, and the Lord taketh away." I wasn't too crazy about that Lord. I've grown up a lot since then, but still when I see things like terminally ill children or hear of tragedy, I wonder why. I find it terribly unfair and want an explanation. Then I run across people like my friend and the lady from church, and I know at least part of the answer, for the glory of God.

A smile on the face of a person who obviously has plenty of room for complaint, a lone hand raised in praise because the other is busy holding a crutch, the mother of a deceased child still showing concern for the child of another, all of that says there is a God; and He loves us so very much. That may not make sense to you. Maybe it only makes sense if you see it yourself, but it is true, and it is awesome in the truest sense of that overworked word.

My friend's battle gave her the spoils of living in the presence of God's healing power. My church lady may have lost a leg, but her spirit is as strong as any Iron Man's body. That mother I see so often carries within her a peace that passes understanding. All of that says to me that whenever I need superhuman strength, all I have to do is ask. I am sorry for the suffering of each one of those ladies and many more like them, but I am grateful that they have shared their silent testimonies with me. They live as I want to live, for the glory of God.

Questions

Search me, O god and know my heart; test me and know my anxious thoughts. Psalm 139:23

"But what about you?" he asked. "Who do you say I am?" Matthew 16:15

When he had gone indoors the blind men came to him and he asked them, "Do you believe that I am able to do this?" Matthew 9:28a

Thomas said to him, "Lord we don't know where you are going, so how can we know the way?" John 14:5

In a small private school, I learned from a fairly young age that questioning authority is not good. In fact, it's pretty bad and certainly frowned upon. Since God is God, the Lord of the universe, Maker and Creator of everything the Authority of all authorities it should follow that I would not question Him, and yet I do it all the time. Where should I go? What should I say? How should I handle this? Why, oh why, did you let that happen? I have no problem questioning Him. The problem is in the questions themselves.

To be closer to Christ, to truly recognize the indwelling of the Holy Spirit, we must ask the right questions. The ones from the Scriptures (above) are a good start. "Search me and know my heart" may not seem like a question but it is a polite way of saying "What's wrong with me?" The other three are about the fundamentals of faith.

Who do you say He is? Not with your words but with your resources, with your time, with your love, who do you say He is? Is he Lord of your life? Does He sit on the throne or do you? Whose best interests do your actions serve?

Two blind men have just asked for healing. They had no trouble with that question. "Can you heal me, Lord?" It is His question that could be the stumbling block. "Do you believe that I can?" Do you believe He can answer that deepest prayer of your heart? Are you truest desires laid at His feet?

Thomas asks, "Where are you going?" We all want to know. Where is he going? Can I come? And by the way, how do I get there? When you think about where your life is taking you, do you think in eternal terms? "Where are you going? How do I get there?"

The answer to Thomas's question seems so easy. Jesus says, "I am the Way." You get there through me, or you don't get there at all. It brings us back to search me and know that I am ready to go. It also brings us back to "who do you say I am?"

We want answers. I know I do. Why? When? How? I have to be sure that I am asking the right questions of myself. Who do I say He is? Do I believe He can answer all of my prayers and do what's best for me. If I know that, then my questions can boil down to one: Lord, what can I do for you today?

The Gift Box

Every good and perfect gift is from above, coming down from the Father of the heavenly lights, who does not change like shifting shadows. James 1:17

I read an account of children in El Salvador receiving Christmas-gift boxes prepared by American children. It was in a book by Max Lucado. He spoke of the excitement the children feel at receiving toys, books, and personal items; but that the part they enjoy the most is the letter that comes from the other child. He made many eloquent and touching points comparing that gift to the gift that God gave to us in the form of Jesus. There was one line though with which I disagreed. He said that for us, the box, which is Jesus doesn't come with toys, books, and the like. He said that Jesus is the gift.

While I agree that Jesus is the main gift and in fact the only gift we need, I believe there are other gifts involved. In fact, I believe that every good thing in my life comes from that gift box from God. My family, my home, my health—all of those are gifts from a loving Father. There are other things too, like a phone call from a friend when I am feeling particularly alone, the knowledge that someone really needed my help or was glad to see my face. Even that extra little bit of cash right when I need it is a precious gift. There are so many things that are gifts from God. I'm sure you can make quite a list of your own, can't you?

The other thing that struck me about the passage was the children's delight with the letter. We too have been given a wonderful letter full of all the ways our Father is here for us. Full of the love he feels for us, enough love to send Jesus to die on the Cross. Each page of the Bible is a blessing just as the letters written from one child to another are blessings.

Those poor Salvadoran children only experience that happiness and excitement once a year; for us, that excitement is at our fingertips every day. We don't have to wait a year; we only have to pick up our Bibles and read God's love letter to us.

Don't wait for a special occasion, reach out now, and let the love of God fill your day.

Daddy's Little Girl

For you created my inmost being; you knit me together in my mother's womb. I praise you because I am fearfully and wonderfully made; your works are wonderful, I know that full well. Psalm 139: 13-14

Some of us, for various reasons may wonder why we were born. Some people were adopted and may feel abandoned. Some were abused or neglected, and some were told outright that they were mistakes. We often hear people refer to the "oops" baby. If that "oops" is said affectionately, it might not hurt, but too often it is said with a negative emphasis. When those circumstances, abuse, neglect, "oops," are a part of our lives; it is easy to ask why we were born.

Thank God, Scripture provides the answer. We were born because God wanted us to be born. In this day of so many unwed parents, we may ask if those pregnancies are truly God's will. I don't have a definitive answer. I know God created marriage as the basis of families. I know that He hates adultery as He hates all other sin and sex with anyone who is not your spouse is adultery. I also know that none of us, not one, is a mistake. The circumstances of conception may be mistakes, but the resulting person is not.

There is a lot of pain in feeling that your presence here on Earth is a mistake. It hurts to know that you were not eagerly anticipated, and you may feel that you are just in the way of the people of real importance. Remember that each one of us is precious to our Father. Other people may treat you with disrespect or outright rudeness. You may feel that you have no value, but that is a lie Satan will use to keep you from achieving the purpose to which you were born.

Each one of us was fearfully and wonderfully made in the image of our Father. We are all Daddy's little girl (or boy). Regardless of our birth circumstances or the way we were treated by our parents or the people around us, we are God's children; and He doesn't make mistakes.

Going Through It

> Now if we are children then we are heirs—heirs of God and co-heirs with Christ, if indeed we share in his sufferings in order that we may also share in his glory. Romans 8:17

> Even though I walk through the valley of the shadow of death,
> I will fear no evil, for you are with me;
> your rod and your staff comfort me. Psalm 23:4

Our pastor gave a very eloquent talk the other day on suffering. Perhaps that sounds odd using eloquent and suffering in the same sentence. Maybe it should read effective. It was certainly challenging and he made his point as he usually does. He rarely, if ever, lets us walk out with a "Jesus loves me this I know" attitude. He gives the kind of talks that demand a response, and this one was no different. During the course of the talk, he used the phrase "going through it" more than once. He made references to the fact that suffering cannot always be avoided. He said, "You can't get around it," again, more than once.

There is a children's song called "Bear Hunt" that, between teaching pre-K, raising four children and now working in special ed., I have heard many, many, many times. To say it is not my favorite is a vast understatement. It's one of those that repeats and repeats and drives me crazy, and it includes that same phrase that David used, "You can't go around it, gotta' go through it." The song takes its little hunters through muck and mire, over trees, and through deep waters only to encounter . . . THE BEAR! Then it's back through weeds, water, and whatever else to dry land and safety. I'm telling you, it's an annoying song. But it is a perfectly simplistic illustration of what Pastor David was saying.

The suffering is there to be endured. The best thing is to learn from it so as not to encounter the same thing again. The problem in the "Bear Hunt" song is that the travelers are looking at each challenge trying to find a way to go around, but there is no around. They fight their way through to worse and worse outcomes. We do the same. In an attempt to forestall the first pain, I bumble my way into something worse. My analogy falls short here because the end result for the hunters is to have to endure the same suffering to get to safety. We need only to hang in, know that we are not alone, and that at the other side of our suffering there is peace.

We go through valleys to rest on mountaintops. Those mountaintops are great, and like vacations, we are reluctant to give them up, but give them up we must. Walking through the valley with our Savior at our side is the best way to grow to be like Him. If we stop fighting and resolve to "go through it" with His help, there will always be both a lesson and a blessing.

Some suffering seems purposeless, but that is because we are shortsighted. We have no idea what God has planned for us, today, tomorrow or ten years from now. Today's suffering may be next decade's miracle.

"You can't go around it." So go through it with God's help.

Image

**Then God said, "Let us make man in our image in our likeness..."
So God created man in his own image: in the image of God he created him, male and female he created them. Genesis 1:26a, 27**

In His image we were created. We are supposed to look like our dad or brother. People should look at us and say, "Wow, she looks just like her brother." So what does that mean? Should we all have Jewish features? Or the darker complexion that comes from living and working in a desert climate? Not at all. The image here has a bigger meaning. We won't necessarily look physically like Jesus, but our lives should mirror His as closely as humanly possible.

That other image, that physical image is sometimes a big problem. Some of us are dark, some lighter, some are chunky while others are thin, some have large breasts or muscles while others aren't sure where to find theirs. All of that becomes terribly important to us as we go through life, and none of it is important. It is our spiritual image that should matter most.

Fads change. Appearance is subject to the passing fancy of dress designers and magazine editors. Look back at the Jayne Mansfield era. At that time women wanted to be busty, but they had the rest of the body in proportion. At my age, I have lived through the straight-hair era (very good for me) and the Farrah Faucett-thick-and-curly era (where I had no chance of coming close).

We watch TV. We look at magazines, and we say, "That's what I'm supposed to look like." Today the trend is to be very thin but still carry around the big bust. How is that going to work? It works because those breasts, lips, and other assorted body parts are for sale. I meet disagreement from many of my friends when I say this, but I think purchasing those parts is dangerous. It may well take our focus off of our spiritual life and place too much emphasis on the physical. We will one day meet the God, who created us in His image, and then we will have to explain how it is that we came to have that new nose. In the same way when we overspend buying clothing or jewelry to improve our package, we are not honoring God with our resources.

God is not concerned with the appearance of our bodies or any individual part thereof. He is concerned with our behavior, our charity, the way we treat His people.

Steven Curtis Chapman has a great song called "Fingerprints of God." There is a part in it that says, "The person in the mirror doesn't look like the magazines but when I look at you it's clear to see . . . you are covered with the fingerprints of God."

Short or tall, thin or fat, with the nose I would like or the one that I have, flat or "blessed"—I want to be covered with the fingerprints of God. I do not want to explain why I thought I could build a better temple than the one God gave to me.

I hear the groans of all of you who "just want to feel better about myself." I hear you, and I would tell you this, **"Clothe yourselves with compassion, kindness, humility, gentleness and patience (Col. 3:12). Rather clothe yourselves with the Lord Jesus Christ, and do not think about how to gratify the desires of the sinful nature" (Romans 13:14).**

A friend of mine says often, "We need to live simply so others can simply live." Too much time and money spent on ourselves prevents us from doing the work God has given us to do. Can we comfortably be well fed, well dressed, and synthetically magazine stylish while our fellow Christians are starving and homeless?

If you have succumbed to the pressures of this world to change your body, don't beat yourself up with this message. Remember Romans 3:23: "All have sinned and fall short of the glory of God." Most women, through actual surgical change, eating disorders, or some other brilliant plan have bowed to the body image issue. Instead of feeling guilty, hold tight to the knowledge that we are always beautiful to our Father; and when our behavior reflects His love, then the world can see that beauty too.

Sacrifices

After that they presented the regular burnt offerings, the New Moon sacrifices and the sacrifices for all the appointed sacred feasts of the Lord as well as those brought as freewill offerings to the Lord. On the first day of the seventh month they began to offer burnt offerings to the Lord though the foundation of the Lord's temple had not yet been laid. Ezra 3:5-6

How do you feel about tithing? I know that many people have different views. In my own church our pastor makes things very clear, but in a church I formerly attended, that pastor made his view equally clear, and they aren't the same. The 10 percent never seems to be an issue as it shouldn't give the word, "tithe." The question arises in where does the 10 percent go? Directly to your home church? So if you are on vacation and contribute to the church you are visiting, that doesn't count? Is that what I have heard called "an extra gift"? It's very confusing, and people get really worried about doing it right.

I don't have an answer. Well, I have an answer for me, but I don't have a definitive answer. This I know. My Father loves me, and He knows my heart. Look at the people in Ezra's account. They made all the appropriate sacrifices, but in the next chapter they are bickering with each other.

Does God want us to tithe? Yes. Is He keeping track of what went to the church and what went to the neighbor in desperate need? Do you think that when He puts a needy soul (truly needy not just lazy) in front of you that He wants you to say, "Can't help ya. This money is going to God but at my church"?

Does He want us to worship Him in a nice building? I don't think He cares. I know He wants us to worship Him, and I think He is happy when we do, whether it's in the beautiful stained glass building or anywhere else. Scripture says where two or more gather, He will be there. It doesn't specify what kind of building is required.

Psalm 51:16-17 says, *"You do not delight in sacrifice or I would bring it; You do not take pleasure in brunt offerings. The sacrifices of God are a broken spirit; a broken and contrite heart, O God, you will not despise."*

The people in the account from the book of Ezra got caught up in the letter of the law. They forgot about the spirit of love. They were eager to secure God's good opinion but not as concerned about doing His will. Our Father is well aware of the attitude with which we give. He does not delight in an empty sacrifice. It is the motive not the means that mean the most to Him.

Under Satan's Radar

> Submit yourselves, then to God. Resist the devil and he will flee from you. James 4:7

"Become so small that the devil can't see you." A friend shared that quote with me that he had heard from a Catholic priest. I've forgotten the context of the original use to be honest because it spoke to me so personally.

Years ago one of my favorite pastors shared a series of prayers we should learn and pray. They had been a huge blessing to him and he wanted us to receive that same blessing. The first one is "pray to be obscure." I remember distinctly his description of his experiences with obscurity and was not certain that I was comfortable with that prayer. I attempted it a few times but without any real conviction.

One day, I decided that I wanted prayer number 3 (to be used by God over and over) so badly that I would walk through 1 and 2. Immediately I was even more obscure than I believed possible. A woman I work with, and know fairly well, literally looked past me to greet the woman behind me. It was as if I were invisible. At first, I was offended and then excited. After a few days stretched into a few weeks, it was way less exciting. I was beginning to truly crave some kind of acknowledgement, any kind really.

I prayed, "Lord, how long does the obscure part last?" He answered, "As long as I need it to last, maybe all of your life." I had to really think about that. I was still thinking about it, trying to come to terms with it when my friend shared that quote with me. "Become so small that the devil can't see you." Can I do that all of my life? YES!

There was a blessing in that obscurity as I knew there had to be. God never asks us to do anything without good reason. He loves us. I knew that if He wanted me to be obscure for a long time there was a reason. I had decided that it was of the "he must be greater and greater, and I must be less and less" variety. That is when I heard that quote, and it confirmed it. The bigger I am in my life, the smaller He is. He must be HUGE, a giant, and I must be smaller than an ant.

Obscurity will have its problems, I am sure. It is not human nature to go unnoticed, but I will remind myself if those people can't see me maybe Satan can't either.

Cruel Words

You have heard that it was said to the people long ago, "Do not murder and anyone who murders will be subject to judgment." But I tell you that anyone who is angry with his brother will be subject to judgment. Again anyone who says to his brother "Raca' is answerable to the Sanhedrin. But anyone who says "you fool" will be in danger of the fire of hell. Matthew 5:22

Are you thinking right now that you are in big trouble? As you read those words did you think about how many times you've done just that. I know I do every time I read that passage. I have a sarcastic tongue. Most of the time, now, it is just nonsense, nothing that would truly hurt; but there were years when I thoroughly enjoyed cutting people to the bone with words. I regret that for more reasons than are mentioned in the Scripture. Thankfully, I regret it because of the hurt it has caused and for the satisfaction that did not come.

Before our Lord rescued me from myself, I was happy to use someone else's shortcomings to bolster my own self-esteem. If I could find a poor soul in worse shape than I, then I had it made. I could point at his/her lack hopefully illustrating my own superior nature. As I'm sure you already know, it doesn't work that way. I am not more successful because someone else enjoys less success. I am not a better person because I view another's sin as larger than my own.

What if I had continued down that unsavory road still having more "clever" things than kind ones to say about the people around me? I may well have developed a personality to go with the talk. We see it happen all the time; negative speech patterns become negative behavior patterns until what is left is a truly miserable person.

I won't pretend that I now wear rose-colored glasses and find everyone else in the world simply adorable. I don't. There are many people I dislike and probably twice that number who dislike me. That's okay. None of us is expected to like everyone we meet. What is expected, commanded really, is that we speak without judgment. None of us ever knows what is behind another person's attitude. Perhaps there is hurt or frustration that we label as snootiness or conceit.

We think that we can say whatever we want as long as the other person can't hear us. Jesus disagrees. In no small part because *He can* hear us but also because other people hear us and are influenced by our opinions. It has helped me to stop and think how I would feel if the other person were saying the same words about me.

Recently I had occasion to be righteously offended by another person. I shared that offense with a couple of close friends. I also took the matter under the microscope of "what if she were saying this about me?" I can honestly say that if I had treated her with the same measure of disrespect, she would be well within her rights to speak unkindly of my behavior. There was no need to cast aspersions on the woman's entire character, just on the incident itself.

Words are very powerful. We need to use them to build up and not to tear down. We need to remember that Jesus is looking at our intentions, at our heart's condition. Speaking the truth in love (Ephesians 4:15), we will build good relationships, show respect for God's people, and fulfill the commandment to "love your neighbor."

Beyond Understanding

At that time Jesus said, "I praise you, Father, Lord of heave and earth because you have hidden these things from the wise and learned, and revealed them to little children. Yes, Father, for this was your good pleasure." Matthew 11:25-26

I have a friend who is taking algebra in college. More than a few of our conversations lately have included her angst over this course. I feel for her. While she is younger than I, she has still been away from this subject for more than a few years. I have no aptitude for Math, and it appears that she is slightly better off. In fact, she seeks help from her son. As I read this verse from Matthew, I was reminded of how I feel when Debbie talks about her class. It is a foreign language in some sense just as these verses refer to things I may never understand.

Debbie and I both spend our days with children who are disabled. Some are simply unable to process information accurately, and others face challenges far more involved. We see a few on a daily basis who neither walk nor talk. We see some who can do both of those and in fact look quite like any other child until you ask a simple question. I look at those children and think, "Why them and not me?" Or more to the point, "Why them and not my children?" The answer I suppose is God's grace, but then that seems wrong, until you read these verses from Matthew.

There are so many things we cannot comprehend, like Debbie's Algebra terms only so very much bigger. Debbie has some understanding of those terms that I do not. The author of her textbook completely understands it. So it is with God's mysteries.

I may have less understanding of Scripture than some people and more than others, but I know one thing for sure. The Author of those words, the true Creator of all knows exactly what it all means and how it all fits together. One day it will be revealed to us and things like precious children who lack blessings I take for granted will all be pieced together in a mosaic of majesty that is beyond anything we can begin to imagine.

It all comes down to trust. I trust that if Debbie applies herself, she will learn those terms in which I have no interest, and the light of understanding will shine for her. I trust that one day, one great day, our Father will reveal the tiny details of His massive plan and the Light of understanding will shine for all of us.

> **"Come to me all you who are weary and burdened, and I will give you rest. Take my yoke upon you and learn from me, for I am gentle and humble in heart, and you will find rest for your souls. For my yoke is easy and my burden is light"** (Matthew 11:28-30).

Vertically Challenged

> **Jesus entered Jericho and was passing through. A man was there by the name of Zaccheus; he was a chief tax collector and was wealthy. He wanted to see who Jesus was, but being a short man he could not, because of the crowd. So he ran ahead and climbed a sycamore tree to see him, since Jesus was coming that way. Luke 19:1-4**

Zaccheus was a short man. His height was an impediment to seeing Jesus. Oh well, poor Z, there's really nothing he, or anyone, could do about height, especially in his day. Being a tax collector, Zaccheus would have been fairly well off, but no amount of money buys height. Today he might be able to get lifts in his shoes, but there weren't any lifts for sandals back then. Give up, Z, it's not going to happen.

Height wasn't the only factor Zaccheus had against him either. He was a *tax collector,* one of the shifty breed, not the type you want at your table or in your pew at church, but Zaccheus had something all of us need. He had desire. He had the desire to see Jesus and the determination to back it up. Zaccheus saw a challenge and tackled it. He saw a once-in-a-lifetime opportunity, and his height was not going to stop him. He climbed a tree.

The rest of the story is that Jesus saw Zaccheus and recognized his efforts. Verses 5-10 tell what happened next. Jesus spoke to Zaccheus, and Zaccheus responded. He turned over a new leaf. The tree climbing was not the rubbernecking we all do at traffic accidents. It was the determined act of a desperate man. Zaccheus wanted more out of life. He wanted to *be* more not just have more, and he was willing not only to climb the tree but also to change his ways.

I am blessed to know another short man who has changed his ways. When faced with a challenge, he took it on, not grumbling but with cheerful determination. Physical height really isn't a factor for him, but the analogy works anyway. The young man is my son-in-law, and he is seriously close to a foot shorter than my youngest son. Actions speak louder than stature, and Mike is a man of action. In being so, he set a standard for his brother-in-law that has had an impact on many lives. In fact, his example may literally have saved one life.

We can all rise above our limitations—be it height, education, or finances. God has a plan for each of us. If you can't see Him, climb a tree or maybe sit down. Some of us may be too tall and refusing to look down at what is real. Jesus is looking for you. Put yourself in his line of vision.

Lost and Found

But while he was still a long way off, his father saw him and was filled with compassion for him. He ran to his son, threw his arms around him and kissed him.

The son said, "Father I have sinned against heaven and against you, I am no longer worthy to be called your son."

But the said to his servants, "Quickly! Bring the best robe and put it on him. Put a ring on his finger and sandals on his feet. Bring the fattened calf and kill it. Let's have a feast and celebrate. For this son of mine was dead and is alive again; he was lost and is found."
Luke 15:20b-24a

It has occurred to me how often my actions with God are similar to the actions of my children that I most dislike. For a year or so, my daughter chose to act against everything she had been raised to hold dear. She had to move away from our home to do it. It was something of an "if you can't see, it can't hurt us" school of thought. She didn't want to be permanently out of the family, but the family values were too tight at that time. She wanted to behave in a very similar fashion to the Prodigal Son. Too often I treat God that way. It is the sin of putting ourselves on the throne and taking God off. "I'll just be over here for a minute attempting to control my own fate, don't mind me." Then when I have royally messed up, back I trot, wanting Daddy to fix it.

It didn't work that way for my daughter, and it doesn't work that way for me. She was forgiven before she ever asked for forgiveness, long before, just as our Father often forgives me before I even ask. She didn't feel forgiven and couldn't act on that mercy because she hadn't received it. I could. I could love her, pray for her, and begin to rebuild our relationship even though there was still a wait for the actual request for forgiveness. Even after she knew she'd been forgiven, the mess was still hers to clean up. She has my prayer support and love, but the broom, so to speak, is in her hands.

The consequences are still there. Some things in our relationship were broken and needed mending; some were beyond repair and had to be replaced.

There are events that should have been a natural progression for her that will never happen. All of that is a result of her choices. So it is with God and each of us. He forgives us before we ask, but we can't feel it until we open that channel. He is always willing to rebuild with us, but the consequences are still there. In His amazing mercy, God walks through all of that with us and sometimes He does allow us to avoid some of the pitfalls we should have had to go through.

There is no place, no time that our Father's eyes are not on us. He doesn't have to wait for someone else to tell Him what we've been up to. He doesn't have to "catch" us at anything. He knows what we are doing, have done, and will do. The good news is His forgiveness cannot be exhausted. Even when we repeatedly break His heart, He is open to trying again.

No Worries

Then Jesus said to his disciples, "Therefore I tell you, do not worry about your life, what you will eat or about your body, what you will ear. Life is more than food and the body more than clothes. Consider the ravens: They do not sow or reap, they have no storeroom or barn; yet God feeds them. And how much more valuable you are than birds! Who of you by worrying can add a single hour to his life? Since you cannot do this very little thing, why do you worry about the rest? "Consider how the lilies grow. They do not labor of spin. Yet I tell you Solomon in all his splendor was dressed like one of these. If that is how God clothes the grass of the field which is here today and tomorrow is thrown in the fire, how much more will he clothe you, O you of little faith! And do not set your heart on what you will eat or drink; do not worry about it. For the pagan world runs after all such things and your Father knows that you need them. But seek his kingdom, and these things will be given to you as well.

"Do not be afraid, little flock, for your Father has been pleased to give you the kingdom. Sell your possessions and give to the poor. Provide purses for yourselves that will not wear out, a treasure in heaven that will not be exhausted, where no thief comes near and no moth destroys. For where your treasures is, there your heart will be also." Luke 12:22-34

My very close friend and prayer partner, Charlene, was at my home the other day. Our conversation went all over the place, as usual, and came back for the most part to trusting in God, as usual. We should understand God's providence very well. Both of us have spent many years trusting in God for our finances, which is a pretty clear-cut way to see God's hand moving in your life. We also both have children, healthy children with only the minor illness, except my oldest son, whom I was told was brain damaged and now has two college degrees, both obtained on scholarships. God provides for Charlene and I all the time. He provided us with each other. Still we worry.

We worry about our kids, spouses, jobs, finances, health, etc., just like everyone else. At least we did until recently. The last year or so, my life has been pretty much a series of questionable events. In one light you see blessing but turn that puppy the tiniest bit and uh-oh. I could really be worried right now except that God has other plans for my time. So in His own inimitable way, He has taught me not to worry. I don't have it down completely yet, but I am getting better. Enter Charlene, who has decided, somewhat out of character, to make worrying her newest hobby. Just the other day she told me, "I worry about everything." She went on to recite her list of worries, and she wasn't kidding. She is worried about everything.

I asked her what God has been asking me for the last few months. "And what effect is your worry having on the situation?" Her answer was the same as mine. None, nothing, not one iota of effect.

The truth of it is on our own, we have no power. We can only accomplish a task through the power of God. God is in control, not us. He is on the throne, and we are, for now, in the cheap seats. The great news is that we have unlimited access to that throne through the person of Jesus. Instead of worrying, we need to pray. That's what I am learning, and that is what I shared with Charlene. I know that one day when I forget, she will remind me. She's great about that, reminding me to practice what I preach, and I love her for it—especially when it is such a powerful truth.

Our best hope—Charlene's, mine and yours—is *not* to worry but to give everything to God in prayer with thanksgiving. The instructions are in **"Do not be anxious about anything but in everything by prayer and petition, with thanksgiving, present your request to God."**

As Charlene said to me, "It sounds so simple." That's because it is. It doesn't seem like it should be, and so we make it harder than it has to be. The truth of it is we can worry ourselves sick literally, and the outcome will not change. Or we can pray with thanksgiving and watch God do amazing things.

So seek God and pray first, and then if there is still time and you absolutely can not help yourself—then worry.

Positive vs. Negative

> You brood of vipers, how can you who are evil say anything good? For out of the overflow of the heart the mouth speaks. The good man brings good things out of the good stored up in him, and the evil man brings evil things out of the evil stored up in him.
> Matthew 12:34-35

Perhaps it is because I grew up surrounded by it. Perhaps it because in my lifetime I have too often caught myself wanting to fall right into it. Most likely it is a combination of those factors, but the truth is I have zero tolerance for negativity. I'm not talking about the occasional complaint legitimate or otherwise. I am talking about an actual spirit of negativity. The other day, I came across a room full of it, and the saddest thing was that the women in the room saw themselves as positive.

I entered the room to hear the first happy comment about another woman and her inability to understand her place in this world. It was clearly not as a part of their group. They went on to discuss her total lack of ability to discern when she was not welcome at the group's function (from what was being said I think the poor woman is welcome on the day after the Twelfth of Never). The oh so thinly veiled venom continued until one woman made a semidecent comment. Well, suddenly she was queen of the hop.

"We have our own little Pastor X," one woman remarked, referring to a very famous preacher known for his amazingly upbeat attitude. That remark took them off into a discussion of how open-minded and positive they are as opposed to the interloper who can never be on time when she is part of the group and never understands that she is usually not wanted. All in all, it was a frightening conversation to overhear.

I happen to be a big fan of the pastor to whom they made reference, and I assure you this is not his line of thinking. It made me wonder if these women truly see themselves as kind, joyful, positive people. How could they after verbally removing another person's skin? Yet they certainly seemed to be patting themselves on the backs for having such good outlooks.

I am also too often exposed to one person who reeks of negativity. I try and try, I pray for her, but still the sight of her makes me uncomfortable. Although I do believe that she is oblivious to the danger of her attitude, I do know that she is completely aware of it, proud of it in fact. That amazes me as much as the gaggle of gals so busy looking at the speck in one woman's eye that they couldn't see the forest in their own eyes.

It occurred to me to say something to the group of ladies so sure they were living according to the words of Pastor X, but having heard how they felt about intruders, I kept silent. I don't think they would have heard me in any case, but I am grateful to them. Every time I rub up against negativity that strong, I remember to check my own attitude and to be grateful that our Lord is teaching me to hold onto my joy. It is imperative that we take stock every now and then. Do our talk and walk match? Are we reflecting the love of Christ? Would our conversations cause someone to rejoice or despair? We never know who is listening to us from the other side of the room.

Law or Love

We also know that the law is good if one uses it properly. We also know that law is make not for the righteous but for lawbreakers and rebels, the ungodly and sinful, the unholy and irreligious; for those who kill their fathers or mothers, for murderers, for adulterers and perverts, for slave traders and liars and perjurers—and for whatever else is contrary to the sound doctrine that conforms to the glorious gospel of the blessed God, which he entrusted to me. 1 Timothy 1:9-11

In this letter to Timothy Paul is preaching to all of us who get caught up in "doing the right thing." Denomination doesn't matter because every single one has laws or doctrines. We may point a finger at one denomination while following our own crazy set of rules and regs. God wants us to follow him. Our Father sent Jesus to show us the way. If we truly believe and are truly saved by grace, the law is unimportant.

As we live to serve God to keep *his* commandment, we will naturally fulfill the law. Anything that tightens the boundaries of the Ten Commandments is unnecessary. Jesus put it as succinctly as possible; you must love the Lord your God and love your neighbor as yourself. (See Matthew 22:37-40.)

We like to put amendments on God's law—don't eat this, don't drink that, don't do this on this day—but it's okay the next day. Some of them are ridiculous. I wonder what God thinks of all our histrionics. He made it as simple as possible with the Ten Commandments, and when that was too much, he sent Jesus to make it all clear; and when we missed the boat, there he offered us the Holy Spirit. That last option of support allows us not to worry about a single detail. All we have to do is yield to the prompting of the Spirit.

Of course we aren't capable of totally yielding with that pesky free will, but that is the goal and if we aim for that, live as closely connected to the Spirit as possible we will be far better off than following a list of checks and balances. Truly feeling the nudge of the Spirit will keep us on the right path. When we ignore it or refuse to even ask for guidance, we fall. Don't worry about that. Don't then go back to keeping some man made rule as a safety net. Romans 6:23 advises that we all fall, all miss the mark. A pastor friend of mine always says, "The difference between the saints and the rest of us is in the speed with which they repent."

Years ago, I learned the acronym OBA, obedience with alacrity. That's a great one to adhere to as long as that obedience is to the Word of God. It is much easier to rely on the advice of a trusted friend than try to keep track of a list of rules. Make Jesus your trusted friend and rely on His Spirit to guide you.

Grateful

Be joyful always; pray continually; give thanks in all circumstances, for this is God's will for you in Christ Jesus. **1 Thessalonians 5:16**

There is great joy in belonging to God. Every day we are blessed to know him and to be known by Him. I was listening to some songs the other day that were based on the themes of thanksgiving and forgiveness. My reaction to them was rather odd considering that each song outlined all that we do wrong, but they did also point out the patience and love of God. As I listened, I thought of how different my life would be if it hadn't been for God.

I know a woman with whom I have a lot in common. At least our pasts are very similar. She's a fun woman with a good heart, but she has built a lot of really big walls around her. She says and does things that come from the hurt she experienced in her past. That happens because she still carries it with her.

It is much easier to see how far you have come when you see what might have been. My friend and I often reach the same conclusions but then deal with the knowledge so differently. Why? The answer is simple. God. I believe He loves me and wants what is best for me and she does not.

Driving down the road today listening to those songs made me think of my friend and once again I wanted her to have what I have. I wanted her to know what I know, which is that if God is for me, no one can come against me and win. He loves me just as I am. He loves her too; she just can't see it.

It is great to be able to praise God when things are good and better still to praise him when they are bad. Things may get bad, but God is good all the time. He knows each of us and every thing we have ever done. He forgives before we even ask, and He never ever leaves our sides. I'm never sure how people who don't know Him get up day after day. I am so grateful that He has called me and that He has allowed me to share Him with each one of you.

Handle With Care

Whoever loves discipline loves knowledge but he who hates correction is stupid. Proverbs 12:1

There's one in every crowd. In every family, workplace, classroom exists that person for whom everyone else has to make changes. You know the type, the one who can't be told things or has to be told oh so gently. This is the person whose most questionable behaviors are overlooked. This is the one displaying an invisible "handle with care" across his/her chest as the Ms. America contestants display the name of their states. Is that person you? Or are you picturing someone else? If right now you are cringing take heart, there is hope. If you are chuckling because you've identified "the one," hang on a minute.

If you've found him/her in the workplace, look around at home. Now is it you? I think each one of us has our teachable moments and our prideful moments. For me, I think there are areas where I accept correction fairly well, and others were I get a little prickly. The Scripture is referring to the more chronic type. The Kid Glove Katie at all times. This is the one who rules the roost as well as the workplace. No wants to upset that one.

God wants to upset all the porcupine people. We need to be able to receive correction from Him and from those people He sends to help us grow. Nobody's perfect except one. In striving to be like Jesus, we will encounter corrective criticism. We all have to learn to take it in without melting down.

As for the Histrionic Hazel in your life, try a little gentle honesty. Take off the kid gloves and speak the truth in love. You'll both be better for it.

Gratitude

Be joyful always; pray continually; give thanks in all circumstances, for this is God's will for you in Christ Jesus. 1 Thessalonians 5:16

There is great joy in belonging to God. Every day we are blessed to know him and to be known by Him. I was listening to some songs the other day that were based on the themes of thanksgiving and forgiveness. My reaction to them was rather odd considering that each song outlined all that we do wrong, but they did also point out the patience and love of God. As I listened, I thought of how different my life would be if it hadn't been for God.

I know a woman with whom I have a lot in common. At least our pasts are very similar. She's a fun woman with a good heart, but she has built a lot of really big walls around her. She says and does things that come from the hurt she experienced in her past. That happens because she still carries it with her.

It is much easier to see how far you have come when you see what might have been. My friend and I often reach the same conclusions but then deal with the knowledge so differently. Why? The answer is simple. God. I believe He loves me and wants what is best for me, and she does not.

Driving down the road today listening to those songs made me think of my friend and once again I wanted her to have what I have. I wanted her to know what I know which is that if God is for me no one can come against me and win. He loves me just as I am. He loves her too; she just can't see it.

It is great to be able to praise God when things are good and better still to praise him when they are bad. Things may get bad, but God is good all the time. He knows each of us and everything we have ever done. He forgives before we even ask and He never ever leaves our sides. I'm never sure how people who don't know Him get up day after day. I am so grateful that He has called me, and that He has allowed me to share Him with each one of you.

In Everything

Give thanks in all circumstances because this is God's will for you in Christ Jesus. 1 Thessalonians 5:18

Is this verse asking us to live like an ostrich? Are we to bury our heads in the sand saying "Everything's fine" when in fact it isn't? No. This verse does not call us to live in denial. It calls us to live in trust. As Christians our ultimate goal is to be as close to God as possible. The closest person to the Father is Jesus. I have never known anyone who has suffered as Jesus suffered. I know people who have endured hardships and terrors that I cannot begin to imagine. I have endured circumstances that others believe to be overwhelming. None of us endures alone. We have the Holy Spirit, and we have Christian brothers and sisters standing by our sides.

Our Lord asks us to give thanks in everything. He doesn't ask us to deny the existence of a problem. Nor does He ask us to give thanks for the suffering. We are not instructed to be thankful *for* illness, loss, hard times, or abuse. We are told to be thankful *in* those times.

How can we be thankful when our bodies are racked with pain, or the pressures of this world are crushing our spirits? We can be thankful because God is still God, and He will not let us be destroyed. We will feel the heat from the fire but we will not be burned. That fire will certainly not consume us.

God is perfect. He knows what is right and best, all ways always. We see a glimpse. He sees it all. We do not have to be thankful for sickness or torment of any kind. We can always be thankful that Jesus left us a Comforter.

Next time you are in the midst of something that you feel you truly cannot endure, try thanksgiving. Say, "Lord, I know you are here. I know you will never leave me. I know you will take this suffering that was meant to harm me, and You will work it for my good." He is. He won't. He will. The Holy Spirit will never leave us. The Comforter is at our service 24/7/365.

Whether you feel love, terror, or desperation, give thanks. God is for you. No one else can win. He is the Victor, and we are His. In everything give thanks.

Overnight Sensation

He said to them, "It is not for you to know the times or dates my Father has set by His own authority." Acts 1:7

You know them well—the performers who formerly unknown are now on every magazine, every talk show, and every billboard. You can't go anywhere without seeing or hearing about this new marvel. We wonder where they were before. Were they pouring coffee somewhere and suddenly decided that performing sounded good? We call them overnight successes.

They call themselves hard working, patient, and broke. Yes they did pour coffee, wait tables, wash floors, or walk dogs the entire time they were pursuing the dream. We never see what went on before the big discovery.

So it is in our Christian walk. One minute we are struggling along simply putting one foot in front of the other praying for that breakthrough—be it spiritual, occupational, financial, or personal. All the people around us think, "Wow! That was quick!" but we know better. We know about the hours spent in prayer, the pruning of our beings, and the days we wondered if anything could ever change. We know the death grip it took to hang on in faith when every thing else pointed away from the dream.

I have no idea why one struggling actress makes it, and the other doesn't. I also have little insight as to why some prayers are answered quickly, and others require more patience. I do know that God is faithful. He is never ever late, and He never changes. If He has promised you something, it will come to pass—suddenly—after days, weeks, months, or years of prayer. Then the people around you will say, "Wow! That was quick!"

Clothing

Therefore, as God's chosen people, holy and dearly loved, clothe yourselves with compassion, kindness, humility, gentleness and patience. Colossians 3:12, NIV

Put on therefore as the elect of God, holy and beloved, bowels of mercies, kindness, humbleness of mind, meekness and longsuffering. Colossians 3:12, KJV

Normally I like the more modern translations of the Bible. The wording is easier to follow in some cases. Sometimes the modern language is a little more to the point, harsher, which draws the line more clearly. This verse is great in both translations, but the wording in the King James leaves no wiggle room at all. "Bowels of mercies . . ." The New King James has changed that to "tender mercies" but kept the "long-suffering."

The use of the word "bowels" brings all kinds of images to mind but mostly the idea of deep-seatedness. We refer to the bowels of a building and mean the darkest, hardest place to find. We refer to the bowels of our body usually in connection with distress. The word does not have a sunny side. It is a sobering expression, but even that pales in comparison to long-suffering.

Patience is tough. Working with small children, being married, driving a car, being a member of any organized group, being a friend—all require patience. We talk about it all the time. We pray for more and admire it in others. Think about the fact that it is interchangeable with the word "long-suffering." Oh dear. Why do we have to talk about bowels, patience, long-suffering?

Our pastor always says that when you are reading and you see a therefore see what it's there for. The answer to that for this verse lies in the verses before it. Verses 5-11 tell us to put to death anything that separates us from Christ. They clearly define what has to be stripped away from us. Having stripped it all away, we would then be naked and *therefore* need to clothed. So, therefore, we are to dress in compassion, kindness, patience, etc. We aren't to do it casually either. We are to dig deep get into the bowels of change and become the people God created us to be.

It isn't easy, and sometimes it really hurts, but the rewards are well worth the effort. The best news is that we don't have to do it alone. Every bit of grace that we need to clothe ourselves this way is given to us by the power of the Holy Spirit. We aren't drawing on our own strength. Then we would surely fall and fail. We are calling on resurrection power. We are "God's chosen people, holy and dearly loved"; therefore, that power is available to us. We would be foolish not to use it.

Five Minutes

Now brothers about times and dated we do not need to write to you, for you know very well that the day of the Lord will come like a thief in the night. While people are saying, "Peace and safety," destruction will come on them suddenly, as labor pains on a pregnant woman, and they will not escape. 1 Thessalonians 5:1-3

What are you doing right now? Is it what you want Jesus to find you doing when He returns to take us home? How about five minutes ago? What were you doing then? Many people swear that they ascribe to the "live each day as if it were your last" theory. Maybe they do. I think if I knew for sure that this were my last five minutes, I would want to be with my husband and our family—not at the grocery store, doctor's office, or work. Yet I have to go to all of those places.

Each of us has a job to do. Most of us have several jobs to do. Are any of them what you would want to be doing if you knew this was your last day here? The truth is, it may be. We don't know the date or time when we will be called home.

When my children were small, I always gave them a five-minute warning before we left a friend's house or the playground. It was a chance for them to do or say that one last important thing. Most of us will not get that warning before we die. We need to live as closely as possible to Christ. Whatever I am doing when He comes for me, I want it to glorify Him.

My husband and I have a really nice marriage. I thank God every day for Otto, but like most other people, we sometimes argue. I still thank God for him, but I usually add something about being irritated. That's okay. God already knows how I feel. The important thing is not to walk away from Otto for work or any other reason without saying good-bye, I love you, have a blessed day. I don't know as I leave if I will ever see his precious face again, and I do not want the last thing he sees on my face to be anger.

Every minute is a gift from God, even when they are unpleasant. We need to be thankful for each minute and live it with the knowledge that it is a priceless gift. It is the one thing people want when they lose a loved one, just one more chance to say something that feels left unsaid. Don't wait until you think it may be your last chance, live well now.

Amazing Love

> Lord, I have heard of your fame;
> I stand in awe of your deeds, O Lord
> Renew them in our day,
> in our time make them known;
> in wrath remember mercy. Habakkuk 3:2

Then Peter got down out of the boat, walked on the water and came toward Jesus. But when he saw the wind, he was afraid and beginning to sink, he cried out, "Lord, save me!"

Immediately Jesus reached out his hand and caught him. "You of little faith," he said, "why did you doubt?"

And when they climbed into the boat the wind and the waves died down. Then those who were in the boat worshiped him, saying, "Truly you are the Son of God." Matthew 14:29b-33

Then he went up and touched the coffin, and those carrying it stood still. He said, "Young man, I say to you get up!" The dead man sat up and began to talk and Jesus gave him back to his mother.

They were all filled with awe and praised God. Luke 7:14-16a

The disciples went and woke him saying, "Master, Master, we're going to drown!"

He got up rebuked the wind and the raging waters; the storm subsided, and all was calm. "Where is your faith?" he asked his disciples.

In fear and amazement they asked one another, "Who is this? He commands even the winds and the water, and they obey him." Luke 8:24-25

It is hard to believe that with day-after-day exposure to the incredible power of Jesus, the disciples could still be amazed, and yet they were. They were amazed that He could calm the waters, heal the sick, and raise the dead. They stood in awe when He spoke to the Pharisees as if they were common men and not very intelligent. They saw His works, His gifts day after day and several times a day, and they were flabbergasted. We read those accounts and wonder how they could be shocked. They were with Jesus who is almighty, all-powerful, and perfect, of course; enormous things are happening around them. But are we any different?

Jesus is in our midst too. He left His Holy Spirit to be with us until He returns to take us home. Daily we see His majesty, and we are worse than the disciples because we aren't always amazed. Someone receives healing, and we credit medical science. A marriage, friendship, or parent-child relationship is restored; and we acknowledge a counselor or therapist. We see the sun rise every day and explain it by planetary movement. It rains, and we look for the high-low pressure system. Once in a while, we call any one of those occurrences a miracle, but for the most part we take it all for granted as part of life.

Rarely are we amazed by God, stunned into speechlessness. We find it odd that the men who traveled everywhere with Jesus could still be amazed. Of course He could heal the sick, raise the dead, calm a storm—why be amazed?

They were amazed because to them, He was a peer, one of the guys. They tended to forget that He was the Messiah, and when He demonstrated that fact, they were amazed. We see that same power at work in our own lives and ignore it or take it for granted. Jesus is the Messiah. His power is dazzling, amazing, awe inspiring, and it is still here. It isn't odd that the disciples who saw that power in action every day were amazed. It is odd that we are not.

Today be dazzled, be delighted by the vast power of God. Stand in awe of the mighty works Jesus has done and can still do. Don't be immune to the extravagant love of Christ.

The Value of Suffering

> Now there were some present at that time who told Jesus about the Galileans whose blood Pilate had mixed with their sacrifices. Jesus answered, "Do you think that these Galileans were worse sinners than the other Galileans because they suffered this way? I tell you, no! But unless you repent, you too will all perish. Or those eighteen that died when the tower in Siloam fell on them—do you think they were more guilty than all the others living in Jerusalem? I tell you, no! But unless you repent you too will all perish." Luke 13:1-5

Suffering is never good. Even when someone has really offended me, I might want him or her to suffer too, but when it happens, I wish it weren't happening. It's hard to go through suffering and harder still to watch someone we love go through it. In order to make it slightly more acceptable, I try to rationalize it, find a reason. Sometimes there isn't any explanation. It is a little easier when I can see that the pain is the consequence of sin, but too often I can't see any value in the suffering. That isn't because there is no value; it is because I am shortsighted.

The image of Jesus that comes to mind easily for most people is gentle Jesus, a meek, mild loving savior who only wants us to eat cake and be happy. Wrong! Sweet gentleness is only a part of Jesus's makeup. He wants more than anything for us to be saved, to live well, and to come home. He hates anything that gets in the way. He is also very realistic. It's easy for him because unlike us, he sees the whole picture. He knows where we will spend eternity if we are saved and where we will go if we are not.

When we see illness or tragedy of any kind, we want to tie it up with a bow of rationalization. We have all learned cause and effect. We want to take an untenable situation and make it plausible. We *need* a reason. We are like the disciples and townspeople who wanted to know why the man was born blind. They asked Jesus, "Was it his sin or his parents?" "Neither," was his answer. We don't look far enough.

All of humanity is connected because God created us all. When Adam and Eve fell, they did it for everyone of us. When we can't readily identify a cause for suffering, when it seems ridiculously useless, we have to remember our family tree goes *way* back. We call it original sin. Look at today's advertising—"better than the original," "new and improved," "advanced"—all those words to describe products or events that have out grown the original. Sin has also grown. We have bigger and better (?) approaches to sin every day. As sin grows, the consequences grow as well.

There will be times when suffering makes no sense at all to us. Be assured if God stays His hand to allow something or even causes it to be, there is a very good reason. Like all of us with our children, He knows what is best for us even when we can't see it. Perhaps it is easier to deal with suffering when we know there is a purpose to the most seemingly purposeless events. The absolute bottom line is that our Father loves us, and at the end of our days He wants us all to come home.

Majestic Skies

And God said, "Let there be an expanse between the waters to separate the water from water." So God made the expanse and separated the water under the expanse from the water above it. And it was so. God called the expanse "sky." And there was evening and morning—the second day. Genesis 1:6-8

The heavens declare the glory of God; the skies proclaim the work of his hands. Psalm 19:1

The sky is so pretty this morning. It's early, and yet the sun is so bright. The sky was very different a few weeks ago as I drove this same path to work. It wasn't as at all pretty, but it was magnificent. There was a heavy gray cloud cover that was moving so fast it caught my eye. Under the rapidly moving clouds the sun tried valiantly to shine. Every so often a glimpse would appear only to be swallowed again by the clouds. The morning had an eerie feel. The sky looked as it did due to shoestring effects of Hurricane Katrina. As I was watching an analogous sky many Americans were dying or being displaced. It impacted me then and I knew there was a message. I didn't fully understand until this morning when I drove through bright blue skies.

God never changes. The sun doesn't either. It is up in the sky shining whether we see it fully or not. Some days clouds roll over it and cover it up; but even so the rays stick out a little, the clouds shift, and for a second we see the sun. Other days it shines so brightly we can barely stand to look up. That seems very similar to my relationship to God. Maybe it does to you too.

There are dark days in every life. We can't see or feel the presence of God, and yet He is there. He never changes. His love never ceases. The sun shines whether we see it or not. On that gray morning, I was awed by how fast the clouds were moving and by the quirky glimpses of the sun.

Just as the clouds move quickly over the sun one day, obliterate it the next, and are obliterated by it the day after that, so is our communion with God. One day our troubles move all around trying to block our view of His majesty, but if we keep our eyes on Jesus, we can see Him in the midst of any storm. The next day those troubles may be just a little more intense, and we will not be able to see our Savior nor feel the comforting warmth of His presence. Another day brings that special blessing of feeling Him at our side all day long and of seeing His mighty hand smoothing everything around us.

No matter how the sky looks, the sun is up there. No matter how our day looks, the Son is in it with us.

The gray sky with the swiftly moving clouds was beautiful in an eerie sort of way. This morning's bright blue sky is more traditionally beautiful. The days that are obviously blessed are more comfortable than those that great present challenge, but there is beauty in pain as well as comfort. Blue skies or gray, happiness or tears—our God reigns.

Shark Bait

> From inside the fish Jonah prayed to the Lord his God. He said,
> "In my distress I called to the Lord
> and he answered me.
> From the depths of the grave I called for help,
> and you listened to my cry."
> Jonah 2: 1-2

We sing a song in our classroom about fish or maybe "sea life" is a better term. It's a cute little song that gently presents the concept of survival of the fittest. Tuna (I think) swallows sweet little slippery fish, tuna by octopus, etc., until the humongous whale is OH NO! swallowed by the Great white shark. That's it, and there is no more. Bye-bye humongous whale, octopus, tuna, and whoever else is fool enough to cross paths with the great white. It may seem crazy to you, but that little song reminded me of our Christian faith.

So many things would like to swallow us whole, consuming us, and destroying our faith; and they would succeed if like the fish, tuna, and even whale, we had no protector. There is no giant hand in the ocean pushing the shark away. In fact, the giant hand set that pattern in motion, big fish feed on little fish. It works for fish, birds, and other members of the animal kingdom. It does not work for the future members of God's kingdom. For us, He has an entirely different plan.

Stronger Christians are called to protect the weaker brothers and sisters (Matthew 25:40) and One greater than anything protects us all. The world is an ugly place right now. Our Lord may well reign with us, but the enemy has a lot of power in this world, and he is not afraid to use it. We are daily faced with choices and challenges that could take our focus off of our Savior. Once the focus has shifted, we are in danger of OH NO! being swallowed by the Great White Shark. The good news is that even then God can rescue us. If you aren't sure, you believe that check with Jonah. All it takes to receive rescue is to sincerely ask for it.

There is a Great White Shark swimming in our water, and he brought his little friends who are not too friendly to us. There is also a fisherman willing to gut that shark and all his little friends to set us free. Don't forget for a minute that if the Son has set you free, you are free indeed (John 8:36).

Get Out of the Way

> Meanwhile, Saul was still breathing out murderous threats against he Lord's disciples. He went to the high priest and asked him for letter to the synagogues in Damascus, so that if he found any there who belonged to the Way, whether men or women, he might take them as prisoners to Jerusalem. As he neared Damascus on his journey, suddenly a light from heaven flashed around him. He fell to the ground and heard a voice say to him, "Saul, Saul why do you persecute me?" Acts 9:1-4

I have four children and three in-law children. I want them all to be close to Christ. I pray for them, and often I will say to our Lord, "Whatever it takes." My son Jeffrey and I have had many chats about ending up under the horse instead of on it. Sometimes it takes something very dramatic. I know that, and I understand it; but when it comes to my kids, I don't know if I can watch it.

One of my sons was very heavy on my heart the other day. I have great concern for much of his current situation. I prayed that our Lord would be bold with him, asking for a Saul experience if necessary. I asked as I often do to stay out of God's way. The love and concern I feel for my children can be a problem when I want to shelter them from the very thing that could wake them up. I thought about Saul. What if his mother had been on that road to Damascus? Would she have run to his side as he lay under the horse? Would her chatter be about seatbelts and horse safety? Would her questions about broken bones and sobriety have drowned out God's voice?

Instead of hearing "why are you persecuting me," would Saul have heard "I told you to get those horseshoes checked"? We all want what we see as best for those we love. Only God knows what is truly best for each of us. When praying for our children, spouses, family members, or friends, it is important to remember the best prayer we can pray is, "Your will be done."

Attitude Is Everything

But my God shall supply all your need. Philippians 4:19

In an article I was reading, Corrie Ten Boom quoted this Scripture. The Scripture is powerful on its own; but when used by a woman who housed the hunted, watched as her friends, and family were tortured and lived in concentration camps, it is magnified to the extreme. Corrie Ten Boom is an example of trust I would love to live up to but doubt that I can even come close. Her life was filled with disaster through no fault of her own. She is the personification of the term "innocent victim," and yet she never saw herself as a victim.

The children I work with are trying to earn the privilege of going on a field trip. To do so each, child must secure a rung on his/her fireman's ladder each day. They obtain the rung by reaching the day's goals. It is a very easily obtainable reward, or so it seems. The rules are simple to begin with and simpler still for those less-capable children. The biggest obstacle is attitude. I have said to them several times this week, "Attitude is everything." I have even had them repeat it back. I'm not sure they get it, but I know it's true.

If the kids would realize that every other child in the room has feelings and desires too, there would be no doubt that everyone would be on that field trip. As it stands, we wonder each day how many are actually going to make it. That puzzles the adults in the group because we honestly thought we had made it as easy as possible. I can't help but wonder if God feels the same way about us. There are after all only ten commandments. When He saw that we couldn't get that, He made it even easier. He sent His Son to die for us so that we don't have to earn a thing. Love the Lord your God and accept His gift.

Just as Ronna, Cheryl, Alaina, and I are puzzled that some of our students cannot understand "just keep your hands to yourself, and others have trouble with no pushing," God wonders why we can't understand His guidelines. It is so simple: Love the Lord your God.

The key for us is the same as the key for our students; attitude is everything. If I have an attitude of faith, if I truly believe that if God is for me no one dare be against me, if I know His will is best, then my attitude will be grateful no matter what comes my way. I won't stomp my feet and yell, "Leave me alone." I will graciously accept whatever comes my way.

Corrie Ten Boom knew that attitude is everything. She lived with an attitude of servitude and love. If you asked her, she would tell you her sister Bessie did an even better job with the attitude challenge. I don't know about you, but if I can even get in Corrie's attitude neighborhood, I will count myself successful. If attitude truly is everything, then it is in our hands to determine what each challenge will bring. Perhaps we should start with answering the call to meet any circumstance with the words used in the Anglican Church's christening ceremony, "With God's help." I think that may be how Corrie did things and it certainly worked for her.

Fear and Trembling

Continue to work out your salvation with fear and trembling, for it is God who works in you to will and to act according to his good purpose. Philippians 2:12-13

With fear and trembling... Often when I see a Christian brother or sister that seems so together, so sure of his/her faith, I feel inadequate. I wonder what is wrong with me that given the same truth I cannot walk in the same level of trust and contentment. That feeling has caused me to miss out on prayer support that was waiting there for me. I didn't want to seem weak, unable to faithfully meet a challenge. That line of thought is a huge tool for the devil, and praise God He has rescued me from it.

Every Christian has moments of triumph and failure, strength, and weakness. The problem starts because we are viewing other Christians from the outside. When the trials come in my life, I feel them, and my reaction to them and being my own harshest critic, I believe that my reaction is unfaithful. I can only see my Christian friends. I have no idea what they are feeling. They appear to be handling challenges better than I do, so I judge myself as inferior. Satan can then reinforce that belief and the slip down the slide to sin begins.

God does not expect us to be perfect. He knows we aren't. In this quote from Philippians, St. Paul uses the words "fear" and "trembling." He knows there is an enemy prowling around him sniffing at that fear wanting to devour him. That same enemy is sniffing around you and me. He would very much like to devour us too, and when we chastise ourselves for feeling fearful, he gets the chance at least to nibble if not devour.

Any Christian who has been in a particularly fearful place will tell you they felt that fear. The difference between those of us who believe and those who don't is simple. We may feel fear, and we may tremble, but those things send us rushing to our Father's side. Those without faith succumb to the fear. Next time a situation arises that terrifies, you don't despair. It isn't a lack of faith. It is an opportunity to exercise your faith and to invite your Christian friends to help you.

Remember in not asking for prayer, we deny our prayer supporters the opportunity to receive the grace that comes from praying for another person's needs. Refusing to ask for help in times of fear and trembling is a position of pride, and we all know that pride goes before a fall. Fear that fall more than any challenge who encounter because that fall, that prideful fall, is without grace. It is okay to feel fear and to tremble as long as that fear and trembling take us closer to the throne.

Disabled?

Not only so, but we ourselves, who have the firstfruits of the Spirit, groan inwardly as we wait eagerly for our adoption as sons, the redemption of our bodies.

In the same way, the Spirit helps us in our weakness. We do not know what we ought to pray for, but the Spirit himself intercedes for us with groans that words cannot express. And he who searches our hearts knows the mind of the Spirit, because the Spirit intercedes for the saints in accordance to God's will.
Romans 8:23, 26-27

The idea of Helen Keller fascinates me. I don't understand how Annie Sullivan broke through nor had the patience to finger spell everything into the child's palm. What intrigues me most is what happened before Annie arrived. Helen was obviously of above-average intelligence, but how did her mind work? My thoughts come in words and mental images. Helen had never heard words. She had no visual images. I wonder where her thoughts came from and can only come up with one answer, God.

There is an account of Annie trying to teach Helen about God. Helen is said to have replied, "I know Him! I know Him!" How did she know Him? I knew Him first through what people told me and then through what I read myself. Helen had neither of those skills, hearing or reading, before Annie. I think Helen is a perfect example of Spirit-to-spirit communication. Her heart and soul could hear her Lord, and her spirit could *groan* an answer.

Often I hear people say they don't have time to read the Bible, or they don't understand it when they do. Some say they don't have time to go to church, or they don't know how to pray. They don't know God because they make no effort to know Him. They do not make themselves available to Him. For those people, their abilities have hindered spiritual progress. Helen's knowing God takes away any excuse a person may use to explain why they can't develop a relationship with God.

Our Lord will be known to any who seek Him. Maybe what we see as Helen's disabilities enable her to be still and hear that small still voice. Perhaps she was way ahead of the rest of us who measure time with God against time on the phone, with the TV, racing here and there. Helen couldn't see God's miracles, hear a worship song or a great sermon. She couldn't read a single word of the Bible. Her spirit called to her Father's spirit, and He answered her. Call to your Father. He will answer you too.

Attempted Deception

> Then Jesus was led by the Spirit into the desert to be tempted by the devil. After fasting for forty days and forty nights, he was hungry. The tempter came to him and said, "If you are the Son of God, tell these stones to become bread."
>
> Jesus answered, "Man does not live on bread alone, but on every word that comes from the mouth of God."
>
> Then the devil took him to the holy city and had him stand on the highest point of the temple. "If you are the Son of God," he said, "throw yourself down. For it is written,
>
> 'He will command his angels concerning you,
> and they will lift you up in their hands,
> so that you will not strike your foot against a stone.'"
>
> Jesus answered him, "It is also written; 'Do not put the Lord your God to the test.'" Matthew 4:1-7

Jesus was fully man while he was on this earth. If a young man were walking around today telling everyone the things Jesus told the people of his time, he'd be committed. In Jesus time, there weren't therapists on every corner. No one had time for psychoanalysis. The true crazies, the truly spirit, tortured were obvious. They had no ability to provide for their own needs. Jesus was different. He had a job. He wasn't running around half naked and babbling. Odd maybe, but was he insane? No. He didn't even seem as bizarre as John the Baptist, but by today's standards, Jesus would be certifiable. Some well-meaning person would stage an intervention and have him locked up.

God never changes. He is the same always. What about Satan? What if his tactics are the same? Consider Jesus's time in the desert. Was Satan telling him he was crazy? He says to Jesus, "*If* you are the Son of God." That little word "if" that causes us so much trouble is there in the desert with Jesus. Twice there in the desert Satan used it with Jesus. "*If* you are the Son of God." There was no "if" in it for Jesus. He knew He was God's own son.

Satan may have more at his disposal, more means to torture us, and get us to succumb; but his main weapon remains the same. If he can get us to doubt that we are truly children of God, then he will win. If we feel unloved by God, it isn't so difficult to hurt Him. We lose the feeling of disappointing our Father because we're convinced that He is not our Father. If he isn't our Father, then He doesn't really care about us anyway. Or so Satan would have us believe.

Satan's maneuvers didn't work with Jesus because He never doubted for a second that He was the beloved Son of God. The spirit that dwelt in Jesus making Him aware of His parentage dwells in us too if we let it. We can bow to the power of the Holy Spirit and live in the assurance that we are God's own, dearly loved children, or we can believe the lies of the enemy. The choice is ours. We don't have to believe Satan's lies even if he uses a family member or a fancy therapist to whisper them in our ears. The world may tell you that you are a little off center. That's okay. Today's world would have Jesus in a padded room. Be willing to be seen as a little odd. Just tell people you take after your Brother.

Knees or No Knees

Be joyful always pray continually; give thanks in all circumstances, for this is God's will for you n Christ Jesus. 1 Thessalonians 5:16-18

A friend of mine reminded me of a very simple truth the other day. It wasn't a revelation because it was something of which I was quite well aware. It was the source from which the information came that made it remarkable. This friend of mine is not a practicing Christian. She is an amazing woman who could and will do great things once God gets a grip on her but at the moment she's almost anti-God. To put it bluntly, she's a little ticked off with God and not ready to get over it. That's okay, she has a plateful of what looks like good reasons. That is why it was so profound to me to hear her affirm a simple truth that many people overlook.

She made a quirky remark to me, and I teased back that I obviously wasn't spending enough time on my knees for her. "You don't have to be on your knees to pray," she said. "Of course not," I replied. I then shared an incident from earlier in the day when I had not only not been on my knees but had been in a bit of a tempest situation.

She's right of course; you don't have to be on your knees. That would make the admonition to pray without ceasing (1 Thessalonians 5:17, KJV) a little hard to attain. Most of us have pretty busy days, and taking a quiet time with God requires planning. To me that quiet time is the most precious part of my day. The rest of the day would be much more difficult without that morning time I spend chatting or just sitting with my dad. That time enables me to cry out for help, praise, and/or bring everything to Him as I am walking through the day.

There are times for me when a situation is so big that the only place I want to be is on my knees. The enormity of the blessing or the challenge takes me to my knees to seek God and either praise or plead. There is a wonderful comfort in bowing before my Lord. The posture itself is prayer.

Pray without ceasing and without any concern about where you are or how your body is situated. Our Lord invites us to seek and find Him all day and all night. Once in a while, try it on your knees; besides pleasing God, it really irritates our enemy.

Empty Spaces

"When an evil spirit comes out of a man, it goes through arid places seeking rest and does not find it. Then it says, 'I will return to the place I left.' When it arrives, it finds the house unoccupied, swept clean and put in order. Then it goes and takes with it seven other spirits more wicked than itself. And they go in and live there. And the final condition of that man is worse than the first. That is how it will be with this wicked generation." Matthew 12:43-45

Once we recognize that what is in us is not good, that it is in fact evil, we want it gone. We pray fervently for whatever it is to be taken away. The idea of being without that pain or sin consumes us. We forget that when a thing is removed, it leaves an empty space.

Whenever I clean out my pantry or even rearrange it, I am amazed at how much space I really have. Of course within a day or two at best that space is filled. While I'm enjoying the look of that nice new opening, my family is putting their stuff in that very space. It goes on and on until one empty space has four occupants. The previous occupants are all shoved together to make room, and the pantry ends up more crowded than before I cleaned it out.

So it is with sin. We pray and pray for God to remove the strongholds, and when He does, we are so thrilled. We feel so relieved to be free of what formerly held us hostage; we forget to fill that empty space with Godly behavior, with prayer, or whatever God has planned for that space. The enemy doesn't appreciate being uprooted, but he does appreciate the nice airy niche we have created for him and back he comes; only this time he is not alone. The thing we saw as a problem now has friends. That one area we were complaining about has introduced its cousins, and now we're complaining even more.

It is important to pray that God will help us clean our spiritual house. It is just as important to pray to God to fill our lives with thoughts, behaviors, and activities that please him. Sometimes what we see as improvement is just breeding ground for more evil. We need to be careful to seek God for all of our decisions, to stand for something so that we won't fall for anything.

We need to attack our own demons one at a time. When we remove them, we need to lock that door.

Mighty Reference

A good name is more desirable than great riches; to be esteemed is better than silver or gold. Proverbs 22:1

"Our Father in heaven, hallowed be your name." Matthew 6:9b

A friend of mine said something the other day that hit me hard and has stayed with me. We were talking about her daughter who had used her dad's name as a reference. After stating that yes, she was trustworthy and that her father would back that statement, she demonstrated that she could not be trusted. When the fallout reached her mom, it wasn't pretty. That man may be dad to the girl, but he is my friend's husband, and she loves him dearly. It hurt her that his good name had been put into question by someone else's behavior. She said, "I told her if you're going to use your dad's name, you better follow through on your promise."

Follow through is tough. My gram was fond of the adage "The road to hell is paved with good intentions." It's a pithy little saying but true. Perhaps the daughter meant to follow through, but when it got tough, didn't even consider the reflection on Dad. Or maybe she knew she wouldn't be true to her word, but didn't care again with no concern for Dad.

Don't we do that with our Father? We call ourselves Christians. We use that label as an indicator of the foundation of our value systems and personalities. People who know us as Abba's children expect us to behave in ways that would please Him. They hold us to a higher standard. We use our Father's name as a reference, and sometimes, too many times, we don't follow through.

It may seem simplistic but it's true, we are only as good as our word. If we put someone else's name behind our words, we're saying I'm as good as my word *and* his word. Then when we fail, we call into question not only our character but also the character of the other person.

Think about your behavior. We can't let our actions bring shame to our Father's name.

Suffering

Some sat in darkness and the deepest gloom, prisoners suffering in iron chains, for they had rebelled against the words of God and despised the counsel of the Most High. Psalm 107:10-11

When we are suffering, we often want to see that as a shared experience with Christ. There are several worship songs that reference knowing the suffering of Christ. Sometimes we are suffering not because of a kinship with our Savior, but because we have sinned. Our pain then is due to rebellion, disobedience, or some other ignorance of Christ's will.

I do not see God sitting in a huge chair somewhere waiting for me to mess up so He can make me hurt. I am certain that is not how it works. No, I think when we sin, we put ourselves in the wrong frame of mind. Sometimes it is one colossal slip, and other times it one small misstep that leads to another and another until we have a very hard time getting up. Once in that place of pain, we find it easy to believe that God can't forgive us. Getting a person to think, "I've gone too far this time," is a great advantage for the enemy. It isn't true. Note **Romans 8: 38-39, NKJV, "For I am persuaded that neither death nor life nor angels nor principalities nor powers, nor things to come nor height nor depth nor any other created thing shall be able to separate us from the love of God which is in Christ Jesus our Lord.** Nothing we do, don't do, say, or think can take God's love from us. We can take ourselves from Him and will if we believe the lies that Satan wants us to believe.

If we allow Satan to convince us that some action of ours will cause Jesus to turn His back on us, we will be lost. We need to remember what that back looked like on Jesus's last day, covered with slash marks and blood. We need to remember His suffering and take part in it for the grace that comes from knowing Him in that suffering.

It is important to understand to the best of our ability the agony of the Cross. That torture had a great purpose. Suffering because of an act of selfishness on our part has no redeeming grace. If we must suffer and Scripture says that we will have tribulation in this world, let us all pray that it is suffering with Christ and not suffering because of offending Him.

Precious Gifts

For God so loved the world that he gave his one and only Son that whoever believes in him shall not perish but have eternal life. John 3:16

Remember this whoever sows sparingly will also reap sparingly, and whoever sows generously will also reap generously. Each man should give what he has decided in his heart to give, not reluctantly or under compulsion, for God loves a cheerful giver. 2 Corinthians 9:6-7

Every holiday and birthdays, it's the same thing. One of my children will tease me about my reaction to their gifts. My children are older now and having been giving me store bought gifts for several years. The joke usually occurs as they discuss the amount of time and thought they put into whatever they are giving me. They tease about how they would give me handmade, lopsided, articles accompanied by cards with misspelled words, and I would be thrilled. They seem to think that delight that I felt in receiving their gifts was put on for their benefit. They believe that because they either don't have children or have children too small to give gifts. It is hard for them to understand the pleasure didn't come from the gift but from the giver. Looking at those unique offerings, my heart swelled with love for the creator of the oddly shaped, off-center masterpiece.

The funny thing is that as they tease me, I know they are thinking how much better today's gifts are than the ones they presented as children. They don't realize that the value of the gifts is the same today as it was then. The significance is not in the gift itself but in the giver. Last year I received my first birthday gift from my first grandchild. He sent me a beautiful flower arrangement. When it arrived, I assumed it was from my husband and was quite touched when I read the card. My son had thought to send flowers from his son. When I called to thank him, he didn't take credit. He said, "That sneak. So that's what he was doing with my cell phone and credit card." Joey was eleven months old at the time. There was joy in receiving the flowers but so much more joy in sharing that silly moment with my son.

In the way I receive gifts, I believe I am a lot like my dad. When we cheerfully offer gifts to God, He is happy to receive them. We have nothing that He needs but everything He wants because what He wants is us, ourselves. Everything else we give Him is extra. Much like when my little ones presented me with gifts they'd made from things I purchased or gifts they had purchased from money I had given, when we give to God we are using His resources.

Our Father gave us the best lesson in giving when He gave Jesus for us. That gift illustrated the willingness He had to give us His all and to be all for us. He uses each of us to teach each other about graceful receiving. We've all been given an odd, unusable gift. What makes the difference in our reaction to it is how we feel about the giver.

Going back to my birthday flowers, the story doesn't have a happy ending. A few days after my birthday, I received some very disappointing news about my son. I wondered if the sweet gesture was just a way to soften the blow. I don't know that for sure, but it certainly took the pleasure out of the gift.

I can't read my son's heart, but our Father can read ours. The Lord loves a cheerful giver, so give Him whatever you can, but make sure you give with a smile and an open heart.

Pigs

When he arrived at the other side in the region of the Gadarenes, two demon-possessed men coming from the tombs met him. They were so violent that no one could pass that way. "What do you want with us, Son of God?" they shouted. "Have you come to torture us before the appointed time?"

Some distance from them a large herd of pigs were feeding. The demons begged Jesus, "If you drive us out send us into the herd of pigs."

He said to them, "Go!" So they came out and went into the pigs and the whole herd rushed down the steep bank into the lake and died in the water. Those tending the pigs ran off, went into the town and reported all this including what had happened to the demon-possessed men. Then the whole town went out to meet Jesus. And when they saw him, they pleaded with him to leave their town.
Matthew 8:28-34

Two men filled with demons call out to Jesus to free them, and He does. He sends the demons into some pigs. I have always wondered what the owner of the pigs thought about that. It would make sense to me if the last verse of the chapter read that the pig man came out and asked Jesus to leave. After all, those pigs were a part of his livelihood if not all of it. That isn't the way it reads. No, the pig man takes off and tells the rest of the town what has happened. It says that after the townspeople heard about what Jesus did for the demon-possessed men, *that* is when they begged Him to leave their town.

It makes no sense. The pig man is not livid because he lost his pigs. He's terrified because Jesus was able to free the demon-possessed men. The loss of income is not foremost on his mind. It is the power of Jesus. Would that we were all inclined to think that way, not of our purses but of the power of God. We aren't anymore inclined that way than the people of Jesus's day.

The people had seen great light shine in their darkness, but they were not drawn to it. No, they were terrified. They wanted Him gone, out, go away! Thanks but no thanks to you, sir. Don't save us anymore. Sometimes we are no different.

We too see the awesome glory of God. We glimpse His magnificence, and we cower. We are frightened. Why? Who doesn't want that kind of power working in his/her life? The answer is people who aren't sure what that means. If God can throw a whole herd of pigs off a cliff what else can He do? What will He do if I mess up?

We are drawn to the Light, but when it shines too brightly, it hurts our eyes. What if we have to make changes to live in that Light? What if I there is something in me that He sees and wants to put into pigs? What if I want to keep that thing?

Majesty is a double-edged sword. God has the power to be merciful and the power to excise anything that causes Him pain. If we are unsure of our actions, we may be unsure as to which side of that sword we will see.

We think if we'd been in that village, we would have run to Jesus side to ask Him to help us. Maybe we would run away, too afraid that He would see us for what we truly are.

Trust in God's mercy. Praise Him for His awesome power that strengthens and saves.

Whatever

I will give you the keys of the kingdom of heaven; *whatever* you bind on earth will be bound in heaven and *whatever* you loose on earth shall be loosed in heaven. Matthew 16:19 (emphasis mine)

Whatever! If you have children, teach children, or have any communication with children, you know the word whatever has taken on a whole new life. It is usually spoken with great disdain and little patience. It says, in a word, "I'm finished listening to you, your words are unimportant, I don't care what you think." And we say it in a myriad of other less-than-compliant things. The connotation now is very far out from the original meaning.

There is another truer meaning of the word "whatever." It means anything and everything. If your response to someone is, "I can do *whatever* you need." You better be ready to do whatever. When we say those words to God, we cannot begin to imagine what "whatever" might entail.

We might feel a little intimidated when we pray, do with me *whatever* you will; but if we truly trust our Lord, it shouldn't be scary. Whatever He wants is what is best for us. We pray whatever assuming that now the test will come. Sometimes it may mean that now we're open to the blessing we formerly thought we didn't deserve. There is the earn-it attitude in some of us that thinks that whatever has to be a challenge or a sacrifice. "Whatever" is simply what it is.

Look at the way Jesus uses the word: whatever we bind on earth, whatever we loose on earth. He is saying whatever in an all-encompassing way too. His words are very promising. If we are his, we have the keys to the kingdom, and *whatever* we do in His will will meet with success.

Don't use it as a throw-away word. "Oh sure, whatever." Use it as a promise. "I am yours, Lord, whatever."

Anno Domini

> **Lord, I have heard of your fame;**
> **I stand in awe of your deeds, O Lord.**
> **Renew them in our day,**
> **in our time make them known;**
> **in wrath remember mercy. Habakkuk 3:2**

I was sitting in a classroom the other day when a child of about eleven asked a visiting speaker if there were people on the Earth in year 1. The man nodded his head yes. The boy repeated, "There were people here in year 1?" The man said yes and quickly moved on to something else. It seemed an odd question to me because I was educated in a school where everything was taught from the perspective of biblical truths. We all understood the way time was counted BC, before Christ, and AD, anno Domini or the year of the Lord. I was raised to know that even time revolved around the birth of Christ. The boy asking the question may come from a Christian home, but the man answering the questions either didn't know BC and AD or was not about to give that answer in a public school.

The episode brought two things to mind for me. First, that though I may not agree with all the "religion" I was taught in school, I am very grateful that I was given a lot of information about God in an historical sense. Second, that the politically correct world can deny God all day long, but time after time He rears His magnificent head, and there is nothing that can be done to stop Him. Time is marked in Christ terms. People love to quote the "Golden Rule." Many cliches are actually paraphrased Bible verses. We even have laws that treat Sunday differently than the other six days.

Anyone who wants to can deny God's existence. Unenlightened people can lobby to remove prayer from schools and the word God from the Pledge of Allegiance and money, but God will still be prevalent in all that we do. In small ways that many people don't even notice, God leaves His mark. His majesty touches everything. Even when things look so awful that we believers wonder where He is; He is there. Nothing is beyond Him.

I wish that child would have asked me his question. It would have opened a door for me and maybe for him. It is sad to me that children are being taught about the mysteries and wonders of life without being taught about the Creator. That question made me even more aware that as Christians we have to live the Gospel to the best of our ability because more and more there are places where we are asked not to talk or teach about it. Walk as loudly as you can and praise God for every opportunity you have to share His truth.

Emotions

I do not understand what I do. For what I want to do I do not do, but what I hate I do. And if I do what I do not want to do, I agree that the law is good. As it is it is no longer I that do it, but it is sin living in me. Romans 7:15-17

If you can relate to this verse, you know there is somewhere within you a place that does not hate the sin. We may hate the fact that it is sin but there is a part of us that enjoys the behavior. We hate the after effects or the shame that comes with it, but in the moment of sin there is some pleasure, or we wouldn't keep repeating it.

The key then is to recognize how we feel when we are engaged in the sin, not how we feel toward the sin. Then we need to be open with our Lord. We need to pray that He will take away the emotion that holds us captive.

Try this prayer:

> Lord, I know that I am offending you in this, and I hate that.
> Some part of me enjoys this, but I want to stop. Please
> help me to give it all to you. Remove it and replace it with a behavior
> that is pleasing to You. Amen.

In that way, we recognize our weakness, our slavery to the emotion, and we give it over to the one who saves us. Nothing is greater than God. He is above all. No matter how tight a grasp any activity or behavior has on us, God can set us free if we trust Him. When we repeatedly fall into the same sin, we begin to hate ourselves. If there is a pleasant side to that sin, we feel even worse. Satan will use that against us to keep us down.

Emotions are a very strong motivator. Often God uses our emotions to get us into the right place. Satan uses them to keep us in the wrong place. The difference is that God takes us past our emotions, into faith, into discipleship. Satan likes us to stay at that surface level where we are so easily controlled. When we give the reins of our emotions to God, we cripple Satan. We know that God is on our side, and with Him on our side we win.

Seeking God's Favor

> Because the gracious hand of our God was on us, they brought us Sherebiah, a capable man, from the descendants of Mahli son of Levi, the son of Israel, and Sherebiah's sons and brothers, 18 men.
> Ezra 8:18

"Because the gracious hand of our God was on us" something they needed was provided. That makes sense. God loves us. Of course He wants to provide for us and protect us. How did the "gracious hand of God" come to be on Ezra and his group? Obedience.

The verses surrounding this one talk about Ezra's conscientious adherence to God's leading. In this passage, he is looking for men to take care of the temple. There weren't any Levites, the people normally assigned that task, so Ezra sought replacements, and they were supplied to him. A few verses later, Ezra is concerned about safe travel. He calls for a fast, a time to petition for God's favor. A little further into the same chapter, he consecrates items and men to God as a freewill offering. Ezra knew who was providing his bread and butter and assuring his safety. He had no problem pointing back to God.

Obedience and a willingness to recognize the favor of God are key to remaining in close relationship with Him. Our flesh balks at fasting. Our wallets shut down at a hint of the word tithe. Our hearts get a little hard when a worthy cause wants our time not our check. Then we need God's favor, and we forget that we have done precious little to stay close to Him.

It isn't a matter of what have you done for me lately? God doesn't work that way. He shows mercy to whom he chooses to show mercy (Exodus 33:19). The obstacle is in our own hearts. It isn't easy to ask for a favor of someone you barely know. When we are close to God, we place everything in His hands, under His protection, as Ezra did. When we don't know Him very well, we aren't even sure how to speak to Him.

Know the Lord your God well enough to be able to cry out with little more than a groan and know that He hears and understands. The more we obey and serve, the closer we will feel to our Father and the easier it will be to ask for His favor. Stay close to him that He may keep His gracious hand on you.

The Power of the Cross

> I pray also that the eyes of your heart may be enlightened in order that you may know the hope to which he has called you, the riches of his glorious inheritance in the saints, and his incomparably great power for us who believe. That power is like the working of his mighty strength, which he exerted in Christ when he raised him from the dead and seated him at his right hand in the heavenly realms.
> Ephesians 1:18-20

The Cross of Christ is the biggest symbol of the Christian faith. We sing songs, write essays and poems, and pray prayers of gratitude for an act we cannot begin to fathom. Every Christian I know understands the saving power of the Cross, but many of us, I would even say most of us, sometimes forget the full extent of that power.

It was not meant just to save us for eternity; although that certainly is more than enough. No, that power is for us to use daily. It is at our disposal when we are weak or frightened. When the challenges of life threaten to undo us, we have only to look to Calvary, and there we will find victory over death and over that nagging back pain. The victory claimed at the Cross unleashed a power that can and does overcome depression, illness, loneliness, poverty, and any other obstacle the enemy throws at us. We are victors because Jesus was willing to be, for a time, a victim.

Too many of us live lives identified by what has happened to or in us. We are the people who used to (fill in the sin) before we truly met Jesus. Who are we now? What does Jesus want us to do today with the power He offers to us? If we will draw on that power and allow it to dwell in us in the person of the Holy Spirit, nothing can defeat us. Circumstances may put us on our knees; that's okay. On our knees in sublimation, we are just that much closer to Christ.

Praise Jesus and thank Him every day for the sacrifice He made for us. Don't let it go to waste. Use the power of the Cross. Don't wait for eternity to enjoy what God has for you now.

The Perfect 911

A man in the crowd answered, "Teacher, I brought you my son, who is possessed by a spirit that has robbed him of speech. Whenever it seizes him, it throws him to the ground. He foams at the mouth, gnashes his teeth and becomes rigid. I asked your disciples to drive out the spirit but they could not."

"O unbelieving generation," Jesus replied, *"how long shall I stay with you? How long shall I put up with you?* Bring the boy to me."

So they brought the boy to him. When the spirits saw Jesus it immediately threw the boy into a convulsion. He fell to the ground and rolled around, foaming at the mouth.

Jesus asked the boy's father, "How long has he been like this?"

"From childhood," he answered. "It has often thrown him into fire or water to kill him. But if you can do anything take pity on us and help us."

"If you can," said Jesus. "Everything is possible for him who believes."

Immediately the boy's father exclaimed, "I do believe, help me overcome my unbelief!" Mark 9:17-23 (emphasis mine)

Do you wonder how often God feels this way about us? How long shall I put up with you? Jesus gave His life; our Father gave his Son so that we could go straight to him. No intermediary is necessary, we seek Jesus, and he takes it from there. Except we don't. We fret and figure trying to find solutions to our problems. In the last few years, I have gotten better about seeking God first, but I still tend to go elsewhere before going straight to the throne. Too often I run to my prayer partners without first seeking God's face.

Our Lord wants us to seek him first, not in a minute after I call the doctor, lawyer, plumber, etc. Seek him first. Even in an emergency as we are dialing 911, we can breathe that perfect prayer: "Your will be done."

How long should he put up with us? How precious is it to him when we say, "I do believe help me overcome my unbelief"? Any acknowledgement that God is in control will go along way to healing or fixing a problem.

The doctor, lawyer, plumber, etc., may be necessary; but how much more calmly can we present the problem when we know we've first given it to the Master? Even the selection of the professional is better when influenced by prayer.

Call the pros and absolutely call your prayer partners but make that first call, the first plea to the Lord. Don't make him ask how long he should put up with you even though we know his mercy never ends.

Better Than the Job

The next section was repaired by the men of Tekoa, but their nobles would not put their shoulders to the work under their supervisors. Nehemiah 3:5

There are historical explanations for this passage that explain the reluctance of these people to work. It isn't the event of the passage that I find intriguing. It is the wording: "The nobles wouldn't work." Before I looked into it further, I read those words as this group of people saw the work as beneath them. "I'm too good for this job." We've all heard someone say at some point and may have even said it ourselves. If you haven't said it out loud, maybe you've muttered it to yourself as you did some menial task. The time that stands out for me is when I was working in a retail store during high school. Believe me I knew I was too good for that job. I'm sure you can see it too. I was a teenager with all the knowledge that implies, and I definitely had better things to do than open a dressing room for boring women with nothing better to do than try on clothes two sizes too small for them.

That may be a slight exaggeration, but I think it makes the point. We can see ourselves as better than the tasks we are given to do. In a worldly sense, that thinking makes us negative and difficult to be around. In a spiritual sense, it makes us sinful in that we question the Creator, the perfect supervisor. He chooses us for certain tasks, and we shouldn't see ourselves as too good to do the work. We pray to be of service to him, and then when we are called, we grumble at foot washing, wanting instead to be a gatekeeper, or anything a tad more glamorous. We scoff at the idea that opening a door for someone we may not like is a sacrifice. We wonder if by smiling every day at that oh so unpleasant coworker we are really serving God. The answer is we are.

In ESE, my colleagues and I are often privileged to help a child eat, tie a shoe, unbutton a button, or wipe a dirty face. All of those are small things, but they answer the call of "whatever you do for the least." It may not seem like a privilege, but I promise you that it is. When we forget that, we can see ourselves as better than the job.

It is okay to want to serve God in a larger sense. I pray for that privilege every day. But while I wait for God's answer, while you wait for him to call you to something bigger, remember that we aren't too good for anything he calls us to do.

Don't be like the nobles. Work when you are called to work. Remember the promise made to those who are faithful in small matters. Big things are ahead.

Hurt Feelings

The third time Jesus said to him, "Simon, son of John, do you love me?" Peter was hurt because Jesus asked him the third time, "Do you love me?" He said, "Lord, you know all things; you know that I love you." Jesus said, "Feed my sheep." John 21:17

Jesus asks three times, "Do you love me?" Peter is hurt. Of course he loves Jesus. They are best friends. His heart is broken over what happened to Jesus and even more so over his part in it. Peter knows how he feels and is saddened that Jesus has to ask. Yet I think he understood that Jesus did have to ask. Just like us, Peter had been saying one thing with his words and saying something altogether different with his actions. Just like He does with us, Jesus gave Peter a chance to redeem himself. Peter had denied him three times, and so three times he was asked, "Do you love me?"

Our opportunities may not be so clear-cut. We stumble through repentance hoping to feel forgiven; sometimes we feel it, and sometimes we don't. Now and then Jesus treats us exactly the way He treated Peter putting us in a position to literally turn a decision or mistake around. Those times are great because, like Peter, we can see God's hand moving us toward the forgiven state. We feel reassured, happily established back in the fold. It's harder when we pray for forgiveness and just have to have faith that we are forgiven.

Maybe we feel the same hurt Peter felt. We wonder why God doesn't choose us for service more often or why we feel so separate from him. Our feelings are hurt, and then we remember what we've done. Our words are saying, "I love you Lord, and I want to be a good servant." At the same time our actions might be saying, "Not with her Lord, she's just nasty."

Peter felt the hurt of having to reestablish a relationship he treasured. We only read of that one time when Jesus called Peter on his sin. We are blessed to read other things about Peter and know that he stumbled often, so eager to please he ended up disappointing. We do it too, over and over, and we are offered the same chance to make our actions line up with our words. Our feelings may get hurt, but it is all a part of the process of learning to let our actions yell and our word whisper.

We all need to be humble enough to accept holy correction and guidance. Peter struggled with that a little, but in the end he was grateful for his second chance. I am grateful for the infinite number of chances that God has given me. It is good to know that his love and mercy endure forever.

Food for Thought

> Then Jesus began to denounce the cities in which most of his miracles had been performed, because they did not repent. "Woe to you, Korazin! Woe to you, Bethsaida! If the miracles that were performed in you had been performed in Tyre and Sidon, they would have repented long ago in sackcloth and ashes. But I tell you, it will be more bearable for Tyre and Sidon on the day of judgment than for you. And you, Capernaum, will you be lifted up to the skies? No, you will go down to the depths, If the miracles that were performed in you had been performed in Sodom, it would have remained to this day. But I tell you that it will be more bearable Sodom on the day of judgement than for you." Matthew 11:20-24

Why do some people get it, and others do not? I look at my own children, raised in the same household with the same moral code, same faith background, and I have to ask what makes them all so different in their response to God? My sons know a young man who has had multiple opportunities to embrace God. He seems to have no real interest in Christ but plenty in Christians.

The reason is that Christians are a great audience. We know we have the answer to any problem because Jesus is the answer. So we listen intently waiting for the right moment to say, "Well, if you really want to feel better . . ." The problem is for some people the solution falls on deaf ears. They aren't paying attention, just looking for the next listener. They don't want to feel better or be saved. They just want sympathy. In the victim state, they desire a soapbox, not a sermon.

In the passage from Matthew, Jesus talks about the miracles that the malcontent cities have witnessed and the lack of repentance there. He says that there are other cities that would have gotten the message given the same evidence and opportunity. I think this gives us a great way to pray for the miscreants in our own lives. We can plead with God to give them open hearts to see the error of their ways and not to be like Capernaum, Korazin, or Bethsaida. We want Ninevehs who once they heard from Jonah, repented and began anew.

I wonder though, what makes the difference? I still have no answer for why one man hears, and another doesn't. Why did Nineveh get it? Why didn't Bethsaida? There was Jesus in the midst of Bethsaida—raising the dead, healing the sick, giving sight to the blind—and still the people wanted something else.

There is a very old joke about a man trapped in a flood sitting on his roof praying for God's mercy. I'm sure you've heard it. The man refuses several viable offers of help because God is going to save him. When he drowns, he asks God about it, and God asks what more he wanted. So many people are like that; miracle after miracle happens right before their eyes, and still they question the sovereignty of God.

Don't sit blind on your roof refusing help. Pray for the stubborn sillies in your life to hear, truly hear the word of God. Pray that the majesty of Christ is evident in you and visible to those who cross your path. Be the rowboat and pray that the reluctant citizens in your life will jump on in.

A Wider View

Each of you should look not only to your own interests, but also to the interest of others. Philippians 2:4

Not very long ago, I was facing a very difficult situation in my life. A very dear sister in Christ made a suggestion to me. She said, "Pray for someone else in a similar position if possible and if not just someone you know who really needs prayer." I chose to pray for my niece who was facing similar hurts from a very different source. The results were amazing. My situation remained the same for a while and then worsened, but my joy in the Lord remained steadfast. Even as my heart was breaking, even in the midst of weeping over my loss, I could still feel the joyful presence of God.

A few months later, another friend was facing a very trying time with one of her children. I passed on the wisdom that I had received. Nearly a year later, she reminded of that wisdom and shared just how much it had helped her.

Too often we fall into self-pity because we believe that we are the only person ever to face such a challenge or catastrophe. No one has ever felt the pain we feel. Of that we are fairly sure. Even if they have, they are clearly better equipped to cope with it. We console ourselves with such drivel as we fall deeper and deeper into self-centered behavior and move farther away from God. Before long, we have lost the ability to see past the end of our noses. The world becomes very small, and our view of it becomes very paranoid.

We need to recognize the needs and feelings of others so that we will not become slaves to our own selfish desires. Pray for your family, friends, and that woman who works down the hall who just never looks happy. Pray for them especially on the days when all you want to do is cry out to God for yourself. There is much joy to be found in caring for someone else even as your own heart is breaking.

Filthy

Come to me all you who are weary and burdened, and I will give you rest. Take my yoke upon you and learn from me, for I am gentle and humble in heart, and you will find rest in your souls. For my yoke is easy and my burden is light. Matthew 11:28-29

For years I wanted to come to God cleaned up and with my ducks in a row. "Look, Daddy, I'm getting it right." That day never came, and it isn't on the horizon. As soon as I clean up one area, another is shown to be filthy. Whenever I get a few ducks walking together, at least one malcontent has to take a little field trip. I got tired of waiting and went to the Lord mess and all. Then I learned that to some extent, we all go to Him in that condition. It's okay. He loves us at our best and worst.

Whenever I think that maybe I've gone too far this time, it helps me to think in terms of my own children. Each of them has come to me in various forms of broken over the years. Perhaps the best illustration is the time my son Jeffrey flipped his truck. He had thirty-two staples in his arm, and the bandage had to be changed. Due to the bandage he had been unable to shower for two days, and it was obvious. Add to that a bloody bandage, a huge scar and thirty-two pieces of metal. Then add to that the fact that the accident was in part his own fault. Then add to that the accident occurred at a time when he should have been safely at home. He was broken, dirty, and guilty; but he needed me. I didn't hesitate for a minute. Later he would be able to clean up. Later the metal would be removed. Still later he would walk through his consequences. In that moment when rebellion or guilt could have kept him away, he put himself in my hands, trusting me to take care of him. Of course I did and got blood and dirt on me in the process. Why did I do it? He's my son.

Our Father feels exactly that way about us but to a degree we can't begin to imagine. He welcomes us into His perfect embrace—filthy, bloody, carrying whatever burden. He holds us close. Then when He opens His arms, we walk away clean, and He stands covered in our filth.

God isn't waiting for pretty polished Christians. He is waiting for human, fallible people. He doesn't care if we are dirty or if we even have ducks to line up. He just wants open hearts. We only have to fall into His arms, and He will do the rest.

Falling Asleep

> But while everyone was sleeping, his enemy came and sowed weeds among the wheat, and went away. When the wheat sprouted and formed heads the weeds also appeared. Matthew 13: 25-26

Do you ever have nightmares? Maybe you have odd dreams that while not quite nightmare caliber are certainly unsettling. We can and should control our thoughts while we are awake (Philippians 4:8), but when we are asleep our guard, is down. Thoughts that we rendered powerless while awake are able to invade at that point. Most people have an occasional nightmare or unsettling dream. I believe that sometimes God uses those unsettling dreams to wake us up a little. For the most part, I believe that God wants to guard our hearts and minds even at night. If we fall asleep listening to music about God or fall asleep praying to God, maybe it will make it harder for the negative thoughts to take hold.

What about daydreams? The word invokes a pleasant image, but not all daydreams are pleasant. If we do not follow the advice of Paul to put our mind on noble, lovely things our thoughts can take over and take us to very negative, uncomfortable places. We may be walking and talking, seemingly awake but our minds are sleeping. At that time, it is quite easy for the enemy to take over. We begin to believe all the lies. All the can't, shouldn't, never lies that can ruin us seem so true because we are "sleeping" by letting our guard down.

Our Lord is gracious, and He waits for us to throw wide our door and invite Him to enter. The enemy is not at all gracious. He is slick and conniving. He slips through the tiniest crack in our spiritual armor. We have to be ever-vigilant and always awake. The awareness that nothing can separate us from Christ needs to be in the forefront of our minds at all times.

If we fall asleep on the job or at the wheel, the consequences *can* be grave. If we fall asleep in our faith, the consequences *will* be grave. Stay awake and alert to guard against the enemy.

Changes

Therefore if any man is in Christ he is a new creation, the old has gone, the new has come. 2 Corinthians 5:17, NIV

Do you have a junk drawer or maybe even a junk room? We have a junk drawer; okay to be honest, we have a couple of junk drawers. Every once in a while, I get that crazy urge to clean them out, especially the one in the kitchen. When it is finished, I feel such a sense of accomplishment. After all, I've just gotten rid of useless stuff (who needs six copies of the Chinese take-out menu?) and created space for something more important. What happens to all that lovely clean space? Give it a day or two, and it is once again filled with useless junk. The same is true of our minds and spirits.

We clean up our act, determined not to gossip, have pity parties, overeat, smoke, lie, etc.; but very quickly we see the same pattern as the junk drawer. If we don't fill that space in our lives with something good, all we've done is create more room for uglier junk. The sin we despised has returned with a vengeance, and angry at having been set aside, it brings reinforcements. The next time we decide to clean our spiritual home, we will find it much more difficult.

A few people have shared with me lately that they don't believe that human beings are capable of any significant change. I disagree. It is true that on our own we are not, but with God's help we can change. The key is that removing the offensive behavior is not enough. We then have to pledge that space and/or time to the Lord and allow Him to fill it with something better. "The old has gone, the new has come." If we want that "new" to also be improved, we can't go it alone. We have to commit that change to our Lord.

Then He who sat on the throne said, "Behold *I* make all things new" Revelation 21:5a NKJV, (italics mine).

Tax Exempt

"Then the sons are exempt," Jesus said to him." But so that we may not offend them, go to the lake and throw out your line. Take the fist fish you catch; open its mouth and your will find a four—drachma coin. Take it and give it to them for my tax and yours." Matthew 17:26b-27

This passage is so strange to me. I have little trouble seeing Jesus interacting with the sick and poor or with the so-called high and mighty. I love the image of His holy anger in overturning the tables at the temple. The images of Jesus holding small children and being patient with thickheaded adults all seem familiar and as they should be to me. Even in the miracle passages, I see Jesus as human, yes, but there is so much God operating. This passage about Jesus finding a way to pay taxes just like we do is different. Here He is just a guy trying to pay His taxes. Suddenly Jesus isn't this otherworldly person who happened to come and pretend to be like us. No, in this picture it is easy to see that He was just like us with the same concerns and same boundaries.

"Then the sons are exempt." The sons of the earthly kings were exempt, but there he was the Son of God and not wanting to cause a feud for the wrong reason he paid the tax. This is a prime example of pick your battles. Jesus could have argued that his Father was Lord of all, and that meant that his Father owned them, and they should pay Him. He made no such argument. He paid the taxes because that was the rule of the land. He didn't come to upset the rulers of the day. He came to save the people and if *that* upset the rulers too bad.

Jesus knew that the people of power were uncomfortable around him and getting more uncomfortable all the time. If he had refused to pay his taxes, the officials would have had at least a slim reason to arrest him. Instead Jesus was a model citizen so that in his arrest and subsequent death, we would all see his innocence and know that it was our sin that put him on the Cross.

Over and over in the Scriptures we read about obedience. We know we are to obey God, but in this passage Jesus shows that we have to obey worldly authority too unless that disagrees with God. We may grumble over rules we find foolish, but as long as they do not go against the Scripture, we need to follow. Jesus did because he knew the value of obedience. We need to know it too. Once again our best course of action is to follow the actions of Jesus.

Written in Heaven

He replied, "I saw Satan fall like lightning from heaven. I have given you authority to trample on snakes and scorpions and to overcome all the power of the enemy; nothing will harm you. However, do not rejoice that the spirits submit to you but rejoice that your names are written in the heaven." Luke 10:18-20

Do not rejoice that the spirits submit to you? Is Jesus serious? Here they are ordinary men who are suddenly extraordinary because of the power of God, and Jesus doesn't want them to be ecstatic over that? No, He doesn't because He knows that even that, feeling the anointing of that awesome power, pales in comparison to knowing that in the end you get to go home.

Have you ever had a really hard day at work? Of course the answer is yes. Well since you know the feeling of just wanting to go home. You almost ache for the comfort of that familiar surrounding. You know just what you want to do when you get there. Maybe your spouse or children will be waiting for you. Maybe when you walk in the door, somebody is going to run up and give you a big hug. Maybe you have a great book to read. In any case, you know that getting home is going to make it all better.

What about on a good day? Home is the same place. Even after a really great day, there is still that pleasure of simply being home.

Imagine if home were something so perfect, so precious you can't really begin to visualize how wonderful it is. Then imagine that the cost of going there is so far out of reach it would be foolish to try. Think about how you would feel if then someone came and said to you, "Don't worry, I paid for you. Enjoy all that is good here, and then when it is time come on home, free of charge."

That is what Jesus is saying to the disciples. He is telling them, "Yes, it is great that the demons submit to you, of course they do because you have my anointing, but it is greater still that you get to come home with me."

We all want to be able to use the power that God has given to us. It would be great to cast out an evil spirit, and we can. The best thing is knowing that when our work is done, good day or bad, we will be welcomed home in Heaven.

Gardening

I planted the seed, Apollos watered it, but God made it grow. So neither he who plants nor he who waters is anything, but only God who makes things grow. The man who plants and the man who waters have one purpose, and each will be rewarded according to his own labor. 1 Corinthians 3:6-8

For several years I led a teen-girls Bible study. Some weeks when they left, I felt as if I'd really made a difference, and some nights I just cried out to God because I felt so useless. I felt that I had failed Him terribly. Over and over as I would share my frustration, friends would tell me, "You're planting a seed." This wasn't any great comfort to me because as anyone who knows me can tell you, plants come to my house to die. As new friends hand me beautiful living blooms, I can almost hear them shrieking at their certain fate. I have many lovely albeit empty planters that are a testimony to my black thumb. If my time with the girls was "planting seeds" we were in big trouble, right up until verse 6 of 1Corinthians 3.

It isn't my responsibility to do it all. In fact, I have neither the wisdom nor ability to do it all. In that season with those young women I was planting seeds and even my sorry gardening will be made magnificent in the hands of the Master Gardener.

This verse is so great because it offers the assurance that no matter what we are called to do—plant seeds, water them, or work in the harvest field—if we dedicate it to the Lord asking for his help and guidance, it will succeed.

It isn't about credit either. It's not as if Jesus is standing off to the side marking how many souls we lead His way and how many we miss. He watches with a loving heart as we make each attempt. The simple bowing of your head to pray in a group that may not pray is planting a seed.

I am death to plants but given the knowledge that God will watch over the seed and bring it to fruition I will plant, water and/or harvest as long as I'm breathing. In His graciousness, He blesses my efforts, and in that, as in all things, the glory belongs to Him.

Praising or Cursing

With the tongue we praise our Lord and Father and with it we curse men, who have been made in God's likeness. Out of the same mouth come praise and cursing. My brothers this should not be. Can both salt water and spring water flow from the same spring? James 3:9-11

As each of my children reached adolescence, there was the need to use the shock language. Each one wanting to see how ugly their words could get before I would speak up. I remember when I was in high school, I kept on hearing the cliché "you kiss your mother with that mouth" from one boy to another after a particularly choice word was uttered. Those words, those shock-value words are often referred to by their first letter; you know the—word is spoken even among adults. There are words we just don't want to say or hear.

I'm not sure those were the words James was referring to in this passage. I can't help but think that he was speaking more about hurtful words. We curse people with words like "you'll never amount to anything," but if I'm repeating that in conversation to a friend, I won't be using euphemisms or first letters. Contrarily I might be quite proud of setting the other person straight.

Phrases like "that's just how Susie is" pigeonhole a person into a place they may not want to stay. Even words spoken in pseudokindness can be hurtful. "We didn't want to bother you with all that you already have going on." That may be concern, but it may be seen as a judgement. It could sound like "we didn't think you could handle it you incompetent mess."

I don't think we please God when we use the letter-specific words, but I think we need to keep in mind that cursing wears many faces. Avoid the obvious curse words but think before saying something that may be just as deadly. We would all be wise to follow the advice I'm sure most of us have heard from our mothers or grandmothers. "If you can't say something good, don't say anything at all."

Broken or Crushed

Jesus said to them, "Have you never read the Scriptures:

> The stone the builders rejected
> has become the capstone
> the Lord has done this,
> and it is marvelous in our eyes.

Therefore I tell you that he kingdom of God will be taken away from you and given to a people who will produce its fruit. He who falls on this stone will be broken but he on whom it falls will be crushed."
Matthew 21:43-44

Can you imagine if a person just beginning to seek God came across this verse? If I fall on the stone, putting everything on God, I will be broken; but if the stone falls on me, I will be crushed. You can almost see them weighing the odds. How many choose to run far and fast so the "stone" won't be able to find them? Where is the "come to me all you who are weary" in this verse? Where is gentle Jesus making it all better? Right smack in the part of the verse that is so hard to take: "He who falls on this stone will be broken."

We fall at his feet, and we are broken then slowly; but surely he begins to rebuild us piece by piece, insult by injury, healing for each wound. No Humpty Dumpty here, this is the stuff of Saul/Paul. Arrogant and determined Saul is knocked off his high horse literally, blinded, and dealt with gently once God has his attention. He then becomes Paul, a powerful force that cannot be stopped. Saul fell off that horse and landed on the capstone. It sounds painful because it was, although Paul later refers to being "saved by grace." I have often thought, "If that was grace, I'm not sure I want any." I was wrong.

The only way we can become the people God wants us to be is to give up who we want to be. Sometimes they are very similar. Some people end up right where they thought they would, but we all have to know it was not our power that got us there.

Humpty Dumpty, the song says, cannot be rebuilt or reborn, but we can. Out of our brokenness God creates something whole and beautiful. The new being is much stronger built for a higher purpose. When we give ourselves, our broken eggshell selves to God, he produces a being with a much truer stock. We are rebuilt for service.

The best part is that although the fall will break you, it won't kill you. God's mercies are always new and never ending. The verse may sound like a once-and-for-all fall, but again look at Paul. He writes about doing things that he doesn't want to do. He writes about slipping into sinful behavior, and he writes about the thorn in his flesh. The rebuilding will not be complete on this side of heaven. After the initial slam onto the stone, we encounter the stubbed toe and bruised knee of everyday Christianity. With every bump and bruise, Jesus stands ready to save us from the enemy, who often is ourselves, and this verse contains the promise that the kingdom of heaven is waiting for us. The news for the broken is great news; the kingdom of God is waiting for us. The news for the crushed is not so great. There is no promise there. Be humble enough to broken so that in your pride you are not crushed.

Perfect Timing

> My times are in your hands;
> Deliver me from al who pursue me. Psalm 31:15

> He said, "It is not for you to know the times of the dates the Father has set by his own authority." Acts 1:7

Lately I have been learning a lot about God's timing the hard way. By that I mean that although I know in my mind that God's timing is perfect, my emotions sometimes forget it. The lessons have varied from truly difficult to just slightly annoying but there must be some urgency in the teaching because they are coming one after another.

Just last night I was out with my husband and went into a public restroom. I found it odd that in the stall there was no where to set/hang my purse. That reminded me of a time I lost a package in a restroom. It was shortly before Christmas; Otto and I were staying at a resort a couple of hours from home. I had purchased a Christmas video that we later found out was only available at that location. We learned this because my husband looked all over trying to find it.

The next Christmas, he was determined to get that video for me, not because it's such a great video but because he loves me, and he knew how foolish I felt about losing it. He took my daughter on a secret (from me) day trip to the resort area and found the video. Maybe that doesn't seem like a lesson in God's timing, but it is.

Our daughter had been through some tough times. The year before while we were away had been a particularly dark time for her. There was a rift between her and her dad that I feared would never heal. When he included her in his mission, she was thrilled. They had a great day together, and that began the healing process for them. They shared a secret (for a few days), they bonded in fixing my gaffe, and they remembered that the bond between them is too big, too important to be broken.

The year before that I felt foolish about losing that video. I wanted it for *that* Christmas season. I also wanted my daughter to be the same daughter I had always known. The next year God, in His wisdom, used that mistake of mine to begin to bring Laura back to her dad. A few months later, some other events would draw us all even closer. Again I would question God's timing, and again it would be perfect. The events may be foolish or even sinful, but God works everything for our good (Romans 8:28).

As this holiday season approaches, my daughter is remembering her secret trip with her dad. She feels loved and accepted by him once again. She may not need as many lessons about God's timing as her mother does. She has felt its perfection.

Often we ask, "Why now?" And the answer comes back, "Because I know more than you do." He does, count on it.

Small Matters

But when you give to the needy do not let your left hand know what your right hand is doing, so that your giving may be in secret. Then your Father, who sees what is done in secret will reward you. Matthew 6:3-4

Whoever can be trusted with very little can also be trusted with much, and whoever is dishonest with very little will also be dishonest with much. So if you have not been trustworthy in handling worldly wealth, who will trust you with true riches? And if you have not been trustworthy with someone else's property, who will give you property of your own? Luke 16:10-12

It is important for all of us to remember that once we have declared a bond with Christ, people will view our behavior in a different light. The more outspoken we are about our faith, the more our actions are scrutinized. There is a woman in my life right now who is quite vocal about her boundaries. She has tight boundaries and looks disdainfully at anyone who doesn't live according to her way. To me that makes her less than pleasant sometimes, but I'm fairly sure she finds me unpleasant too. In fact, I know it.

My problem with her is that I have seen what she does in secret, and it is not good. The first Scripture always makes me think of those little things we do for people that go unnoticed, that we want to go unnoticed, but that God sees. I believe that because we aren't seeking any reward beyond the good feeling that comes from giving that God is pleased with those actions. There is another point to this Scripture. It says, "Then your Father who sees what is done in secret."

Unfortunately I have seen something this woman thought she was doing in secret. It was illegal as well as sinful, but it was a very small thing. In fact, it was the smallness of it that hit me so hard. There was a financial aspect to it, but it was so minuscule it was almost ridiculous. I was quite, frankly, shocked. Here was this woman who wants to sit in judgment of everyone compromising her faith for pennies. I walked away from the incident feeling very differently about her. It wasn't until later that I realized the effect seeing that act had really had on me.

We are in fairly close contact, and I am often able to observe her behavior. On more than one occasion, I have seen actions that are most likely leading to the same sin that I first witnessed. I notice other corners being cut as well, nothing exactly illegal but not truly above board either. This woman may have something great to share with me. She may be a spiritual giant in some way, but I may never know that because of her petty behavior. I can't look at her without seeing a person whose talk is so far off from her walk. I see a person who is not trustworthy with worldly wealth, so I wonder about her heavenly treasure.

Some good has come from it though. It has made me very aware of the small things in my life, those things in which I must be faithful if I want anything bigger. When I find myself wanting to walk in a little gray area, I see that same questionable incident in my mind's eye. I know that even if no other human being can see me, God can, and I don't want to disappoint Him. I am reminded that one small misstep can easily lead to another and another until we are steeped in little sins. We may never do anything blatantly sinful or hurtful, but that pattern of little compromises is just as deadly.

Be careful in the small matters. You never know who can see you.

The Understanding of the Centurion

> When Jesus had entered Capernaum, a centurion came to him asking for help. "Lord," he said, "my servant lies at home paralyzed and in terrible suffering."
>
> Jesus said to him, "I will go and heal him."
>
> The centurion replied, "Lord I do not deserve to have you come under my roof. But just say the word and my servant will be healed. For I myself am a man under authority, with soldiers under me. I tell this one 'Go' and he goes; and that one 'Come' and he comes. I say to my servant, 'do this' and he does it."
>
> When Jesus heard this he was astonished and said to those following him, "I tell you the truth, I have not found anyone in Israel with such great faith."
>
> Then he said to the centurion, "Go! It will be done just as you believed it would." And his servant was healed at that very hour.
> Matthew 8: 8-10, 13

I have heard many preachers speak about this passage and the great faith of the centurion. They speak of his boldness in asking for help and in his great understanding of Jesus's authority. I agree with all of that, but something else strikes me every time I read or hear these words, "For I myself am a man under authority, with soldiers under me." Again, I have heard pastors talk about how the centurion would understand Jesus's authority over the demons due to his having authority over his men. The key to me is "I myself am a man under authority."

He knows what will happen to his men if they disobey him because he knows what will happen to him if he disobeys his commander. He obviously knows Jesus's reputation by either having seen the miracles or hearing about them. He knows that Jesus has the power to change things and knowing that perhaps he can't imagine anyone or anything that would be foolish enough to cross Jesus. So he takes his problem to Jesus sure that no one, no thing, would dare incur the consequences of disobeying Jesus.

He might not understand Jesus's teachings. He might not think Jesus is very politically correct, but he does understand that one would have to be mad to defy Jesus. He believed that if Jesus so much as gestured to the demons plaguing his servant, they would have to disperse. They wouldn't dare defy Jesus anymore than he would defy his supervisor.

When you know you are right in God's will approach him with confidence, knowing that nothing dares to defy God and expects to be victorious. The centurion clearly understood protocol. He was willing to live Romans 8:31. He was willing to put his faith to the test knowing that only a fool would dare go against God and knowing that the fool could not win.

The centurion was not raised in a Christian home. He did not have a car/home full of praise and worship CDs, but he knew all he needed to know, that in Christ we are more than conquerors. Obedience is key. The centurion knew it, and we need to know it too.

Neighbors

On one occasion an expert in the law stood up to test Jesus. "Teacher," he asked, "what must I do to inherit eternal life?"

"What is written in the Law?" he replied. "How do you read it?" He answered, "'Love the Lord your God with all your heart and with all your soul and with all your strength and with all your mind,' and 'Love your neighbor as yourself.'" Luke 10:25-27

Our pastor gave a very strong teaching on this passage a few weeks ago. The following week he spoke about the parable of the Good Samaritan (verses 30-37). As he was talking about neighbors, about who is our neighbor and what makes a neighbor, I thought of our military people. They are sent to foreign countries to protect not only our country but also the innocent citizens of the country where they are fighting. It is their sworn duty to protect us, their fellow Americans, and they do an admirable job. It is my opinion that many of us take the strong presence of our military for granted. I know I did before I moved to a navy town. I had no idea what kind of sacrifice went into military service. Now years of living here, marrying a marine brat and watching my little sister turn into an air force major have taught me a lot about what military service is all about. I understand it, and I am so grateful for it, but there are those who are not grateful, those who treat military people with great disdain.

When our military personnel are in other countries, they see atrocities from which the rest of us are sheltered. I have seen many magazine or newspaper stories with accompanying pictures that detail the way our military treat the innocents. We've all seen the pictures of the big guy kneeling to speak to a small foreign child or carrying a so-called enemy to safety. In those instances they are living this parable. In Vietnam, in Desert Storm and today in Iraq, Americans are not welcome. We aren't seen by all as the great white hope. Our military men and women are seen as the enemy. They are feared, and yet when it is necessary, they step in to bring aid to the innocent. Sometimes it costs them their lives.

Those brave men and women are neighbors to the people of the country that has been invaded. Sometimes they may be helping a true enemy, and other times they may be helping a victim of circumstances. They are also our neighbors—watching out for us, protecting us, and caring about what we care about. We need to remember that as the Good Samaritan made a difference for one man, our friends in the military make a difference for all of us. It is the difference between freedom and oppression, and we need to acknowledge that not just a couple of times a year on designated days and not just when there are big news stories. Find someone who is serving or has served our country and thank them. They deserve at least that much.

Fan the Flames

> **By day the Lord went ahead of them in a pillar of cloud to guide them on their way and by night in a pillar of fire to give them light, so that they could travel by day or night. Neither the pillar of cloud by day nor the pillar of fire by night left its place in front of the people. Exodus 13:21-22**

Moses and his people needed help. They had to get to the Promised Land, get away from Pharaoh, but they had no clue where they were going or how to get there. God knew their hearts so well. He knew they would discourage easily. He knew slavery wouldn't look so bad, and Pharaoh might even seem like a decent guy if things got rough. So He led them with clouds by day and fire by night. God's presence was with them every minute. Can you imagine?

We have the Holy Spirit brought to us and left with us by Jesus. The presence of God is with us every minute, but how do we know that? We know it by faith. There are no cloud or fire pillars in our day to day. We pray, discern, and walk by faith toward all of our goals and through all of our circumstances. God is with us, but we can't see Him. Wouldn't it be nice to have a pillar of clouds leading us through the day?

Look at our brothers and sisters in the Old Testament. They didn't fare any better than we do even with the pillars. They wandered for forty years in circles even with clouds, fire, and the ever-present help of God. In the next chapter of Exodus, God set up questionable circumstances to show the people that Pharaoh hadn't changed. He was the same evil manipulator they had always known. Still later on there is grumbling, maybe slavery wasn't so bad. We read that and think how ridiculous they are, but we are guilty of the same behavior.

We don't have pillars of clouds or fire, but we might not see them if we did. We see unpleasant, even tragic circumstances, and we question the presence of God forgetting that He sees the whole picture. What looks so wrong, so awful to us may well have a purpose in God's plan. In those times, we have to hold tight to Romans 8:28 and 31. God will and does work things for our good, and nothing can defeat Him.

There may not be pillars of clouds and fire in front of us, but inside of us dwells the consuming fire of the Holy Spirit; all we need to do is fan the flames.

Prayer Changes Things

"O Jerusalem, Jerusalem, you who kill the prophets and stone those sent to you, how I have longed to gather your children together, as a hen gathers her chicks under her wings, but you were not willing. Look your house is left to you desolate. For I tell you, you will not see me again until you say, 'Blessed is the name of the Lord.'"
Matthew 23: 37-39

This verse could very easily become my prayer for one of my sons. "O Joseph, Joseph, you who kill your own spirit, ignore your God and forget your faith, how I long to gather you and your children together and make you see." I can't gather Joseph anymore than Jesus could gather Jerusalem, far less in fact are my chances than His. After all, it is Jesus I appeal to on Joe's behalf, and I, like Jesus with Jerusalem, encounter that pesky free will.

If only I could grab my son and lock him in my house until he gets it. If only, but how long would that take? Would it even be possible? He lived in my house. He knows the *truth*. He simply chooses to ignore it because it doesn't fit his current lifestyle.

My pastor gave me great hope when he compared my son to Jacob, one of the great names in the Old Testament. Jacob made some pretty lousy choices. His life was not always so clean and tidy either, and look what God did with him. That helped me and shortly after that conversation I read these verses. Jesus is heartbroken over Jerusalem, and that was in the neighborhood of two thousand years ago. Jerusalem is still a mess, but I know God hasn't given up on Jerusalem, and I'm not giving up on Joseph.

If you have a Joseph in your life, someone with such a great heart, so much to offer but so much to clean up, remember this verse. Jesus wants to gather Jerusalem and Joseph and your person too. Keep praying. God hasn't given up on Jerusalem or Joseph or your person. Prayer changes things.

Whitewash

> "Woe to you teachers of the law and Pharisees, you hypocrites! You are like whitewashed tombs, which look beautiful on the outside but on the inside are full of dead men's bones and everything unclean. In the same way, on the outside you appear to people as righteous but on the inside you are full of hypocrisy and wickedness."
> Matthew 23:27-28

Jesus is not happy with these people. His chief complaints are centered on how they view themselves and how that effects those around them. He compares them to whitewashed tombs so pristine and beautiful on the outside, so full of death within. To what would he compare us? An enormous amount of money is spent on clothing, makeup, hair care, and now plastic surgery. Today's society is very much into looking good on the outside. You aren't pleased with your looks? No problem, for a few dollars and/or a little nip tuck we can make you anything you want to be. Most of us buy into that at some point or another in our lives. If we can look good, we will feel good. We will feel successful. We will exude confidence, and we will be the envy of all the people who see us. How? By buying the latest miracle cream or doing the latest exercise.

It extends so far beyond the physical too. We want to "look good" as in appearing to have a strong moral character, a deep faith, or a serious commitment without actually having any of it. The Pharisees all wanted the biggest phylacteries (see verse 5), but they didn't want to actually live the Scripture contained therein. They believed themselves to be men of God—strong, moral, faithful men. They believed it because it was what they were selling everyone else.

The same thing happens to us. We build a façade layer by layer until one day we truly believe that is what we are. We carry the biggest, heaviest Bible, sure that it will prove our deep faith. We become prey to our own hype. For some, life goes on, and everything seems to be fine. But for others, there comes a day of reckoning, a day when we realize that all we have done is build a wall between Jesus and ourselves.

We need to remember that just because something looks good doesn't mean it is good. It is important that we are honest enough with ourselves to see the whitewash we may be wearing. God doesn't care what we wear or how we style our hair. He cares about what our hearts look like, and He wants our actions to reflect a faithful heart.

Impress Your Children

These commands that I give you today are to be upon your hearts. Impress them on your children. Talk about them when you sit at home and when you walk along the road, when you lie down and when you get up. Tie them as symbols on your hands and bind them on your foreheads. Write them on the doorframes of your houses and on your gates. Deuteronomy 6:6-9

I had dinner with a couple of friends the other night. Early in the evening we spoke about our children, of course, and Sally shared some concerns about her children's spiritual growth. She is concerned that they do not take God seriously. They aren't interested in being in church or even in a youth group. It is a common concern I've heard it and certainly expressed it, but it wasn't until later in the evening that I gained some insight on the subject.

As we talked about our latest events, Ann asked Sally how getting her doctorate had changed her life. Sally answered talking about her confidence level in her job and in life in general. Then she said, "The biggest bonus is what it has done for the kids. They are so proud. In fact when I visited him at college Keith introduced me as Dr. Smith to one of his friends." That's when it hit me.

Sally is a very hard-working women, very dedicated, and very organized. I am sure that her children witnessed a strong work ethic and commitment to task as she studied and worked to get the higher degree while already working in that same field. Of course they are proud, being in school they know all the things they would rather do than study. Still they saw her put pleasure aside and put hard work first. In addition they saw her do it without benefit of a helpful husband as hers has decided marriage is not for him after all.

So I wondered why do they see that commitment and not the same level of dedication to God? Sally loves the Lord, but she is rather private about it. It isn't something her kids would see or hear. She may incorporate her faith in all she does, but it is a very subtle thing. It may in fact have been her faith that sustained her while she studied and dealt with personal issues. I doubt that she shared that with her kids.

Sally wants her children to love God, and she wants to be able to see it. I want the same thing, most people of faith do. The question is, can they see it in us? Do they hear us praise God and thank Him for everything? Are we living our faith out loud in front of our families, or do we save that for Bible-study groups? Our children, spouses, and friends need to see and hear our faith. The devotion we feel to God should be evident in everything we do. A friend's young son referred to me as his mom's "Bible friend" until he learned my name. I wouldn't mind my kids introducing me as a "Bible friend," a "Jesus freak," or anything else that announces my faith. How about you?

Strengthen Me

**They were all trying to frighten us, thinking, "Their hands will be too weak for the work, and it will not be completed."
But I prayed, "Now strengthen my hands." Nehemiah 6:9**

The people around Nehemiah want him to feel weak. They want him to see the task as too daunting to handle. They clearly want him to see himself as less than he is in God's sight. Nehemiah may not have been strong enough in his own power. The people around him were determined that he sees and accepts that fact. Nehemiah had broader knowledge. Nehemiah knew that he wasn't up to the task alone, but he also knew that he had God's favor. Lest he or anyone around him forget that his response to the taunting was to pray, "Now, strengthen my hands."

Can you relate to Nehemiah? Are there times when you feel God calling you to do something even you believe is bigger than your ability? Then you have felt that pressure of the taunting used by the enemy to defeat us. Whether it comes from our inner fearful self or from others outside of us, that constant drip of negativity has the power to shut us down.

Picture an IV dripping life-giving fluid into a dehydrated patient. It is so comforting to see it there restoring the health of that severely ill individual. Now picture it full of a solution created just to suck all the life supporting cells out of that body. As each drip goes in, you see the patient shrivel bit by painful bit until there is nothing but a shell.

That is what Nehemiah's detractors were trying to do, and it is what the enemy tries to do to us. Those drips of "you're no good," "you'll never finish," "you can't do it," and "who do you think you are anyway?" are all from Satan. He picks and picks at us usually using our own worst fears to defeat us. So what do we do?

We take a page out of Nehemiah's book; and we pray, "Strengthen my hands, back, mind, resolve, or whatever else needs straightening." God heard Nehemiah, and He hears us too. We need to remember to cry out to Him and listen for His response to drown out our detractors. Try it next time you feel defeated. Pray simply, "Now, strengthen me."

Shoulder to Shoulder

Then I will purify the lips of the peoples, that all of them may call on the name of the Lord and serve him shoulder to shoulder. Zephaniah 3:9

My son Paul loves the movie *Mary Poppins*. He has loved it since he was a child, so I have seen it numerous times. Whenever I read these words from Zephaniah, I hear that song from the movie about "shoulder to shoulder and bolder and bolder." The woman in the movie is a suffragette. She is fighting for the rights of women, but she is not fighting alone. There are lots of cliches about strength in numbers and standing together, and they all come from Scripture.

The media uses those cliches all the time and would like us to think that these are original, secular thoughts. I would encourage them to look at the New Testament where Jesus admonishes his disciples to go two by two or where we are promised that where two or more gather, he is in their midst. The idea of working together is a biblical concept. In the secular world, we see the strife of each person wanting the control, but when a group comes together under God's leadership with a strong covering, success is a given. He is there with them as they battle shoulder to shoulder.

Of course we need alone time with God to learn and to be refreshed. We can't grow in relationship with him if all of our time is a group date so to speak, but there are times when we need a brother or sister beside us.

I am blessed to have a small ministry at this point, one I believe will grow larger, but even now in the early small stages I don't do it alone. My friends Charlene and Karen laugh at me because I say "we" all the time when referring to something that to them, I did alone. The truth of it is without their prayer support, without the example of Christian behavior that they show me and without their shoulders against mine, I couldn't do even a small thing.

It is God's plan that we work together. In your prayer life, in your Christian service, find someone who is willing to stand shoulder to shoulder with you. Stand shoulder to shoulder with them and bolster each other in faith.

Thank You, Lord

Let us come before him with thanksgiving and extol him with music and song. Psalm 25:2

In my Bible concordance, I noticed a very interesting thing. The number of references for love, as in the myriad of ways God loves us, are just that, myriad. They take up one page and three quarters of the next, and my concordance is not that extensive. Then I looked at the references for the word "thanks." There are *very* few. To me that says it all.

God loves us and loves us, and then he loves us some more, but when it comes to thanks, well, we thank him and move on. There aren't nearly as many accounts of someone thanking God as there are of God loving someone. Love is all over that book. Thanks is scattered here and there. That is bad enough; but to make it worse, thanksgivings are scattered in with grumbling, from the Israelites, from Lot and Sarah, from David, from people who received miracles, even from the apostles. The first thought that came to me was, "Are you kidding me?" It was quickly replaced with shame when I realized I am as guilty as every one of them. I am most likely circling my own desert right now whining about the manna instead of being grateful that it is there. I won't recognize it until I stop grumbling and gratefully receive God's blessing, but I have a sick belief that somewhere I am behaving that exact same way.

This is the time of year when we count our blessings, and I have been richly blessed this year. I am praying to grow in gratitude so that if ever there were to be a concordance of my life, the love column and the thankful column would run neck and neck.

Let's all try to thank God as much as he loves us. It's a lofty goal we will never achieve, but in the effort we will get much closer.

Beauty by God

So God created man in his own image,
in the image of God he created him;
male and female he created them.

God saw all that he had made, and it was very good. And there was evening and morning—the sixth day. Genesis 1:27 and 31

My daughter now has a daughter. Faith is just a few weeks old, and she looks just like her mommy did when she was that age. She is a pretty little girl, and people tend to comment on that. Whenever someone stops Laura and says how pretty Faith is, Laura thanks them. When they mention that she looks like her mom, Laura responds that she did all the work getting her here. It's funny to me because I said the same thing when she was little, but now if someone compliments Laura's beauty, I respond differently. I might say, "Yes, she is very pretty," but I don't usually say thank you. They are complimenting her not me, right? Hmm . . . maybe not, where Laura is concerned, I did the work getting her here.

So it is with God and us. He did all the work getting us here, *all* the work. I may have carried Laura for nine months just as she carried Faith, but the real work was done centuries ago when God created us in His image. Nothing about us is our, own and yet we take the compliments as if we had some input to the color of our eyes, the shape of our ears, or the quality of our hair.

In the past five weeks my husband and I have been blessed with two new granddaughters. Both of them look just like their mommies, except Faith has her daddy's ears, and Isabelle has her daddy's chin and toes. When the babies were born, we were constantly looking for each parent in those tiny faces. Our grandson is a bit older. He physically looks just like his daddy, but he sometimes sounds more like Mommy. The difference between toddler Joey and the newborn girls is that now we are looking at Joey's heart. Who will he resemble there? Will he be kind and merciful? Will he imitate his pop-pop in choosing to follow Christ?

We all want to see our good qualities in our children and grandchildren just as God wants to see His qualities in us. Anything we have inherited from our Father is good. The next time someone compliments you, remember that just like my angel granddaughters, you can't take any credit. Whatever it is that is being admired is a gift from your Father. Answer your admirer politely, but don't forget the glory really belongs to God.

Selfish Prayers

Yet I considered It necessary to send to you Epaphroditus, my brother, fellow worker, and fellow soldier, but your messenger and the one who ministered to my need; since he was longing for you all and was distressed because you had heard that he was sick. For indeed he was sick almost unto death but God had mercy on him and not only on him but in me also lest I should sorrow upon sorrow. Philippians 2:25-27 NJKV

It is my express privilege that people ask me to pray when they are ill or when someone they love is ill. I feel blessed to be called on for such an awesome task. When the person is somewhat removed from me, I have to leave myself notes. It is my habit to keep a list of prayer request and consult it now and then to remind myself of the request. When the person is close, it is easier to remember because I pray every time I think of them, but those prayers are harder.

When I am asked to pray for an extended family member or friend of a friend, it is easy to pray the request adding, "Not my will but yours." It gets more difficult when the person in need of prayer is in my family or my close circle of friends. Then I want to direct God's efforts. I want that person healed for them but also for me.

Over the past year or so, two people that I dearly love have battled cancer. As I pray for each one, I pray exactly what she had requested. Then I would find myself pleading my own case. "Lord, you know how much I care about her. You know I want her well. Oh, please, Lord, don't let this defeat her." And on and on. Eventually of course I would pray for God's will to be accomplished because I know His will is right and best. What I'm not sure of is whether or not God knows how much it means to me. Of course logically I know He does, but I *need* to say it to Him, stressing what a gift that person is to me.

Right now my one friend is still in her battle. I am always amazed when she is at work after a treatment, but when she isn't, there is a part of me that just feels broken. I know God will work His perfect will for her. I know she will be victorious, but when her precious face is not where it's supposed to be, my heart sinks.

I think God understands this. Read the story of Lazarus. Jesus wept over his loss. He wanted his friend back, and his Father, our Father, heard his prayer. He hears our prayers too, and he understands that sometimes even though the prayer is for someone else, there is an element of self-involvement. It's okay to tell God how we really feel. He already knows anyway. Just believe that God wants what is right and best and will accomplish His will in us if we just trust Him.

God First

> "So do not worry saying, 'What shall we eat?' or 'What shall we drink?' or "What shall we wear?' For the pagans run after all these things, and your heavenly Father knows that you need them. But seek first his kingdom and his righteousness and all these things will be given to you as well." Matthew 6:31-33

A month or so ago we had "backwards day" at our school. In an effort to drive home a point about drugs, we did all kinds of silly things, and backward day was one of them. It was cute and funny to see how far some kids and grown-ups were willing to take the challenge. Backward was okay for a day to make the point that we really are too good to do drugs. Backward faith is not as clever an idea.

In this passage, Matthew exhorts us to seek God first. I wonder if I, if any, of us really get that. We know we need health, money, protection, and we seek God for it. Those of us who are evolving as Christians, growing daily may see the need and take it straight to God. That's great. It is several steps in front of those of us who run around trying to get or achieve something on our own and then when that fails seek God's help. What Matthew is saying goes beyond that. He is telling us to seek God first. Seek God. Not seek God first for—(fill in the blank). Just simply seek God.

The verse explains that if we seek God first, then everything else will be added. If we are approaching God with our hands out, we are not seeking him first. We are seeking what he can do for us. There needs to be a relationship built over time. A trust develops, and then we know that in all things God is able to help and save.

Running directly to God in our time of need is the perfect response, but we need to be sure that we know him. He knows each one of us very well, and he sees us coming before we know we're going to go. For our part we need to know him well enough to know when we've arrived at his side. We do not want to run right past him to an imposter. Seek God first know his face before you ask to see his hand.

The Only Thing

But by faith we eagerly await through the Spirit the righteousness for which we hope. For in Christ Jesus neither circumcision or uncircumcision has any value. The only thing that counts is faith expressing itself through love. Galatians 5:5-6

Too often we make ourselves sick, stressed beyond our limits trying to please God. We volunteer for every committee and say yes to every request. From the outside we look holy and devoted by on the inside we're a mess. No matter how many times we hear that salvation is a free gift, it seems most of feel at one point or another that we have to earn our place in heaven. There is another group that believes they have to make up for past sins. An unfortunate few fall into both groups jumping through self-imposed hoops yelling, "Mea culpa," at the top of their lungs.

The question is why. Why do we not get it? This Scripture makes it abundantly clear; "The only thing that counts is faith." Paul is talking to the Galatians about circumcision, but we can substitute any word, neither heading the committee or not heading the committee, neither washing cars for charity or not washing cars, etc. Anything can be service to God if He is asking us to do it. If He is not asking, then we are just chasing our own tails trying to look good, trying to be saints.

We aren't getting into the Kingdom any faster by serving meals to the homeless when we should be serving a meal at home. We need to understand that while faith without works is dead (James 2:17), works done outside of faith are useless.

If you are called to serve, by all means serve, but if you are serving to get a feather in your heavenly nest, don't bother. Our Father knows our hearts. That smile we wear as we suffer through the latest sacrificial project we've taken on is not fooling Him. He hears every syllable of unspoken irritation. By faith we eagerly await Jesus's return, and by faith we'll be ready for it.

Gentle Victories

Every high priest is selected from among men and is appointed to represent them in matters related to God, to offer gifts and sacrifices for sins. He is able to deal gently with those who are ignorant and are going astray, since he himself is subject to weakness. Hebrews 5:1-2

And what more shall I say? I do not have time to tell about Gideon, Barak, Samson, Jephthah, David, Samuel and the prophets, who through faith conquered kingdoms, administered justice, and gained what was promised; who shut the mouths of lions, quenched the fury of the flames, and escaped the edge of the sword; whose weakness was turned to strength; and who became powerful in battle and routed foreign armies. Hebrews 11:32-34

When we have been subject to a weakness we can go one of two ways. We often hear the jokes about the reformed smoker/drinker/drug addict/adulterer, etc., and how tough they are on the people who still engage in the behavior they themselves have rejected. Others are more tolerant because they have felt the grip of that same sin.

The high priest is said to be gentle having been subject to weakness. Jesus's immense mercy comes in part from dealing with the same problems we face daily. This verse is not about tough love. I do believe that sometimes tough love is all we can give, but most often I think we need to adhere to the "treat others as you want to be treated" verse. Real tough love is a last resort, but often the concept is abused, used by one to gain control over another. Our heavenly Father is not about control. He is mercy, justice, and truth.

It is hard to stand by and watch someone we love falter. We try to tell ourselves that we can browbeat them to a better way. God says no. He says love gently until there is no other option but to turn over some tables. Jesus was righteously indignant when he had to be, and we can be too if we are careful.

So how do we determine when to be tough and when to be gentle? The answer is in Hebrews 11. It is the same answer every time problems arise, by faith. The words "by faith" are used in the eleventh chapter of Hebrews approximately twenty-four times. It worked for the Bible greats, and it will work for us. How were the events in the second Scripture accomplished? By faith. How did Abraham have Isaac? By faith. How did Moses overcome his poor speech? By faith and the list goes on.

Try it before you throw in the towel. Try dealing gently and living by faith.

Prophet

Jesus said to them, "Only in his hometown, among his relatives and in his own house is a prophet without honor." He could not do any miracles there, except lay hands on a few people and heal them. Mark 6:4-5

These two short verses are full of wisdom. First there is the idea that we really have the hardest time reaching the people closest to us. Those are usually the people we want to reach most, but for many reasons, they are the ones we can't reach. Living in the same house we see each other's best and unfortunately worst. Our family members may not hear us because they are with us when the talk isn't matching the walk. It may be a simple matter of hearing our voices too much. I know my husband and children tune me out quite a bit, and of course there is the pigeonhole problem. Those closest to us are sure they know exactly who and what we are. Even if we have an anointing or a special word for them, it can go unnoticed because that's just Mom/Grandma/wife talking, and what does she know?

It is hard to believe that there could have been anyone who didn't take Jesus seriously. He was Jesus after all. Yes, but, JESUS, all capital letters, neon-print JESUS to us is the kid next door, the older brother who wouldn't let his siblings do some dumb thing, that man that once was a tiny babe in arms to all of them. When we look at him, we easily see a prophet, healer, Son of God. They saw brother, neighbor son of Joseph and Mary. The difference is not in who he is but in how he is seen, and the same is true of us.

The other thing that catches my eye is "He could not do any miracles there except lay hands on a few people and heal them." Oh, is that all? Darn! I hope and pray that some of my prayers are a small part of a healing process.

As in many aspects of life, it is all about perspective. The way we perceive each other and the way we perceive our influence. Jesus was wrongly perceived and saw himself as less than effective in his hometown. We see him as amazing no matter where the story is set.

Today be grateful to God who wants to do so much for us that healing seems like a small miracle. Given that view, can you just imagine what big things He wants to do?

Exceeding Great Joy

When they heard the king they departed; and behold, the star which they had seen in the East went before them, till it came and stood over where the young Child was.
When they saw the star, they rejoiced with exceeding great joy.
Matthew 2:9-10, NKJV

It seems to me that we do Christmas a little backward. We buy gifts and plan meals from October or earlier, but when it comes to Jesus, to really thinking about the story of Christmas, we wait until the 24 or even the 25. We read the story of the birth of Christ on Christmas eve or Christmas morning. It gets thrown in with the gifts, meals, eggnog, and candy canes.

The other night I was blessed to hear a recitation of the birth of Jesus intermingled with hymns from an enormous and amazing choir. I was most touched by one song they sang. It is called "Exceeding Great Joy." The chorus says, "When they saw the star they rejoiced with great joy, they rejoiced with exceeding great joy." I love that hymn and that expression with exceeding great joy.

My church is great. It is a very friendly, open place. We have a pastor who is very intelligent but speaks on a level that educates, edifies, and often entertains. The musicians we have are good and somewhat spirited. Given all of that I have still decided that maybe I am in the wrong church. I want to be in a place where the people are rejoicing with exceeding great joy and proud of it. Maybe my church family is rejoicing, but if they are, it is a quiet rejoicing, a proper form of joy.

I am finished with proper. I'm over it. Our Father in heaven sent His one and only Son to live and die so that we could live and not die. In a couple of weeks we will celebrate that, sort of. There will be plenty of loud "ho ho hos" and lots of "Merry Christmases." We will ooh and ahh over some little something given to us by a friend or family member, but will we rejoice with exceeding great joy?

Think for a minute, what did the person closest to you give you for Christmas last year? Can you remember? Did it take you a minute? Jesus gave his life for you, and he would do it again. I want this Christmas to be loud with exceeding great joy. I want to be full of the *CHRIST*mas spirit. I want to see the star and be wild about its meaning, and I want you to be wild about it too.

I am quite Christmas crazy in a secular sense too. I love wearing my crazy socks and odd jewelry. This time of year when you open my door, you are greeted by my ever-growing snowman collection. I love it all, but what I love most is knowing the reason behind it all.

I know you'll see dollar signs, budgets, messy rooms, and empty menus; and I know you'll feel stressed. Relax! The real meaning isn't in paper or bows, and it isn't on platters. It's written in the stars. See the star and rejoice with exceeding great joy.

For Such a Time

"And who knows but that you have come to royal position for such a time as this?" Esther 4:11b

Mordecai is encouraging Esther or maybe inflaming her. He wants her to go to her king and stand up for the Jewish people. King Xerxes is listening to lousy advisors and it has to be stopped. Mordecai seems fairly sure that Esther has been put in a position to influence the king. His words are helpful and affirming to her. They strengthen her resolve. They can strengthen us too.

Whenever we are in difficult or questionable times and we feel helpless, we need to think that we may be in the perfect place. I'm sure that Esther didn't feel that she was in a good place. Her king, her husband, was solidly behind the plan to annihilate her people, the Jews. I'm sure she wondered how she could live with a man who was willing to kill all of her people. What she didn't know until later was that she was the deciding factor. Her faith and her boldness saved the Jews from certain death. While God was lining up the other factors Esther felt doubtful and afraid. In verse 16 she says to Mordecai, "I will go to the king, even though it is against the law, and if I perish, I perish."

It is hard for us to see what God will do with our circumstances. We may feel as frightened as Esther must have felt. Like Esther, we may be where we are for such a time as this. It may be that we are the small piece that makes the puzzle work. We have to have faith that if we are allowing God to guide our steps then all will be well. Later in the book of Esther the truth comes out Haman is a snake in the grass. King Xerxes sees the light, and the Jews are spared. Esther was in the right place at the right time.

When things go well for us we see the timing of the moment and call it good, but when things are questionable, we wonder, "Where is God in this?" The answer is in the question. He is in this, in all of this, with us and our momentary fear or suffering may be as Esther's for such a time as this. In good times or hard hang on in faith knowing that God will work it all for our good.

The Most Wonderful Time of the Year

> For to us a child is born, to us a son is given and the government of the world will be on his shoulders. And he will be called Wonderful Counselor, Mighty God Everlasting Father, Prince of Peace. Of the increase of his government and peace there will be no end. Isaiah 9:7

It's the most wonderful time of the year. The song says so which means it must be true. Look around you. Everything is all pretty and sparkly, decorated to celebrate Christmas or Xmas or "the holiday season" preferably, "the holiday season." The powers of the world are all about celebrating and spending. Holidays are a great excuse to raise prices and call it a sale, but they don't want to call it Christmas. After all some people are offended by that. Those people who don't believe in Christ don't want His name mucking up their holiday. Too bad!

It's the most wonderful time of the year. Look around you. People who are normally very calm and nice are now harried and hassled. They snap rather than smile because they are thinking about what to buy for whom and how many more chores await them. Wonderful, isn't it? During this celebration of the birth of the Prince of Peace instead of peace many people are feeling stress.

It's the most wonderful time of the year. The Scripture says so which means it is true. For to us a child was born, a child called Prince of Peace, Wonderful Counselor. He is the Lord of all life, and he is willing to be the Lord of my life and yours if we let him.

It is the most wonderful time of the year. It is a time to remember that the Virgin Mary had a baby boy, and she named him Jesus. Just a brief while later he gave everything he had for us, and he didn't stress about it. He didn't wrap his gift in silver paper or top it with a big red bow. He wrapped his gift in flesh and topped it with his blood.

It's the most wonderful time of the year because *Christ's* birth is remembered. Don't wish a single person "happy holidays." Wish everyone you see Merry *Christmas* and wish them blessings in the New Year.

Beheaded

**The king was greatly distressed but because of his oath and his dinner guests, he did not want to refuse her. So he immediately sent an executioner with orders to bring John's head. The man went beheaded John in the prison and brought back his head on a platter. He presented it to the girl and she gave it to her mother.
Mark 6: 26-28**

The politically correct world constantly challenges the rights of Christians. It seems that people of other religious affiliations need to be protected by the government and the Constitution while those of us who follow the truth need to be censored. They are certain we need to be watched and monitored for offensive behavior. Right now we are sitting in the midst of the Merry Christmas debate. It's been recurring for the last several years, and every year it gets more ridiculous.

Just the other day, our school principal shared the official ruling on what can and cannot be displayed in our classrooms as per some lawyer's office. It's insane. The world wants us all to be so careful not to offend that here in America, a country founded for religious freedom, there is a chance that people will not hear the Good News because we fear the repercussions of sharing it. Here in America what's the worst that could happen? I might get fired. If I offend the wrong person, I may not have a job, but I would still have my head.

Herod didn't like John the Baptist. He didn't want to hear John's words because John's words convicted him, so he put him in jail. One sin led to another, and John paid the price. I remember quite vividly a picture in my parent's Bible of that very scene, a wild-eyed head on a platter. Those people were so barbaric, so ridiculously afraid of the truth that they were willing to torture people who believed.

Is it any different today? Look at Iraq, Afghanistan, and so many other countries. People there are losing their lives because of their desire to know Christ. Here in America we may be risking our livelihood, but we aren't risking our lives yet. Stand firm in what you believe and be grateful to the men and women who are defending our right to believe it and say so wherever we please. Don't be intimidated by the politically correct. Push the envelope as far as you can. I'm fairly sure it won't cost you your head.

Mary Had A Baby

> The angel answered, "The Holy Spirit will come upon you, and the power of the Most High will overshadow you. So the holy one to be born will be called the Son of God."
> "I am the Lord's servant," Mary answered. "May it be to me as you have said." Then the angel left her. Luke 1: 35, 37

> Mary had a baby born in a manger. Mary what to do Mary what to do? Before a vow was made, in your belly lay the King. Jennifer Knapp, "Sing Mary Sing"

The angel said the Holy Spirit would come upon her. She's a girl, a teenager. From our human viewpoint, we decide that young Mary must have been terrified. The best guess puts her age at about fourteen. We cannot begin to imagine the fourteen-year-olds we know handling that situation. I don't know about you, but I can't imagine anyone I know, regardless of age, handling that situation. The problem is that we look through fully human eyes at a spiritual situation.

I pray constantly to see things and people as God sees them. I pray for more awareness of the Holy Spirit in my life. Knowing that the Spirit of the Lord dwells in us is amazing, but it is something that we all have to take on faith. I can't show you the spot where the Holy Spirit lives. I certainly can't blame the increasing size of my midsection on the Holy Spirit, but Mary could.

Maybe Mary wasn't as terrified as we presume. Maybe, like any other woman who has ever had a baby, she was concerned but perhaps not. Each time that I was pregnant, I had to wonder what the baby would be like or if in fact the pregnancy would go to term. Mary knew that God had a purpose for her child. She knew that God would get him here. Society was definitely against her and would be against him but she had concrete knowledge that the Spirit was in her. I think that may be what strengthened her to endure what was to come. The baby-crazy killing king, the lunatics that threatened and eventually took her son's life, all of that which was in front of her may have been bearable because she spent those nine months housing the literal presence of God.

That may be the best lesson we can learn from Mary, to sit and feel the Holy Spirit within us. When times get crazy, get pregnant with the Holy Spirit. Sit and wait to feel the movement of the Spirit within you. Know that through that Spirit our Father will strengthen you for whatever is ahead.

Mary's baby was born in a manger and died on a cross. Mary was chosen to do great things for God. Perhaps the difference between Mary and the rest of us is that Mary was humble enough to know it had nothing to do with her. She was a vessel, and because she was a willing vessel God was able to use her in a way we still talk and sing about.

We can all relate to what we assume to be Mary's horrified reaction. Can we relate to her humility? I think we should all try and praise God for whatever He calls us to do.

Feliz Navidad, Maybe

> He said, "Go and tell these people:
> 'be ever hearing but never understanding
> be ever seeing but never perceiving.'
> Make the heart of this people calloused
> make their ears dull
> and close their eyes." Isaiah 6:9-10a

Feliz Navidad. For years these were the only Spanish words I knew. Due to my neighbor and friend base, I did pretty well understanding Italian and Greek; I could even speak a few phrases of each, but my Spanish was limited to feliz Navidad. I heard it every year during the Christmas holidays. Jose Feliciano was enlarging my vocabulary. He had no idea that those two words would become two treasured, silly memories for me.

My son Jeffrey, who later became rather proficient in Spanish, first heard those words as "Fleece Navinah." I have a precious handmade Christmas card that says just that. When he was little, "Fleece Navinah" was Jeffrey's favorite song, and he sang it at the top of his lungs, *a lot.*

A couple of years after receiving Jeffrey's sweet card I was working in a rather stressful environment with my friend Ginger. In an effort to bring a little Christmas into our otherwise harried workday, we had Christmas tapes playing as we worked. When "Feliz Navidad" started Ginger sang along, quite seriously, "Fleas on a dog, fleas on a dog." It is important to note here that she was kidding, I think, but her demeanor was not at all silly. She went right on working while singing about fleas. It did just what we needed it to do. It lightened the mood.

With Scripture, it is important that we understand the true meaning. It is very important that when we share God's Word, we do our best to represent it well. We can't turn those sacred words into nonsense sounds or "fleas." Pray to have minds and hearts that are ever hearing and understanding. Share the wisdom that God gives to you. When you hear someone misrepresent the Word, correct them gently. Fleece fleas are amusing, but when Scripture is twisted, it becomes dangerous. Any time you hear a talk or read a message about what God says, make sure it matches the Scriptures.

As for me, I want to wish you a merry Christmas from the bottom of my heart. Feliz Navidad, a.k.a. fleece Navinah or fleas on a dog. In any case, be blessed and enjoy!

Anguish or Freedom

In my anguish I cried to the Lord and he answered by setting me free. Psalm 118:5

The thought that came to me when I read this verse was "don't go there." I feel a little under qualified to talk about anguish when I think of what some of my friends are going through or have gone through. At this time of year, I am reminded in particular of a friend who lost a very young child. I have never known that kind of anguish. As I prayed about it, I realized that just like sin, it is all the same. Each one of us experiences agony in varying degrees. The answer is the same for us all, give it up.

The verse says that the psalmist cried to the Lord. If we cry out to our Lord, we will be free. If we are humble enough to say, "I can't take it anymore," the grip of the agony will lessen. It is the realization that we are not alone. We will still endure the pain, but it will not own us. We will be free. Focusing on Jesus, on the strength of our God, helps us to know that we can endure. Like all the things of this world, our current pressure is here but for a season. It will pass.

Sometimes once we realize that we are free we rejoice, and at that moment we take away every last vestige of power that the enemy has in the situation. Our enemy finds his power in our weakness. His is strong when in our weakness we accept defeat. When we cry out to our Lord, his strength becomes available to us, and in our weakness, He is strong. Then we can rest in his embrace until the agony subsides. Defeat the enemy by realizing where freedom lies. Cry out to the Lord and let him set you free.

Shivering

And there were shepherds living out in the fields nearby, keeping watch over their flocks at night. An angel of the Lord appeared to them, and the glory of the Lord shone around them, and they were terrified. But the angel said to them, "Do not be afraid. I bring you good news of great joy that will be for all the people. Today in the town of David a Savior has been born to you; he is Christ the Lord. Luke 2:8-12

This morning I was singing along with one of my favorite Christmas songs, "Do You Hear What I Hear." As I sang the words "a child shivers in the cold," I was shivering too. It is important to mention that it was fifty-two degrees at the time, not exactly freezing. While my formerly Yankee blood has become quite nicely accustomed to the kinder weather of the South over the past twenty years, I still remember what subzero freezing is all about. I remember it with great disdain. The word "shiver" doesn't accurately describe what your body does in those temperatures. It is more like your own personal earthquake. I remember stiffening every inch of my body in the false belief that stiffening would ward off the bite of the frigid air. I was sort of laughing at my new definition of "cold" and "shivering" when the image of one of my brand-new granddaughters crossed my mind.

I pictured her tiny body cold and shivering. I thought of how awful my daughter would feel if there were no way to protect Faith from the elements. The night before in the shivery cold fifty-degree weather, Faith looked a little like an Eskimo baby as she left my house. Her cousin Isabelle had left just a few minutes before her with a tent of blankets encasing her carrier. Our baby girls are kept warm and protected, but at the time of his birth, our Savior was shivering in the cold, a cold I'm guessing was a lot more like Syracuse, New York, than Orange Park, Forida.

We are all quite used to our creature comforts. We forget that each and every one of them is a blessing from a God who loves us enough to watch His Son shiver in the cold. We hear the cliché about being born with a silver spoon. Jesus was born with no spoon at all.

My little angels Faith and Isabelle have nurseries full of soft, cozy blankets and clothes and toys that they won't use for months to come. Mary did not have the luxury of that kind of prepping for Jesus's birth. We do. Today Jesus doesn't need a literal blanket, but it might warm his heart to be covered up in praise. Don't let your Savior shiver in the cold of neglect this Christmas. Praise his name every chance you get. Celebrate his birthday by offering him yourself. Wrap him in your love. You may be assured you are wrapped in his.

Glory to God

> Jesus commanded them not to tell anyone. But the more he did so the more they kept talking about it. People were overwhelmed with amazement. "He has done everything well," they said. "He even makes the deaf hear and the mute speak." Mark 7:36-37

These verses come right after two miracle stories, Jesus has healed a very ill girl and given hearing and speech to a deaf and mute man. There are many accounts like this through all four Gospels. Jesus doesn't say, "Go tell everyone you see." He says, "Be quiet." Every time I read those accounts, I wonder why he wanted them to be quiet and how he thought they could. I don't know many people who could keep quiet after receiving a miracle. Whenever God blesses me, I want to tell all about it. Besides, why didn't Jesus want the people to know what he was doing?

I think I may have begun to understand the answer to that. Jesus was here on earth to bring people to his Father. He wanted the focus to be on the gift of eternal life and not on the here and now miracle. Maybe he didn't want to become a sideshow. Certainly his compassionate heart compelled him to heal and restore, but that was a small part of what he was doing. The main goal was to lead people to the Truth, to get them to live not just exist. In John's Gospel, Jesus tells the people, "I am the Way and the Truth and the Life." He was here to bring us all home whether we could see, hear, or walk was unimportant in the big picture. When people ran off telling about their miracles the focus was off the main mission and on the what can you do for me today.

Jesus wanted all the glory to go to the Father. It may be his hands touching the deaf or the lame, but it was the power of his Father that was responsible for the healing. Too much emphasis on the acts would take away the attention given to the Source. It is so wonderful when our prayers for healing or any kind of help are answered, and we do want to share it with everyone. We just have to remember to give all of the glory to God. Of course we are thankful for all of our prayer warriors who stand in the gap for us, but they do not cause the miracle to happen. The rescues all come from one place, our heavenly Father. While he was here with us, Jesus wanted us to learn one simple truth, to God be all the glory.

Flowing Through

And if anyone gives even a cup of cold water to one of these little ones because he is my disciple, I tell you the truth, he will certainly not lose his reward. Matthew 10:42

He who gives to the poor will lack nothing, but he who closes his eyes to them receives many curses. Proverbs 28:27

Each man should give what he has decided in his heart to give, not reluctantly or under compulsion for God loves a cheerful giver. And God is able to make all grace abound to you, so that in all things, at all times, having all that you need, you will abound in every good work. 2 Corinthians 9: 7-8

Giving is an interesting thing. When we give as God directs us to give, we are always rewarded. We may let go of a cherished item only to receive something much better. Blessings were never meant to be stagnant. They are meant to be shared. We joke at work sometimes about our paychecks simply passing through our bank accounts. Sometimes before the money even gets there it is on its way to the next destination. It should be with the same with blessings.

Each day God blesses us. If you don't believe that, begin to look over your day each night before you sleep. Even if you can't see a single positive thing in your day, you are obviously still alive to recap it, and that is a blessing. Most days you can see at least one or two events that were gifts from God. If God is willing to bless us every day, we should also be willing to bless those around us. God is never outdone in generosity. Whatever we give returns to us a hundredfold. It may not come in the exact same way we give, but it always comes.

There is a worldly cliché that says, "No good deed goes unpunished." We can all relate to that. Most people have offered a helping hand or a kindness only to have it slapped away. We all know how it feels to have a gift rejected.

So what? That is from the world. The intended recipient may not have been gracious receiver, but our Father in heaven sees our actions and our motivations. The reward comes from Him. It is never about how the gift is received here in this world. It is all about how it is seen from heaven.

Let God's blessings be like those much-needed paychecks. Let them flow right through you, and do it with joy, knowing that you are storing up heavenly treasures. If the blessings don't flow out, there won't be any room for more to flow in. Don't let that happen to you. Be a channel not a trap.

Your Own Petard

Then Hebona, one of the eunuchs attending the king, said, "A gallows seventy-five feet high stands by Haman's house. He had it made for Mordecai, who spoke up to help the king."
The king said, "Hang him on it!" So they hanged Haman on the gallows he had prepared for Mordecai. Then the king's fury subsided. Esther 7:9-10

Haman had a plan. He didn't like the Jews; in particular, he didn't like Mordecai because he could not intimidate Mordecai. He wanted Mordecai and all of his people dead. He wanted to make an example of Mordecai. So he built a gallows and prepared to hang Mordecai in front of all of Persia. It was a great plan as far as it went. When Haman came up with it, he had the king's ear. The king was listening closely to Haman's advice unaware of how self-serving it was. Haman was unprepared for Mordecai and Esther. He didn't know that they had a close connection to each other and more important to God.

This story is from the Old Testament, but it is evidence of the verse in Romans that says, "God works for the good of those who love him" (Romans 8:28). Esther and Mordecai were God's people. They loved and trusted him, and he was not going to let them perish. In the end, the person to hang on the gallows was Haman himself. His own deeds put him there.

That is so hard when we find ourselves swinging from a gallows of our own making. When we know that it was our own choices, our own pride that put us in the situation. My grandmother was fond of the expression "hoisted by his own petard." As a child, I didn't fully understand the words, but I knew it meant that the person had brought the disaster on himself or herself. I realize now that while the exact meaning of petard is not pride, in most cases that is the active ingredient in the hoisting. Pride and vengeance, both of which were at work in Haman, are the terror twins. Too often they backfire, and we are the ones left dangling. We all need to heed the words of that simple children's hymn "be careful little mouth, eyes, ears, etc.," because the Father up above is looking down with love; and sometimes love means discipline, the discipline of having to live out the consequences of our actions. Don't get hoisted on your petard.

Did I Ask You a Question?

> O Lord, you have searched me and you know me. You know when I sit and when I rise; you perceive my thoughts from afar.
> Psalm 139:1-2

We are all God's children. The fact that some of us respond to His call, and others do not does not change his relationship to us. The quality of one may be better than another, but He is father to all of us. Most of the time, He doesn't need our help in parenting His other children.

When our children were younger, we were called on to be their parents. It was our duty to lead and guide them, to provide them with discipline as well as love them. When one of them would interrupt a conversation between my husband and another sibling, to accuse or defend, Otto was known to say, "Did I ask you a question?"

I was reminded of that when shortly after promising to get out of God's way with my now-adult children I heard myself, not once but twice giving spiritual prompting. I could almost hear God asking me, "Did I ask you a question?" I believe that God calls us all to support each other and to hold each other accountable but He chooses the right partner for each person in each circumstance. Perhaps there are times when we are the best people for God to use to bring someone closer to Him, but often we are not the ones called on when that person is a family member or very close friend. The problem there lies in being able to set down our own agenda and truly be a channel for God's word.

We need to understand that God loves each of us better than anyone else. It is hard to believe that anyone could love our spouses as much as we do. It is harder still to believe that anyone could come close to loving our children the way we do. (Mothers, is there anyone that is good enough for your prince/princess?) God loves us better than we can begin to comprehend. He always has our best interest at heart. He loves our family members and dear friends beyond our understanding and, more to the point, He knows them better. He has no need of our input. He won't be asking us any questions.

Pray for those near and dear to you and remember that they belong to God even if they don't know it.

Job's Example

His wisdom is profound, his power is vast. Who has resisted him and come out unscathed?
He performs wonders that cannot be fathomed, miracles that cannot be counted. Job 9:4, 10

To be perfectly honest, I try to avoid the book of Job. The immense pain and suffering coupled with all the back and forth about why there is such pain and suffering is too much for me. Yet every time I do read it, I find something new. There is a lot to be learned from Job.

These two verses hit me today. *"Who has resisted him and come out unscathed?"* That part reminded me of a conversation we had in our teen girl's Bible study a few years ago. After relating a very questionable decision, one of my angels said, "But I didn't get caught, and I didn't get hurt, so it's okay, right?" Wrong. Maybe her parents were still unaware of the event, but her Father knew all about it. Maybe her body appeared to be physically unharmed, but years later will she still feel that she didn't get hurt? When her own daughter or son asks if that behavior is okay for her/him how will she answer? Things may seem "okay," but the aftereffects may not come for a while. God is good to us, and some of our deeds may go unpunished, but at the very least we always have to live with the knowledge of our own choices.

Like Job, it is good to understand that resisting God is a fool's mission. It is also so very good to know that *"He performs wonders that cannot be fathomed."* Wonders and miracles are available to us every day. I am always taken aback when I hear people say that God is not doing the miracles He did in Jesus's time. It is one of those "I would believe but" *s*tatements. If they could see a healing or watch an evil spirit being cast out, then they would believe. I say, "Look around." There has to be someone in your circle who has received healing or rescue. If there isn't, then take a look at yourself. Are you walking and talking? Do you have healthy family members? Have you experienced a tragedy and are you still standing? Well, those are miracles. We live and move and breathe. That is miraculous.

Resist the devil, not the Lord. Look around. Find the miracles in your life. Job had his doubts and fell into despair at times, but he was always aware of God's power and through it all he held on to his faith. Maybe that is why I avoid his book. It shows me where I fall short, but miracle of miracle God loves me anyway, and He loves you too.

Do Whatever He Tells You

> When the wine was gone, Jesus's mother said to him, "They have no more wine."
>
> "Dear woman, why do you involve me?" Jesus replied. "My time has not yet come."
>
> His mother said to the servants, "Do whatever he tells you."
> John 2:3-5

Beside this passage in the Quest study Bible there is a note that asks, "Is Jesus being rude to his mother?" It clearly answers that no, he is not. Jesus understood timing. He was fully yielded to his Father. He waited to be prompted. He was not following his own agenda but that of his Father and therefore the time was not for him to choose. When we look at it that way, the whole section makes more sense. I have often wondered why he said no just to turn around and do exactly what she asked him to do. After reading that footnote, I can only suppose that in the seconds or minutes that passed between the no and the yes, Jesus felt the nudge from God saying, "Now is the time."

When Jesus responded to his Father's prompting, the bridal couple was rescued. People wonder all the time if God cares about the little things. I remember a woman I know telling me that she prayed for God's help every morning as she styled her hair. A friend or hers told her God didn't care about her hair. The friend was wrong. God cares about our hair, our toes, our jobs, our finances, our children, our very lives, every tiny or huge detail; and this story proves that.

Wine at a wedding may seem a trivial thing when compared to pestilence, murder, adultery, illness, etc.; but to our loving Father, what makes it important is that we bring it to Him. Maybe He doesn't care what your hair looks like today because He doesn't see you for your hair. He does care that you care what your hair looks like. He cares because we ask Him to care. God will be involved in any part of our lives to which we invite Him. He loves each of us as if there were only one of us. Whether it's wine, hair, broken heart, or terminal illness, give it to God and like Jesus wait for the prompting, for the answer that will surely come.

Rabbi, I Want

> "What do you want me to do for you?" Jesus asked him.
> The blind man said, "Rabbi, I want to see."
> "Go," Jesus said, "your faith has healed you."
> Immediately he received his sight and
> followed Jesus along the road. Mark 10:51-52

There is an old VBS song about this man. "The blind man stood by the road, and he cried, 'Show me the way, the way to go home.'" Here in the Scripture we see the blind man asking for his physical sight and getting it, immediately. Jesus said to him, "Your faith has healed you." Certainly he had to ask and Jesus had to respond, but I think those words are so important, "Your faith has healed you." Coupled with the words from the song, it is a key to powerful prayer. Faith and the desire to go home. The blind man wanted to see; of course he did. I can't help but think that physical sight was secondary considering that he could already see the Truth.

In contrast to James and John (verses 35-39), the blind man's request is an easy one for Jesus. The man isn't asking for power or glory. He doesn't appear to be concerned with a spotlight. He just wants his eyes to see what his heart has seen already. He wants to see Jesus.

When we pray, can we pray with the humility and openness of the blind man? Can we say simply "Rabbi, I want _____?" We should. The most important thing for us to know at the end of the day is that God is God, and we are not. This life is the means to an end. Do you want to see, walk, and talk while you are here? Of course, we all do. Most of us already have those blessings. So what do we want? To enjoy the big event without some mild illness? To have a happy family? To be married? A little quiet time? Some company? Sure, there are any number of things that can come after the words "Rabbi, I want," and Jesus encourages us to ask for them. Our Father wants nothing more than to bless us. We need to want nothing more than Him, and the blessings will freely flow.

Secret Living

And when you pray, do not be like the hypocrites, for they love to pray standing in the synagogues and on the street corners to be seen by men. I tell you the truth, they have received their reward in full. But when you pray, go into you room, close the door and pray to your Father who is unseen. Then you Father who sees what is done in secret will reward you. Matthew 6:5-6

There are many versions of the cliché that says character is what we are in the dark. They share the theme that we are our truest selves when no one is looking. I hope that's true. When I am alone with God, I am my best self. I have no need for posturing or exaggerating to impress Him. He doesn't ask for my opinion, so I never have to soften it to preserve His feelings or favor. He doesn't gossip, so I never have to choose to go along or walk away. Alone with God, I can relax and be the person I would like to be all the time.

I understand the clichés. I know they refer to the little choices we make when no one is looking. It is true that sometimes we all cut a corner we wouldn't cut if we knew we were being observed. In my life, that isn't as much of an issue as the fitting-into-the-world issue. I'm far from perfect, and I'm pretty sure everyone around me knows that. I don't expect anyone to be surprised if I make a nasty remark or compromise where compromise isn't the best choice. When we have the confession at church, my biggest guilt comes in the "things left undone" category. It isn't the dark or alone time that is the big problem for me. It is the social/work world light and the crowds that are my enemies.

Maybe you fall into that group too. We know God loves us. He knows what we're thinking and doing all the time. When we are alone with Him, we are aware of that, but when we add a crowd it gets a little more difficult. I could live my faith 24/7 if people didn't annoy/harass/irritate/disappoint/tempt me. Couldn't you?

There is a freedom in being alone with God that does not exist in the world for me, at least not yet. Maybe you feel the same way. For us these verses can be reminders that if God can see what we do in secret, He can surely see what everyone else sees too. When will He be pleased? What will disappoint Him? Surely we can develop character in the dark, but then we need to present it to the world. Strive to be the person who God sees and try not to worry about what anyone else thinks they see.

Tools of the Trade

Flee the evil desires of youth, and pursue righteousness, faith, love and peace, along with those who call on the Lord out of a pure heart. Don't have anything to do with foolish arguments, because you know they produce quarrels. 2 Timothy 2:22

This verse is talking about temptation. The word is not included, but it's there all the same. When we desire something we can be tempted by it or whatever means it takes to get it. We can also be tempted to join in a foolish argument that has nothing to do with us. It is clear what we are to do instead of giving into temptation. We are to pursue the truly good things in life—faith, love, and peace. I think the key is in the words "pure heart."

Lately I have been tempted to involve myself in other people's foolish arguments. I have also been tempted to judge the speck in my sister's eye while ignoring the board in my own. Thank God I have been aware of those temptations and am able to fight them with prayer. God supplies us with an armor (Ephesians 6:10-18) and the weapons we need to battle the *"spiritual forces of evil"* as well as our own sinful nature. He also promises to be our protection.

When the temptations seem too big and the pull is just too strong, ask for that hedge of protection. We remember it when we are ill or in imminent danger, but that same protection is available to us when we are facing the small matters. The next time you're tempted to say something unkind or expose another person's faults, pray for that hedge to separate you from evil.

Life is full of temptations, some obvious and some subtle. We need to keep our eyes on Jesus and try to maintain a pure heart. The tools we need are at our disposal. We just need to pick them up.

Important Opinions

> **As for those who seemed important—whatever they were makes no difference to me; God does not judge by external appearance—those men added nothing to my message. Galatians 2:6**

The men around Paul were challenging his authority. They wanted him to prove his anointing. They were doing their best to make him feel inferior to Peter, John, and James. To their way of thinking Jesus, didn't handpick him. He had a reputation, and it wasn't pretty. There were a lot of factors that they could and did use against him. None of it had any effect because Paul knew that God had chosen him. He also knew that God's opinion is really the only one that counts.

I remember when my children were younger and would have some great idea or plan for the family. They would plot and plan convincing each other that the plan would work. Then they would present it to me. Sometimes they were successful, and sometimes they weren't. If their requests were achievable and seemed appropriate, then I went along but sometimes what they saw as possible went beyond ridiculous. They were children and their view was limited. In the end mine was the more farseeing vision, and mine was the only opinion that mattered.

That is how it is with God and us. We see the externals, the here and now. We do not see the future. We cannot see the effects one event could have. Looking at people we see through our own perspective not what is real. Our view is limited and clouded by what we think we know.

Just as the people of Paul's day thought they knew him by one, former, aspect of his character, we think we "know" someone when we know very little about them at all. God knows us inside out. He knows our hearts and our motivations. He judges us on the whole picture, not on the pretty face or phony friendliness. We don't fool God when we smile while thinking, "Oooh, I can't stand her!" Nor do we fool Him when we volunteer to help then resent the person or people we are helping.

It does us well to remember that our view is limited. We aren't expected to know or to judge. That is God's job.

Treasures

My purpose is that they may be encouraged in heart and united in love, so that they may have the full riches of complete understanding, in order that they may know the mystery of God, namely Christ, in whom, are hidden all the treasures of the wisdom and knowledge. Colossians 2:2-3

Wouldn't you like to have *"all the treasures of wisdom and knowledge?"* I would. It would be great never to have to question a decision or wonder about a plan. This Scripture, the written Truth, says that we can have it through Christ. Can't you just hear the groans? We were all hoping for something to just be dropped in our laps. "There you go, there's your wisdom with a side of knowledge. Oh, would you like mercy with that?" Yes, we would. We would like mercy, compassion and infallibility if you've got some.

The good news is that it is all available to us in Christ. We are never going to feel fully wise or knowledgeable. We will continue to question our levels of mercy and compassion. While I have met many people who believe they are infallible, I don't know anyone who is truly without blemish. In this life we are striving for wisdom, knowledge, mercy, etc. We won't achieve them here, but with Paul we can continue to strive until Jesus calls us home.

The key to obtaining any level of wisdom or knowledge is right here in these verses, Christ. Knowing Christ, loving him, sharing in his triumphs and his sufferings will bring us wisdom, knowledge, mercy, and anything else we need. We can't purchase these traits. They are gifts. We can receive them simply by drawing close to the One who embodied everything we strive to attain. Get to know the One who loved you first, even before you were born and will love you forever. Jesus Christ is our key to all things worth having, and he wants us to have it all. Isn't that Good News?

Life Lessons

He said to them, "It is not for you to know the times or dated the Father has set by his own authority." Acts 1:7

I have spent the last year conversing with the Lord on mainly two topics, joy and timing. Those two don't seem to be a good mix, but you can't have one without accepting the other. So in His infinite wisdom, God is graciously teaching me about the one right alongside the other.

It is important to note that joy and happiness are two different things. Happy is a fleeting feeling easily deterred by the slightest change or challenge. Joy is deeper. It is the recognition of a presence larger than we are that supports us and gives our lives direction. I may not *feel* happy, but I can still *know* joy. Joy is more of a security issue. If I know that the God of the universe has my best interest at heart, I know that nothing can defeat me, and in that very protected position there is great joy.

Timing is much more difficult issue, and it causes great problems for joy. When I question God's timing, I question that He has my best interest at heart. That dents my feelings of security, and that robs me of a little piece of joy.

We live life according to schedules most of the time. Working a Monday-Friday job, I lose track of the day of the week during vacations. Without a firm schedule, I sometimes find it more difficult to accomplish things. I, like many people I know, am a prisoner of time. God is outside of time as we know it. His time is not the same as ours. As events occur and sometimes collide, we wonder why. The answer to that is not always clear, but when we can understand the level of our security, tank rises. That little collision is then seen as God's providence while the unexplainable one remains a problem. Whenever an interruption turns into a blessing, we see God's timing as good, but when we feel we are waiting too long, we rage against God's timing.

The lessons I am learning about joy and timing aren't always pleasant, but they are all valuable. Don't let a clock or calendar steal your joy. Try to see God's hand of providence in all things, even delays.

Big Mountains

Then the disciples came to Jesus in private and asked, "Why couldn't we drive it out?" He replied, "Because you have so little faith. I tell you the truth, if you have faith as small as a mustard seed you can say to this mountain, "Move from here to there" and it will move. Nothing will be impossible for you." Matthew 17:19-20

On my way to work each day, I pass the billboard of a small company. They use the board to offer political views, community announcements, and now-and-again uplifting statements. These past few days I have seen these words every morning:

Don't Tell God How Big Your Mountain Is

Every day I finish the statement as I drive by, "Tell the mountain how big your God is." We all forget from time to time that the size of the mountain is irrelevant. God is greater than anything and everything.

This little sign has at times irritated me and at times amused me. The positive thinking statements they've shared prior to this one have been of the simple cliché form and not terribly enlightening. This one isn't significantly different on some levels. However, the missing last half has forced me to not only complete the statement but also stay mindful of it. It's a pithy little cliché unless you truly believe it.

We've encountered a rather large, seemingly insurmountable mountain in our family during this time, but the size of the mountain is insignificant. God is huge. Our God wants the best for us. We are blessed with the ability to say to any circumstance, "You have no power here." We are gifted with the weapon of praise. We can say with great confidence the favor of the Lord is on me and my family/job/finances/marriage/health. Name your mountain. Look it straight in the face (pun intended) and say, "My God is a big God."

Don't tell God the how big your mountain is; He knows. Tell the mountain how big your God is and watch it disintegrate. God is for you, and no one dares come against you (Romans 8:31).

Authority

On the seventh day, when King Xerxes was in high spirits from wine, he commanded the seven eunuchs who served him—Mehuman, Biztha, Harbona, Bighta, Abagtha, Zethar and Carcas—to bring before him Queen Vashti, wearing her royal crown, in order to display her beauty to the people and nobles for she was lovely to look at. But when the attendants delivered the king's command, Queen Vashti refused to come. Then the king became furious and burned with anger.

"This very day the Persian and Median women of the nobility who have heard about the queen's conduct will respond to all the kings' nobles in the same way. There will be no end of disrespect and discord.

Therefore, if it pleases the king let him issue a royal decree and let it be written in the laws of Persia and Median, which cannot be repealed, that Vashti is never again to enter the presence of King Xerxes. Also let the king give her royal position to someone else who is better than she. Then when the king's edict is proclaimed throughout all the vast realm, all the women will respect their husbands, from the least to the greatest." Esther 1:10-12, 18-20

King Xerxes calls for his queen Vashti, but she refuses to come to him. This was much more than an ordinary wife saying, "Just a minute, dear." This was the queen refusing the order of her king in a way that was not simply disrespectful but also set an example for all the women of the region. If the queen doesn't have to answer to the king, why should Mrs. Y answer to Mr. Y? She shouldn't, and she won't, basing her actions on the standard set by the queen. King Xerxes response is to banish her and to find a queen who will come when he calls, a woman who will understand what it means to be summoned by the king.

This passage is full of lessons for us. It isn't just about marriage but also an analogy of Israel and God. The Israelites did not come when God called. They denied the Messiah and that opened the door for us, the Gentiles. This passage teaches that just because you are holding something in your hand today does not ensure that it will be there tomorrow. The privilege will be taken from you if you don't appreciate it. It is about authority.

Some people are great with authority. They understand the need for it, and though they don't always agree, they know there are times when they have to comply anyway. I have slowly come into that group and I believe that I have finally arrived with the help of a very learned pastor who said, "If you want to prosper, you have to accept authority." It helps that I know he gleaned that knowledge from Romans 13:5 and Matthew 22:18-21. Jesus taught the importance of submitting to authority.

I guess this passage gets sticky for some because the authority here is a husband. It brings up the whole "wives submit to your husband" issue. The truth of that is the same for us as it was for Vashti and for the Israelites. We must all first submit to the authority of God, and then everything can fall into its rightful place.

The consequences for Vashti and for the Israelites were the same and yet different. Xerxes replaced Vashti, giving her no second chance. God replaced the Israelites but continues to offer them a second chance. We need to be grateful for the opportunity that is given to us by God and gently invite our friends and neighbors to come along. We can make the best invitation by imitation. We can submit to God and any authority He places in our path and in that, show His sovereignty to those who are watching us.

Bold Questions

> Then James and John, the two sons of Zebedee, came to him. "Teacher," they said, "we want you to do for us whatever we ask."
>
> "What do you want me to do?" he asked.
>
> They replied, "Let one of us sit at your right and the other one at your left in your glory."
>
> "You don't know what you are asking," Jesus said. "Can you drink the cup I drink or be baptized with the baptism I am baptized with?"
>
> "We can" they answered.
>
> Jesus said to them, "You will drink the cup I drink and be baptized with the baptism I am baptized with, but to sit at my right or my left is not for me to grant. These places belong to those for whom they have been prepared." Mark 10:35-38

The behavior of James and John here seems impudent to me, to have the audacity to speak to Jesus that way. *"We want you to do for us whatever we ask."* It's demanding, but even as it makes me wince, I remember that Jesus said over and over that we should ask for whatever we want in his name. The wording is just harsh. Of course the request is huge, and as Jesus answers, not his to grant. It makes me wonder how often my request/demands are out of line.

When we get a no answer, there is often the temptation to think that God doesn't care about us. Our needs are unimportant. That couldn't be farther from the truth. When James and John asked this of Jesus, they were thinking of two people, James and John. They weren't thinking of Peter or Matthew. They had no idea that Saul/Paul would enter the picture. They gave no thought to Elijah, Moses, or any of the other great men that had gone before them. They only knew what they wanted. Beyond that, they didn't understand that Jesus couldn't make that promise. Father God is in charge on that question.

Jesus *"being in very nature God"* (Philippians 2:6a) understood that he couldn't grant that request. Could he heal them? Yes. Feed them? Certainly.

But he couldn't say, "Oh sure, you can sit wherever you want when we get home." The Father has assigned those places.

Are we still able to ask for anything in Jesus's name? Yes we are. We do have to understand that our requests are subject to God's sovereignty. We know that God is right and that His will for us is best. Sometimes it is hard to accept that when we aren't getting the answer we want, but it is true. Even Jesus in his time with us knew there were some things that just couldn't be negotiated. It comes back to the usual place: God is in control. We just need to trust and obey. Everything will fall in place one day, and it will all be well.

Sheep

The miracles I do in my Father's name speak for me, but you do not believe because you are not my sheep. My sheep listen to my voice; I know them, and they follow me. John 10:25b-27

Do you know Jesus? Do you want everyone you know to know Jesus? So many of us do. We read all about evangelism. We listen avidly to preachers who are determined to foster evangelists. We mimic actions that have been successful for others and then we realize the truth. You can lead a horse to water, but you can't make him drink. Maybe the horse is not thirsty. We are excited about Jesus because we know him. We are thirsty for his presence in our lives because we have lived both with and without it.

It is frustrating when we know the difference a relationship with Jesus could make in the life of a person who is happy to live without it, but what can we do? We can still talk about Jesus, and the miracles in our own lives. Even more than that, we can live it. We can smile more often. We can face adversity without falling to pieces and without making everyone in our circle aware of it. The joy of the Lord can and should emanate from us. That will draw others to Christ much faster than cajoling.

Remember the children's story *Green Eggs and Ham*? The more Sam pedaled those green eggs, the more his intended convert resisted. Imagine if Sam had sat himself down and eaten those eggs just as happily as possible with all the requisite ooohing and ahhhing. The other guy would have been drawn to a meal that could inspire such great enjoyment.

Maybe we should be more obvious in our enjoyment of our Lord and let that pleasure do the talking.

Speaking Heartese

You brood of vipers, how can you who are evil say anything good? For out of the overflow of the heart the mouth speaks. Matthew 12:34

And God raised us up with Christ and seated us with him in the heavenly realms in Christ Jesus, in order that in the coming ages he might show the incomparable riches of his grace expressed in his kindness to us in Christ Jesus. Ephesians 2:7

Out of the overflow of our hearts our mouths speak. We say we are followers of Christ. We say we believe that he always has our best interests at heart. Unfortunately we also use the words never and always. "I never win anything." "I'm always the last person anyone thinks about." "My life is so hard, and it is never going to get better." "I always get the short end of the stick." I have heard these sentiments far too often lately. Too many people with whom I have spoken believe the enemy's lies that nothing good is ahead and no one cares. The worst part is that in a couple of situations of my own, I have used the same terms.

The wake-up call came to me the other day when I heard a wonderful sermon about the kindness and grace of God. The preacher continuously reiterated his belief that God wants to do the best for us and give the best to us. I absolutely believe that, but I realized that there are areas of my life where I don't apply that belief. That was a tough-enough truth. Then I realized that by my affirmative head nods or sympathetic murmurs I have encouraged a few friends to carry on without regard to the Truth.

It is true that life will hand us bad apples, but we have to believe in the orchard full of good fruit waiting for us up ahead. We know God has a plan for us, and we know His plans are perfect. We have to believe and not just silently believe but verbally express the belief that God is about to do miracles in our lives. We shame the devil when we declare our faith in God's providence. Conversely we empower the enemy when we give into his whispers that we are never going to see light at the end of the tunnel.

As we say the negative never and always statements our enemy dances with joy, but our Lord's heart is saddened. Those statements tell God we don't believe He will deliver us. When we acknowledge our hurt feelings or fears but follow that with a statement of faith, we put ourselves in line to receive even more grace.

Declare today that God is for you. Say right out loud that no matter how hard someone or something is trying to defeat you that victory is yours in Christ. Let faithful words flow from your heart of love for God and receive His kindness.

Comparisons

Each one should test his own actions. Then he can take pride in himself, without comparing himself to somebody else, for each one should carry his own load.
Anyone who receives instruction in the word must share all good things with his instructor.
Do not be deceived; God cannot be mocked. A man reaps what he sows. Galatians 6:4-7

Reading these verses I was reminded of many of the young people in my life. Just the other day a friend at church shared a story with me about a young man we both know. He had elicited her sympathy by telling her how another had wronged him. I know she expected me to be immediately sympathetic, and she was quite taken aback when instead I told her that he had committed the very same act against the very same person.

These verses in Galatians remind me of a few other places in the New Testament. There are several where we are advised not to think of ourselves too highly but to understand that all our value is a gift from God. Two stories stand out to me when I read this, the story of the speck and the plank and the story of the tax collector and the Pharisee.

Though I quite often hear young people making comparisons that they believe makes their sin less significant, I know that we are all guilty of it. The difference is the younger people haven't caught on to the fact that it doesn't make them look any better. It in fact reminds us of the wrong they have done. When we get older, we may get quieter about it, but many of us still justify our own behavior in light of what we perceive as someone else's greater sin.

Here Paul tells us to judge our own actions. He reminds us that God is well aware of our heart conditions. God loves each of us as if there were only one of us, and He judges us that way too. It doesn't matter what Jane and John Doe are doing. It matters what we are doing and why we are doing it. At some point in our lives we will all realize the truth of the words "a man reaps what he sows." Try to ensure that your harvest will be a pleasant one.

Stepping Stone

Jesus said to his disciples, "Things that cause people to sin are bound to come, but woe to that person through whom they come. It would be better for him to be thrown into the sea with a millstone tied around his neck than for him to cause one of these little ones to sin. So watch yourselves." Luke 17:1-3

There is a lot of responsibility in these verses. They state clearly how our actions can and will effect those around us, especially the impressionable ones.

Wouldn't you resent a person who stepped on you to get to the top? We don't feel kindly toward those people who use our talents to make themselves look better. As with most things that theory is different in God's hands. I long for people to use me to get closer to God. I feel honored, privileged, when someone asks me to pray for them or with them. On the other hand, when someone tells me they are following my example in some way, I get a little nervous. I better be on my toes, doing it right, not casting a bad light on my Lord.

The verses from Luke leave no question as to how God will deal with those whose actions cause others to sin. They also open the door for us to see how we can lead people to Christ. We can't force anyone toward God. We can't convince anyone who doesn't want to be convinced, but we can be available to those who are seeking.

Most of us resent that social climber or professional back stabber who uses us or a relationship we may have to better his/her own circumstances. When someone wants to use my relationship with Christ to get to know him better, I am all for it. Ask me anything. I'll answer if I can, and if I can't, we'll find the answer together. The image of someone climbing me to get closer to God is quite acceptable. If that person gets closer, he/she can share the knowledge with me.

The problem in these verses for me is the fear that my stumble or fall will topple that seeker right back to the starting gate. A friend recently asked me to pray for an issue close to her heart. I agreed, and I did pray. I realized a few days later that I hadn't checked back with her. This is a person taking baby steps of faith, and she was counting on me. I immediately went to her and asked about her request. What if I hadn't? She may have seen me as all talk, and it may have been the deciding factor in her approach to God. At this moment in time in her life, I am God's ambassador. It is a huge responsibility and honestly one that I desire, but I need to do it to the best of my ability. We all do.

We need to make sure we are stepping-stones and not stumbling blocks. Prayer will give us the strength and ability to represent our God well.

Word Bites

Speak to each other with psalms, hymns and spiritual songs. Sing and make music in your heart to the Lord, always giving thanks to God the Father for everything, in the name of our Lord Jesus Christ. Ephesians 5:19-20

It must be my season for clichés because the other day I read one that really hit home. It said, "Keep the 'bark' out of your bite." I thought about the number of times I have snapped at my husband and/or children. It's so easy to make the quick biting comment and so hard to undue the damage. I am not suggesting that we sing to each other or only quote Scripture just that we realize how easily the way a word is spoken can change a whole conversation.

Even when we don't have any intention of offending, we can manage to do it. Once a coworker shared that she would be taking a day off. I asked her if it was for a good reason. My actual words were, "I hope it's for a good reason." What I meant was I hoped she would be doing something enjoyable as opposed to a doctor's appointment or obligation of some sort. The look on her face told me that what she heard was very different. To her, it sounded as if I were asking if she *had* a good reason as in "was it really a worthwhile endeavor?". We laughed about it once we got on the same wavelength, but it is a perfect example of how things go wrong simply by vernacular or tone. If we hadn't cleared up the misconception, she may well have resented me for asking. I in turn would not have understood her coldness, and the results could have been quite different.

Sometimes it is so hard to keep a pleasant tone or even just a monotone, but we really have to try. Harsh words are very hard to forget. If I slap your face, you'll feel it for a minute; but if I belittle you or minimize your feelings, you may never forget it.

We need to follow the advice in Ephesians 4:15 and speak the truth in love. We don't have to sugarcoat every word, but we do have to remember that everyone has feelings. Often we hear people say they are just joking. It's only a joke if both parties see the humor in it. We need to keep the bark out of our bite and the bite out of our speech.

Patterned Behavior

Join with others in following my example, brothers, and take note of those who live according to the pattern we gave you. Philippians 3:17

The verse says to take note of people who are *living* according to the pattern set by the disciples. We need to watch those who are living it, not talking about it not lecturing about it but living it.

There are tons of people who would love to advise everyone around them on how to live and breathe, but are they living according to the pattern? Advice is fine if it is solicited, but unsolicited, it is often interference or worse criticism disguised as kindness. Worse than that even is the backhanded slur.

Have you ever been thrown together with someone who feels that they know best? If the rest of us aren't living according to his/her plan, we are wrong. Sometimes he/she uses words to let us all know this as in the "well, I would never" or "I always" statements. Never and always statements are a little suspect in my book, so that would be bad enough, but there is always more. There are also the looks. You know the kind. There is no sound but the thunder is still mighty loud. The eyes roll. The jaw takes on a very disparaging tightness. Then the headshakes relay all the disgust and disapproval such a small move possibly can.

It is no fun coming across people who communicate in those ways. Even in this God is good. Watching those behaviors we can learn to live the speck and board Scripture (Matthew 6:3-5). We may not behave that way on a regular basis, but it never hurts to question our own motives more carefully. It doesn't make those chronically critical types any easier to be around, but it does teach us to live what we believe as graciously as possible.

We are all much more useful to God when we come humbly and attempt to live according to the pattern to the best of our ability. Our behavior should draw others to Christ, not push them away. Look at the pattern of your life. Does it affirm or condemn?

Fearful

And as he taught them, he said,

> "'My house will be called
> a house of prayer for all nations'

But you have made it a den of robbers."
The chief priests and the teachers of the law heard this and began looking for a way to kill him, for they feared him, because the whole crowd was amazed at his teaching. Mark 11:17-18

They feared him because the people were listening to him. When we share our faith in a less than receptive crowd we too may be ridiculed. It is highly unlikely that it will cost us our lives, but it may cause us some uncomfortable moments at work or in our social circle. Fear is a nasty thing.

The authorities in Jesus's day feared him because the people were listening to him, and because if he were right, they would have to make some major changes. Does that second half sound familiar? We all know someone who loves to argue about faith with us, don't we? They have to argue, and they have to prove us wrong, or else they have to make some changes and no thank-you.

Jesus encountered this opposition in the religious sector, and we do too. It is one thing to run across reluctance in our nonbelieving friends or coworkers. It's much different when we are speaking to a person who claims to share our belief. Much like the Pharisees those people want to pick and chose the Scriptures that work for them. They have no problem with the ones that allow them to live as they please, but those others are to be ignored. I love the rationalization that you can't take the whole thing literally. Hmm . . . and how do we decide what is truth and what is filler? Apparently, as it suits our lifestyle.

Don't be afraid to be feared or to show a little righteous indignation. Jesus sets a fine example here in these verses. He invites us to stand with him and to keep worship pure. Let's do it.

Joke or No Joke

Those who sit at he gate mock me. I am the song of drunkards.
Psalm 69:12

When it comes to jokes about any person in particular, I am uncomfortable. Generalized joking is okay, but when you put a name to it, then it becomes personal. I am a huge figure-skating fan. When a talented skater develops and displays a certain new twist on an old move or creates an entirely new move, the element takes the skater's name. That is an honor. There seems to be a trend now that when a person makes a huge public gaffe, that gaffe takes on that person's name. There is no honor there.

The words from the Psalm are comparable to political jokes of today. As Christians whether we like them or not, we should pray for our politicians/leaders because we don't know the whole story, and because again like it or not they do have power, and we want that power directed correctly. It isn't amusing to make a joke out of a person of that position. What if they begin to see themselves as a joke? How seriously will they take the job? When we implore them to pass or not pass legislation, we want them to take it all seriously. How can we ask for that when later they will be the featured joke of some late-night talk show?

This isn't a modern issue or a new sin. In Ephesians we are warned against coarse joking. (Ephesians 5:4) Joking minimizes the sting of an issue and the value of a person. There should be taboos. There certainly should be things about which we do not joke. When is a joke not a joke? When at the end of it someone or something will be devalued and/ or look foolish. It isn't funny when sin that grieves the heart of God is thought of so lightly that we even have a fun quirky name for it. Jokes should be amusing not abusing.

Naming Names

We give thanks to you O God, we give thanks, for your Name is near, men tell of your wonderful deeds. Psalm 75:1

The name of the Lord is a strong tower; the righteous run to it and are safe. Proverbs 18:10

We praise God. We sing songs to and about Him. We flinch when we hear people abusing His name and all with good reason. The name of the Lord is a strong tower.

How often do you feel that your prayers are inadequate? When someone presents me with a very serious prayer request, there is that moment when I feel the cold grip of fear that my prayers will not be sufficient. I wonder if I will even find the words to draw God's attention. That moment is fleeting because, thank God, my prayers have precious little to do with me.

I have spent the last few days in prayer for three very dear friends. I promise you my words aren't going to help them, but my prayers will. The difference is that my words are just that, words, but my prayers are gifts, from God and oddly enough back to God. In the last few days, I have begged God, praised Him, and questioned Him on behalf of my friends. For two of the three I have a little knowledge of their situation for the other I have none. It doesn't matter because the truth of it is that sometimes all we need to know is the name of the Lord.

We worry and fret about the quality of our prayers, but any prayer offered in the precious name of Jesus goes directly to our Father's ear. He doesn't care what words we use or how long or short our prayer may be. He cares that we trust Him enough to call on His name.

In our most desperate situations we sometimes have no words. We rely on the help of the Holy Spirit to pray for us. Even then we can simply shout or even whisper the name of the Lord, and He will hear us. The people of the Old Testament had all kinds of variations on God's name all adapted to their particular circumstance. Find one or a few you feel you can lean on, and when words fail, just call on that name. Run into it and be safe.

Be Yourself

They came to him and said, "Teacher, we know that you are a man of integrity. You aren't swayed by men, because you pay no attention to who they are; but you teach the way of God in accordance with the truth. Is it right to pay taxes to Caesar or not?" Mark 12:14

Does the tone of your conversation change depending on your audience? Do you speak one way at home, another at work, and still another when you are with your friends? Many people do. It's okay if it is the difference between professionalism and just hanging out. The trouble starts when the beliefs or opinions take on different colors according to the hearers. No one should be able to sway you if you know what you believe is right.

Here in Luke the Pharisees wanted to catch Jesus doing something wrong. They say they know he is a man of integrity. That is their way of letting him know he better give the right answer. They were so very eager to pounce on any answer that didn't adhere to the law. Jesus's answer to them "give to Caesar what is Caesar's and to God what is God's" left no room for argument. Jesus encourages us to live under the authority of the world wherever it does not violate Scripture.

The right answer is always the right answer. If we answer any question according to our belief, in agreement with Scripture there is no room for argument. That doesn't mean there won't be one. It just means that it will be pointless.

People who do not believe will always try to pick at what we do believe. We just need to be true to our Lord regardless of our audience. In worldly matters there is room for opinion. In matters of morality and right living, only one opinion counts, and it is well represented in the Bible.

Jesus paid no attention to who the listeners were. He spoke the same way regardless of his audience. We need to follow his lead and not be swayed by the opinions of others.

Shout or Whisper

> Shout for joy to the Lord, all the earth.
> Worship the Lord with gladness;
> Come before him with glorious songs.
> Know that the Lord is God.
> It is he who made us, and we are his,
> we are his people, the sheep of his pasture.
> Enter his gates with thanksgiving
> and his courts with praise;
> give thanks to him and praise his name.
> For the Lord is good and his love endures forever;
> His faithfulness continues through all generations. Psalm 100

There are times in life when it is very hard to believe that there is a reason to shout with joy. The admonition comes at the front of the Psalm, but the reason comes at the end: "For the Lord is good and his love endures forever."

Maybe it helps to know that King David mostly likely is the psalmist here. If anyone knew about sin and hardship, it was David. So these words come from someone who knew how to find joy in the midst of sorrow, fear, pain, and shame.

Joy is different from happiness. It doesn't have the same feeling. Joy is more settled, as much a cousin to confidence as to happiness. We can feel joy even as our hearts are breaking. The power of joy is released when we recognize its presence, when we shout out that the Lord is good. Those shouts are so effective when the enemy would have us believe that we are down and out. We give glory to God, and somehow the situation seems better. We know that we are not alone. We remember that God's faithfulness has no end.

No matter how low we feel, we need to summon the strength to shout with joy even if that shout is only a whisper.

Famine

"The days are coming," declares the sovereign Lord, 'when I will send a famine through the land—not a famine of food or a thirst for water, but a famine of hearing the words of the Lord." Amos 8:11-12

Famines, thank God, are not something with which we are familiar. America has not experienced famine. I remember gasoline being an issue when I was younger but never food or water. Surely we have people who are better off than others, but as a nation we have not experienced a situation of no food or water and no means with which to obtain any. It must be terrifying, but these words from Amos are more terrifying to me than any famine I can imagine. What could be worse than a famine of hearing the words of the Lord?

My own family has gone through thick and thin times as many families have, but we have never been completely destitute. If we ever had been or ever are, I know that I have extended family and friends who would help me. In times of famine, no one can help.

Think about what that means spiritually. We all have our dry days. We pray and read Scripture, but we still feel empty. There is no spark. The desire remains unanswered. In those times I usually turn to one of my prayer partners and ask for their help. What if the answer that came back brought no relief, no comfort? What if my prayer partner said, "I'm not hearing from God either"? We might go together then to another believer and get the same response. Consider that pattern just repeating and repeating with no one being able to offer spiritual food.

It's an awful thought and one I am glad will never be for us. Our Father sent his Son to die for our sins. The Son left us with the comfort and grace of the indwelling Holy Spirit. We may at times feel alone and all dried up, starving for some insight or comfort, but we won't starve, and we are never alone.

Thank God "the words of the Lord" are always available to us. His Spirit gives us life. It is in Him that we live and move. He will never leave or forsake us. We should be very grateful for that and be so thankful that the famine discussed by the prophet Amos will not happen to us.

Healing Power

And a woman was there who had been subject to bleeding for twelve years. She had suffered a great deal under the care of many doctors and had spent all she had, yet instead of getting better she grew worse. When she heard about Jesus, she came up behind him in the crowd and touched his cloak, because she thought, "If I just touch his clothes, I will be healed." Immediately her bleeding stopped and she felt in her body that she was freed from her suffering.

At once Jesus realized that power had gone out from him. He turned around in the crowd and asked, "Who touched my clothes?"

"You see the people crowding against you," his disciples answered, "and yet you can ask, 'Who touched me?'"

But Jesus kept looking around to see who had done it. Then the woman, knowing what had happened to her, came and fell at his feet and, trembling with fear, told him the whole truth. He said to her, "Daughter, your faith has healed you. Go in peace and be freed from your suffering." Mark 5:25-34

Power went out from Jesus. He felt power go out from him. The poor guys with him are confused. They can't believe he expects to identify the person who touched him, but it isn't surprising that he could. They had an enormous connection. She was suffering. She touched his cloak. His healing power washed over her and her suffering ended. It is amazing, and we all want to be able to use that same power.

At this moment I am begging for that power for two friends of mine. One is facing surgery that is supposed to save her life. The other is just clinging to life and no one knows how to adequately help him. For me the answer for both is the same. We need a miracle.

When Jesus left us the gift of the Holy Spirit, he left us with the ability to do all the things he was enabled by Our Father to do. Through Jesus we have access to that same power—the power that resurrected him, the power that healed the bleeding woman, and the power that calmed the raging sea all come from the same place, the Father of the heavenly lights.

The woman in this Scripture knows something about healing that we all need to know as well. Touch is important. Whenever it is possible, we should put our hands on the people for whom we are praying. We open a channel so to speak. We create a pathway and if our Father sees fit to anoint us with the power to heal or comfort it can flow right through to the person for whom we are praying.

I am blessed to be able to touch my friend heading to surgery. For my other friend, I have to pray and hope that God sends someone else to put his/her hand on him and pray. I trust that He will. I encourage you to reach out and touch someone with whom you are praying. It really does make a difference.

Well Dressed

Be dressed ready for service and keep your lamps burning, like men waiting for their master to return from a wedding banquet, so that when he comes and knocks they can immediately open the door for him. Luke 12:35-36

Have you ever been taken by surprise by a knock at the door? Of course you weren't dressed, right? It never fails. I very rarely have anyone just drop in, but if they do, it is always when I am still in pj's having a lazy day or wearing my oh so attractive grungy work clothes. There is always the temptation not to answer the door. At that moment I am not dressed or ready for company, but am I dressed and ready for service?

The "dressed" referred to here is not about pretty blouses or nice skirts. Jesus is not admonishing us to be June Cleaver. This "dressed" is about our spiritual clothing. Are we decked out in selfish ambition, or are we draped in the fine silk of compassion? Are we wearing pride, or are we cloaked in humility?

When the Master comes and knocks, we want to be able to throw the door wide open. If we are covered up in laziness or anger, we will hesitate. If we are wrapped up in finger-pointing or greed, we will be less than eager to greet Him.

We need to be dressed in kindness, faithfulness, gentleness, joy, and peace. Then we will be ready to throw the door wide open to welcome our Master. It's okay if we have to take a second to pull off that apron of pride or self-righteousness as long as we are well dressed underneath.

Cheer Up

A cheerful heart is good medicine but a crushed spirit dries up the bones. Proverbs 17:22

When I was younger, I thought religion and anything that involved religion had to be serious. I thought that because it was what I was taught. When I began to develop my own relationship with Jesus, I still believed that I had to be serious, almost solemn, about it. My views on religion were bleeding all over my faith. I am not by nature a very serious person—responsible, yes—but not serious. There is a touch of humor to be found almost everywhere, but to be a *good Christian* I had to forget that and take life more seriously. It was rough going for a while as I tried so hard to be *good*.

Eventually, through Scriptures like this proverb and truly getting to know Jesus I realized I had been right all along. There is a touch of humor in most things. Sometimes we have to be serious, and tragedy is just that tragic but whenever possible find something to smile about. There are some amazingly blessed people who find some little foible and laugh about it even in the midst of their very worst days. We all need to find things to smile about or better yet find something to giggle about and take that further to laughing out loud.

If you think there is nothing to smile about, visit a preschool and listen to the little ones or watch teenagers interact. From very different perspectives, both are comical. God wants us to laugh and relax. Without frequent bursts of humor or downright silliness, we begin to take ourselves too seriously. We can become too heavenly minded to be any earthly good. Watch a silly movie, hang out with a two-year-old, or just sit and people watch but find something to laugh about. It will definitely improve your spirit.

Useless Backpack

Humble yourselves, therefore, before God's mighty hand that he may lift you up in due time. Cast all your anxiety on him because he cares for you. 1 Peter 5:6-7

There are many people in my life about whom I have great concern. I read an analogy the other day that is helping me to pray for them, and by the way I wish this analogy were my own. The author wrote of a man caught in a raging river. Several young men came along and formed a chain managing to pull him out. He was told that no one had ever survived being caught in the floodwaters of that river. The author said that is how our lives are without God. We are caught in the floodwaters of the world anchored by the heavy backpack of sin.

When I read that I pictured those for whom I am praying literally wearing their sin in a big cumbersome bag on their backs. It is impossible for them to work themselves free of that pack nor can they continue forward motion while carrying it. It makes praying for them so simple. I only need to pray that God will give them the grace to set that pack down and then replace that heaviness with the featherweight of his love and mercy.

Surely you know someone who carries a great package of sin. In fact, we all want to hang onto to certain sins, tucking them away in a pack on our backs. They bow our spines and hurt our shoulders, but we won't set them down. It is so freeing to know that God offers us His grace daily. He will gladly receive our pack of poison and replace it with love. Give him your pack and pray that those you love who are bowed under the weight of sin will hand Him theirs too.

Citizenship

Do not let your hearts be troubled. Trust in God, trust also in me. In my Father's hours are many rooms; if it were not so, I would have told you. I am going there to prepare a place for you. And if I go and prepare a place for you, I will come back and take you to be with me that you also may be where I am. You know the way to the place where I am going. John 14:1-4

Tradition is a great thing. It lends continuity in families, churches, and even small towns. Like any good thing, we can sometimes get too much. When the way things used to be becomes more important than the way things are, we have a problem.

I am a Yankee transplant who has lived in Florida for twenty years. I like it here—now. I didn't at first. In fact, I was rather rude. You know the type, the person who is always telling you how they do things up North. Adapting to the Southern lifestyle was not on my agenda until I had lived here for two years and went back "home" to visit. I came meekly back to the South quite ready to adapt to the slower pace and more laid-back lifestyle. There are things however that I will never be able to embrace. Terms like "might could" and "cent" where we mean "cents"—as in "can you lend me thirty cent?" No, but I can lend you thirty cent*s*. In verbal terms, I think it is still pretty apparent that I am not "from around here," at least not originally.

In a more serious way, I believe that is how God calls us to live in this world. To adapt enough to be approachable and able to serve but not so much that we blend right in with all the worldly behaviors.

When immigrants come to this country, there is no fault if they want to continue to cook the things they did at home. There is a problem if they refuse to live by our government's laws. Many of them speak their native language in their homes but speak English when in the community.

We too need to speak our native language, the language of God's love at home, but we also need to bring that language into the community. There are places where God will call us to adapt, to make ourselves accessible to people who are seeking Him and need guidance. There are other places where He never wants us to go. Words he does not want us to speak.

We need to remember that we are citizens of heaven. We are just visiting here, just seeing the sights and maybe trying to improve them a little. Speak your native language and feed people with the spiritual food of your homeland.

Consumed

> When you pass through the waters I will be with you;
> and when you pass through the rivers they will not sweep over you.
> When you walk through the fire you will not be burned;
> the flames will not set you ablaze.
> For I am the Lord your God.
> the Holy One of Israel, your Savior;
> Isaiah 43:2-3a

Sometimes the water seems pretty high, and the fire gets awfully hot. We turn to these verses, and we read them trying to hang on in faith. These are God's words through the prophet Isaiah. They are not Isaiah's words. We are not relying on a mortal man to keep such a huge promise. Still the water rises, and the flames lap. It's wet and it's hot and we're frightened. Those times are when we may experience a crisis of belief.

It doesn't make us any less Christian or any less committed to Christ. It just makes us nervous, scared, and anxious. If the words told to us through Isaiah and repeated in similar fashion through Jesus are true, then we have nothing to fear. Still the water rises and the flames lap.

We fall to our knees and shout or whisper, "Lord, help me." He often responds, "I am helping you." We can't see it. All we can see, hear, or feel is wet and hot. A pressure comes against us that we feel too small to resist. We are very correct. We are too small, but God is not.

The waves touch our shoulders, and the flames lick our cheeks. "Are you sure, Lord?" we cry. "Are you sure this isn't going to defeat me?" Oddly we can almost see Him smile. "I'm sure."

We give in. After all there is no alternative. "Okay then, Lord, have your way." The water rolls back, and the flames die down; eventually or perhaps immediately, we see what He saw all along. We weren't consumed. We were strengthened. We feel a new flame, but it comes from within. It is the call of the Holy Spirit. Now it is time for us to answer the call in our newfound strength, with faith that withstood the latest test.

We rise up, and we praise God. With each flood, with each fire, we choose to believe God or the enemy. The choice should be clear, but it rarely is which is why we have to keep making it every day.

For I am the Lord your God.
the Holy One of Israel, your Savior. Isaiah 43:3a

Blind Faith

As he neared Damascus on his journey, suddenly a light from heaven flashed around him. He fell to the ground and heard a voice say to him, "Saul, Saul, why do you persecute me?" Saul got up from the ground but when he opened his eyes he could see nothing. Acts 9:3-4, 8a

We've all heard the term "blind faith." The last few days nature has given me a taste of what that means. When I am on my way to work the sun is just coming out. As I leave my house, it is still pretty dusky, but as I get closer to work, there are spots where the sun is right in my eyes. In one particular place, the sun can be quite apparent. At that point I pull out my sunglasses and drop my visor. Then I round a very heavily shaded curve. For the past several days when I've reached the other side of that curve, the sun has been blinding. For a few seconds, I could not see a thing. One morning I turned the corner just praying that I hadn't missed a car coming at me. Thank God I had not. Thank God. That's when I started to see that corner as quite significant.

I was faced with a choice. I couldn't rely on my own sight. The sun, even with the sunglasses, was so bright that I couldn't see. I have to turn the corner to get to work so there wasn't much of a choice unless I wanted to sit there until the sun shifted and be very late. The truth is none of that ran through my mind at the time. I looked to the best of my ability and then trusted God to get me around that corner. He did. The next day as I was driving, I could see the sun burning the fog away. I've always heard that fog lifts, and maybe it does, but it certainly looked as if the sun were burning it away. The same light that had blinded me the day before was now making the way much more clear.

It made me think about life. How many corners do we have to turn where we really can't see if the way is clear? There are so many uncertainties in life, but God sees the whole picture. Perhaps the secret is in keeping our eyes on Him. With the sun so bright and so dominant, I only see sun at that corner.

Maybe we should make God's light so bright and so dominate in our lives that it becomes all we can see, and everything else is seen in the haze of that precious Light. Then our "corners" or decisions might be easier to handle. Perhaps we should all be blinded by the Light of Truth, taking all actions based on trust alone. The world asks us to be self-sufficient, but I believe God asks us to be fully yielded to Him. After all, for Saul/Paul true sight came after he was blinded by the Light. It's certainly something to think about.

God's Good Work

To him who is able to keep you from falling and to present you before his glorious presence without fault and with great joy—to the only God our Savior be glory majesty, power and authority, through Jesus Christ our Lord, before all ages now and forevermore! Amen.
Jude 24-25

I was rereading something that I believe the Lord had given me to write some time ago. Rereading it I found it to be something very different than I remembered which affirmed my belief that God is the author, and I am just the fingers. I said to the Lord, "You do nice work." I promise you I felt the reply, "Remember that the next time you look in a mirror."

It will help you to know that I avoid mirrors. I have never been one of those people who seeks out reflective surfaces, cameras, or anything that will force me to come face-to-face with well . . . my face or any other part of me for that matter. It has never seemed like sin or lack of gratitude, just an honest assessment of what is real. I see me very differently than God does, and apparently He has a problem with that.

I say that because just the evening before this encounter with God, I heard a teaching on loving ourselves. The pastor said that we cannot love our neighbors unless we first love ourselves. I was nodding in agreement thinking how much healthier my self-image has become just about the time he started hitting my issues. That's when I realized I have heard similar statements from my own pastor, my prayer partners, and have read the same type of teaching in two different books. Do you think God is trying to make a point with me?

So now ask yourself this question, what is God repeating to me? What am I hearing over and over? Do you, like I do, find too much fault with yourself? Are you too hard on you? Or is there another issue?

Do not think for a minute that I ran to a mirror and was oh so pleased. That is a long way off and may not happen until I reach home. I did stop and asses all that God has done in me, is doing in me, and will continue to do. The bad news is I'll probably still avoid mirrors and cameras. The good news is God will not give up. He is still working on me and on you. And you know what? He does great work.

Plenty

Then the Lord said to Moses I will rain down bread from heaven for you. The people are to go out each day and gather enough for that day. In this way I will test them and see whether they will follow my instructions. Exodus 16:4

Do you like zucchini? I do. You can make all kinds of things with it. It goes nicely with almost anything. I learned just how many ways you can cook and eat zucchini the summer after my first son was born. I was able to use that knowledge for the next four years until I moved to Florida. In those four summers, my neighbor Carmella blessed me with more zucchini than I thought it would be possible to consume. Truthfully, it was more than my little family could ever eat. We shared it with our extended family and still had enough to make bread, quiche, cookies, stews, and soups. I promise you if you need a recipe that involves zucchini, I have it somewhere. Carmella was generous with all the produce that she grew in her garden, but the zucchini must have been the most prolific. After a while as I was gracing family members with the overflow of my bounty, I would complain, "I don't know what she thinks I'm going to do with all of this zucchini!" Then I moved to Florida.

Suddenly my appreciation for Carmella's gifts to me grew. Not only was the zucchini here much (and I mean much) smaller than what she had grown, but the price was ridiculous. I'd gone from what will I do with it all to how badly do I really want it in a matter of minutes.

My history with zucchini is not unlike the Israelites and the manna or my history with so many other things. We want something, or we may even need it, but when it is provided so easily with no effort on our part, we forget to be grateful. As I said, Carmella gave me lots of things: tomatoes, beans, cookies, pizza, and advice. Carmella was great for giving little Irish me lots of old Italian wisdom. While it was all being dispensed, I semiappreciated it; but when it was gone, it became much more precious.

The produce was an obvious blessing. Carmella herself was less so. Sometimes the woman downright annoyed me. Then I moved to the *friendly*

South and didn't have a friend or neighborly neighbor. That is when I appreciated Carmella the most.

We look at the Israelites and think those stubborn, ungrateful fools. We see what God had in store for them and wonder why they couldn't. Most of us are pretty sure we would have seen it. Then we face reality. I don't know about you, but sometimes I don't need to read Exodus to find the stubborn, ungrateful fools. There's one right in my mirror.

Surprise!

Praise be to the Lord, to God our Savior, who daily bears our burdens. Psalm 68: 19

Has anyone ever given you a surprise party? I've had a couple. With one I remember trying so hard to pretend I didn't know what was going on, but with the other one, the first one, I really didn't know. For weeks my closest and dearest friend seemed weird. It seemed like she didn't want to talk to me. It was the classic scene where as soon as I would walk up to her and another person, conversation would stop. Where every other year we would discuss my birthday and how we thought we ought to spend the day, that year she never said a word. You can bet I was hurt.

The day of the party, the day before my birthday, she invited me to an event with her as if it were any other Saturday. I was so happy that she was acting "normal" that I didn't notice that she was acting like there was ginger ale rather than blood in her veins. That afternoon when we arrived back at her house, SURPRISE! Suddenly all the hurt feelings were worth something. It all made sense. I know Mary felt awful in the planning process. She knew my feelings were hurt. She knew I felt left out, but she also knew that my joy would outweigh the hurt.

Is that maybe how it is for God when He has to tell us no because there is a greater yes down the road? Our feelings get hurt. We cry out, "Don't you even care about me?" He responds, "Oh, just wait and see how much I care." But we don't hear that part. All we know is that we aren't getting that most prized answer, and we cannot believe how disappointing it is, how much it hurts.

Next time it seems that God is ignoring your pleas, when you are hearing that no or not now, remember that there may be a surprise in the works. God may well be plotting a much bigger gift than the one for which you are asking.

It was hard for me to believe that Mary would hurt my feelings. I knew she loved and cared for me. Our Father loves us deeply, more than we can ever love each other, and He will never let us down. We just have to remember that our vision is limited, and His is infinite.

A Christian FCAT

> Hear O Israel; the Lord your God is one, love the Lord your God with all your heart, and with all your soul and with all your strength. Deuteronomy 6:4

> Jesus replied "'Love the Lord your God with all your heart and with all your soul and with all your mind.' This is the first and greatest commandment. And the second is like it, 'Love your neighbor as yourself.' All the law and the Prophets hang on these two commandments." Matthew 22:37-40

Our pastor joked yesterday saying that we should put those words from Mathew in the back of our minds. "There's going to be a quiz later," he said. "A little mini-Christian FCAT." Everyone laughed because whether you go to school, work in a school, have a child in school, or simply drive by a school, everyone knows it is that time of year. There are Girl Scouts in front of every store in town, and there is fear in the heart of every teacher and student. It's FCAT time. From the second students walk in the door up to this week and then some, everything is about this test. It's sad in a way because there are things that get shortchanged because they aren't important to the test.

When Pastor David made his joke, I realized that if it were true, if there were some sort of test given to us to see if we were legitimate Christians, then what he had just read is really all we would need to know. There is one God, and He sent his Son to save us. If we live to honor him, if we love him with all of our heart, soul, mind, and strength then we are **A** Christians.

When schools do well on FCAT they get bonus money and the right to wear t-shirts that proclaim their status as an **A** school. It says we taught our students what was important according to the current standard. If the standard changes, we may have to change our t-shirts too.

With God the standards never change. Hear O Israel, O USA, O anybody who is listening: there is One God, love Him and your neighbor, and you pass the test.

Healing

And prayer offered in faith will make the sick person well; the Lord will raise him up. If he has sinned, he will be forgiven. Therefore confess your sins to each other and pray for each other so that you may be healed. James 5:15-16

There is some dangerous ground here in these verses from James. Are we sick because we sin? Are we not healed because we didn't confess and/or have enough faith? I think if we take these verses absolutely literally, we might get a little crazy. The truth is we don't fully understand the connection between faith, sin, and healing. We do know there are connections. We just don't see the whole picture.

In terms of serious illness, I don't think we can say that it is all a result of sin. I've known too many incredibly good people who have suffered terribly debilitating illnesses, and I've known too many, um . . . hmm . . . let's just say not so nice people who never seem to suffer from even the slightest cold.

There certainly is evidence in my own life though of sin's involvement with illness. Maybe it's not always physical illness but a sickness of the soul. Spend too long with unconfessed sin, and it begins to show. If it doesn't show up in the form of headache or gastric distress, it will show up in a bitter spirit. No sin is without consequence.

Too often lately I have had people trying to convince me of how different they had become. I have heard the expression "turned over a new leaf" from several different people lately. I wanted to say to each and everyone, if you had truly turned over a new leaf or rounded a new corner, it would show.

All of life is a journey and change takes time. When we let go of a sin that has crippled us for any length of time, there is a lightness that is visible to the people around us. Unconfessed sin is devastating if not in body then certainly in spirit. Perhaps that is what James is referring to here when he talks about healing. Some of us will arrive home with a package sorely damaged from disease, but when we get there, we will get a shiny new package without blemish or stain. Healing doesn't always mean just what we think it means.

Faithful Friends

> Some men came carrying a paralytic on a mat and tried to take him into the house to lay him before Jesus. When they could not find a way to do this because of the crowd they went on the roof and lowered him on his mat through the tiles into the middle of the crowd and right in front of Jesus.
> When Jesus saw their faith, he said, "Friend, your sins are forgiven."
> He said to the paralyzed man, "I tell you, get up, take your mat and go home." Immediately he stood up in front of them, took what he had been lying on and went home praising God. Luke 5:18-20, 24b-25

In the verses that I didn't include above there is a petty exchange with the Pharisees who once again want to point out Jesus's flaws. It is important to the big story of Jesus, but to me it isn't so important here. There are two things I find very intriguing about this passage. "Take your mat and go home" Jesus doesn't say, "Okay I healed you now sit down and listen to all the important things I'm saying." He knows that the man has just received a huge portion of grace. The healing was not just for his legs but for his spirit. "Go home," Jesus says, perhaps hoping that what he has done will speak to the man's spirit and bring him around again. He does that for us too. "Here's your miracle, sit with it and get back to me."

The man left praising God. Jesus had to know that he would have been a distraction in that room. "Look I can walk! I'm forgiven, and I can walk." Jesus had other things to accomplish: "Take your mat and go home."

The other detail that grabs me every time is that Jesus saw the faith of the man's friends and forgave the man. He saw that the paralytic's friends believed in him enough to haul their buddy up to the roof, tear it open, and lower him in. That is desperate faith right there. "We know Jesus can heal him. We just have to get him in there." Faith is not the issue; proximity is.

The former paralytic goes off praising God, but was he praising God as his pals lowered him through the roof? Was this guy as convinced as his cronies before he received healing and forgiveness? We don't know.

For years I have prayed that my children (and now grandchildren) would have good Christian friends. I wanted them to have the security of at least one other person who believed that Jesus had saved him/her and would continue that rescue effort for as long as he/she needed it. When our own faith falters, we need believing friends to hold us up. I know because I know that God has a plan for me and that He wants what is right and best, but sometimes I doubt. That is when I count on Mary, Char, Karen, and so many others to bolster my sagging faith. That is when I want my pastor to have something really strong to say. Other days those same people are seeking my strength to bolster their drooping faith. It is important to have strong Christian friends. One day we may need to count on someone with enough faith to drop us through a roof.

Jesus Is My Copilot?

This then is how we know that we belong to the truth, and how we set our hearts at rest in his presence whenever our hearts condemn us. For God is greater than our hearts, and he knows everything.
1 John 3:19-20

So many cars on the road carry a bumper sticker that boasts: Jesus Is My Copilot." Hmm . . . if there is a possibility of Jesus taking an active roll in my travel, a discernable from any angle role in getting me from *A* to *Z*, then by all means let it be the main role. Think about it. If Wolfgang Puck is in the house, who should be doing the cooking? And who should be the assistant? It only makes sense that the person with more talent and ability should take the lead role. To have a bumper sticker that says the car is being operated by God's grace, that I get, but copilot? That doesn't seem as logical to me. It does seem rather evocative of how we live.

In our day-to-day lives, many of us make decisions and then pray about it. Or we pray for guidance while scanning for the answer we've already somewhat formulated. It is so hard to just understand that we have *no* control. In all things, Jesus should be the pilot.

Consider the number of times you have taken things entirely into your own hands. You don't need help, not even a copilot. Most often haven't those things ended up the topic of your next "oh, dear God, can you fix this" prayers? I know mine have. It gets old having to go back and redo something or make amends simply because I didn't slow down long enough to hear that still small voice. It is pure arrogance to think we know better than God, and I am guilty of it more often than I care to think about. Most often I am guilty of feeling not up to a task. If I would understand that I am not and let Jesus be the pilot, there wouldn't be any need for hesitation.

Whether we're driving, walking, in conversation, or even in prayer, Jesus needs to be the pilot; and we need to be the copilot or better yet the passenger. I wouldn't board an actual plane and tell the pilot to move over. In like fashion, I think my life "flies' better when the control is in the right hand.

House Calls

Here I am! I stand at the door and knock. If anyone hears my voice and opens the door I will come in and eat with him, and he with me.
Revelation 3:20

Do you remember house calls? If you don't, house calls meant the doctor came to you. I remember every spring Dr. Klapetski (try saying that at four!) would arrive with his black bag. I vaguely remember going to his office. The office trips involved lollipops, so that was a plus, but those visits aren't as vivid in my memory as the ones he made to our house. There was a definite security in being in my own home, in my bed most of the time, and having Dr. Klapetski come to me. When I was about ten, Dr. Klapetski retired, and that meant no matter how sick I was, I had to be taken to the doctor's office. It was much more traumatic then to get the annual tonsillitis. The new doctor's office was big and noisy. It most certainly wasn't home. Doctors don't make house calls anymore. That little bit of security has been stripped away.

God still makes house calls. He stands at the door and knocks. He is willing to come in regardless of the condition of our home. Today we go to the nice, clean doctor's office where they can sterilize everything before and after we are seen. Dr. Klapetski came to our home. Sometimes just for me but sometimes for me and one of my sisters. I don't remember, but I have to wonder what our house might have looked like when he arrived. It wasn't sterile. As Dr. K and many like him went into homes regardless of their condition, God comes to us regardless of ours. He doesn't barge in. He knocks. If we are smart enough to open the door, he enters and is willing to sit and eat with us.

We don't have to go to God. Prayers don't have to be said in church or in prayer groups. God is knocking on our door, the door of our homes, but more importantly the door of our hearts. He makes house calls, car calls, workplace calls, and any other place calls. Our circumstances will not keep God from us. Nothing will except our refusal to answer the door. Time doesn't matter either. God doesn't keep office hours. Answer the door: it's your dad.

Walk Right Through

All the people in the synagogue were furious when they heard this. They got up, drove him out of the town, and took him to the brow of the hill on which the town was built, in order to throw him down the cliff. But he turned and walked right through the crowd and went on his way. Luke 4:28-30

These few words are so powerful. The people took him to the brow of the hill *"in order to throw him down the cliff."* There is no secret motivation. They are taking him there to kill him. I don't doubt that Jesus was well aware of their intentions. Yet he walked along undisturbed. He knew that it wasn't his time, but more important than that he knew that whatever the people may have planned his Father's plan was going to take precedence.

I love the power and the confidence in the words *"but he turned and walked right through the crowd."* This is no docile group. This is an angry mob. Think of the hordes of strollers in an amusement park and go even farther, edgier. They are getting through and getting their way. You are not walking against that tide. Jesus did. He walked right through.

So often the enemy is just like that crowd, pushing and shoving us leading us to believe that we are going to be killed, at least in some sense of the word. I have a friend who is right now fighting for life. The doctors keep telling his wife all the awful things that could happen or might be part of his future. Just as the crowd didn't really know Jesus, those doctors don't know JJ. My guess is that they also don't know Jesus. The enemy would like to defeat JJ and destroy his family, but God has other plans. I don't know what the outcome will be, but I am sure of one thing, God will prevail. The power that allowed Jesus to slide right back through the angry throng is available to JJ and to us. The enemy may bruise us a little or even a lot, but he cannot take our lives. We have to give it to him. Instead give your life to God every day and refuse to give the enemy a victory.

Prizes

For the kingdom of heaven is like a landowner who went out early in the morning to hire men to work in his vineyard. He agreed to pay them a denarius for the day and sent them out to his vineyard.

About the third hour he went out and saw others standing in the marketplace doing nothing. He told them, "You also go and work in my vineyard and I will pay you what is right. So they went.

He went out again about the sixth hour and the ninth hour and did the same thing. About the eleventh hour he went out and found still others standing around. He asked them, 'Why have you been standing here all day long doing nothing?"

"Because no one has hired us." They answered.

He said to them, "You also go and work in my vineyard."

When evening came the owner of the vineyard said to his foreman, "Call the workers and pay them their wages, beginning with the last ones hired and going on to the first."

The workers who were hired about the eleventh hour came each received a denarius. So when those came who were hired first, they expected to receive more than a denarius. When they received it they began to grumble against the landowner. "These men who were hired last worked only one hour," they said, "and you have made them equal to us who have borne the burden of the work and the heat of the day."

But he answered one of them, "Friend, I am not being unfair to you. Didn't you agree to work for a denarius? Take your pay and go. I want to give the man who was hired last the same as I gave you. Don't I have the right to do what I want with my own money? Or are you envious because I am generous?

"So then the last will be first, and the first will be last." Matthew 20:1-16

The other night at Bible study, I was teasing about giving the members gold stars for good answers. When one of them made a really great point, I teased the others that they only had a chance at silver. We joked about

Olympic fever and moved on. The next day something reminded me of that conversation, and that got me thinking about competition in general. I am not the least bit competitive. I have never been involved in sports, and I play games for the fun of it. I really don't care if I win. Given all of that, I am on the side of the argument that says you should have to win to get the trophy. This new way of giving every participant an award is hardly analogous of the world those young athletes will enter. In the world, in college, and in work, the competition will be real and fierce. Not everyone will get the promotion.

Thinking of our little quips in Bible study, I realized that while everyone getting a trophy will not prepare the semicompetitors for the world, it will prepare them for heaven. God does not care if we win the game. He only wants us to do our best. Those soccer and T-ball coaches may be saying that, but we all (including the tiny athletes) know that coach wants to win. In that forum, winning is everything. The only place where effort and heart truly mean more is with God.

It is comforting to know that though I may never be the best at anything. That even if there were gold medals for every single event in life I most likely still wouldn't win one, my Father loves me. He loves me just as much as the person who wins Olympic gold, a Nobel Prize, or anyone else. My successes don't matter to Him. The way I handle failure may touch His heart, but in the end, He loves you and me even if we never succeed at anything. He loves because we are not because of what we do.

As I said, I believe we misrepresent the shape of things when we give everyone a prize. We set those little ones up for a very harsh and rude awakening, but then they also get to hear the good news. They get to hear that God is just like the peewee basketball teams, and everyone gets a prize.

Deserving

> There a centurion's servant, whom his master valued highly was sick and about to die. The centurion heard of Jesus and sent some elders of the Jews to him, asking him to come and heal his servant. When they came to Jesus, they pleaded earnestly with him. "This man deserves to have you do this because he loves our nation and has built our synagogue." So Jesus went with them. Luke 7:2-6

We read about the centurion's faith, and that is always the main focus of the story, but here it says the elders told Jesus that he was deserving of help. How often do we pray for our friends saying but he/she is such a good person? We make the same mistake of feeling at least somewhat that we have to be deserving. I realize that what we deserve has absolutely nothing with the way God works. If it I can accept that on the blessing end, I have to accept it on the curses end too.

Unfortunately we all know people who have had cancer, lost a loved one, or suffered some other tragedy. Don't we all also know people who have been blessed with healing, given birth, or were otherwise blessed beyond measure? Every day we speak to someone who is struggling with a buildup of the little stresses of life. If we were all as quick to mention God's blessings on our lives, we'd hear about those every day too. In any case, deserving is not a part of the equation.

The centurion's elders note that he loves the nation and helped build the synagogue. Is that what mattered to Jesus? Maybe, but only because He could see the man's faith. If the centurion were a "hey, look at what I can do" type with no faith behind his works, the story might end differently.

When answering our prayer, I do not think for a minute that God pulls out a checklist. I don't think it is a what have you done for me lately issue. I believe that we are blessed and tested not as we ought to be but as what God sees is best for us.

In the blessing moments that is easy to believe, but in the challenges or curses we often ask why me? I am always awed by the people who sincerely say, "Why not me?" The elders believed the centurion was deserving of a miracle,

DESERVING

and the centurion saw himself as unworthy. So who was right, the elders or the centurion? It doesn't matter. The truth is Jesus is right. God chooses who will receive His mercy (Exodus 33:19). We can never be deserving, but on the other hand we don't have to be deserving. We just have to be faithful. It was the faith of the centurion that saved his servant. It was his willingness to say, "I'm not worthy." Jesus was amazed at that faith and humility. He answered the prayer of the centurion, and he will answer ours too. We just have to faith enough to accept the answer.

One God

*I am the Lord your God, who brought you out of Egypt,
out of the land of slavery.
You shall have no other gods before me.
You shall not make for yourself an idol in the form of anything
in heaven above or on the earth beneath or in the waters below.*
Deuteronomy 5:6-8

You shall have no other gods before me.

God made it very apparent to the Israelites just who was in charge. He let them know that He expected all of their devotion to come His way. It sounds arrogant but consider all that He had done, was doing and would continue to do for them. He asked very little of them, and He asks the same of us. To their defense perhaps they got confused. Maybe the cows and the really nice tree branches did start to take on a godlike appearance. They weren't sure so they messed up. Not likely. They were selfish and ambitious, stubborn. They didn't want to be told how to live. Sound familiar?

In our case, God sent us Jesus. This is what God looks like. This is how God behaves. This is the person to whom you place all your trust, to whom you give all glory and honor. The wandering Israelites may have been confused by unfamiliar territory and desert heat, but we have no excuse.

So why do we choose other gods? Why do we idolize the insignificant? We do it because it is easier. Idols of metal or stone or of human flesh do not cause us to take a closer look at how we live. They are not absolute, so we can change them at our own whims. We can stay in a bad place, continue a bad habit, and not regret it. We can live anyway we choose because those false gods cast no light of truth on our lousy choices.

When we craft false idols, we can even convince ourselves that we are living according to God's plan and deny the existence of the false god. Calling ourselves Christian, memorizing a verse of Scripture here and there does not make us true followers of God. It does not make us people who put nothing before God. We all have to check our priorities and make sure that God is number one and that He is standing there alone.

Casting Aspersions

To what then can I compare the people of this generation? What are they like? They are like children sitting in the marketplace and calling out to each other;

> "We played the flute for you,
> and you did not dance;
> we sang a dirge,
> and you did not cry."

For John the Baptist came neither eating bread nor drinking wine and you say, "He has a demon." The Son of Man came eating bread and drinking wine and you say, "Here is a glutton and a drunkard, a friend of tax collectors and 'sinners.' But wisdom is proved right by all her children." Luke 7:31-35

This Scripture is not unfamiliar to me. Yet when I was reading it the other day, the same words kept going through my mind, "at my church." It is a great thing to love your church. I love my church. I love the people, the pastor, the teachings, and the way we do things. My friends are well aware that I love my church, and I am well aware of how they feel about their own churches whether it is love or ambivalence. The words "at my church" come out of my mouth pretty often too. As do the words, "our pastor says," but I certainly hope I am not saying them the way I was thinking them as I read this passage.

Here Jesus is talking about the way the Pharisees behaved. It wasn't their way of doing things, and therefore it was wrong. Their feelings had nothing to do with righteous living and everything to do with being right. As I read this, it sadly reminded me of how different denominations or even churches within the same denomination treat each other today.

My husband and I have a friend whose wife attends a church he does not understand. He told Otto he knows everything they are against, but he has no idea what they are for. That is because they sling mud instead of teaching from the Gospel. Nowhere in any Gospel that I have ever read does it say, "That person will never get to heaven because they don't—like we do."

God calls us to love our neighbor. When Jesus walked this earth, he reminded the people with words and with actions. Jesus didn't ask questions about religious practices before deciding if he would eat, chat, or walk with someone. He knew that the Father loves all of us. He knew that the form didn't matter anywhere near as much as the function.

All Christians claim to love Christ. It's the other Christians that cause us such problems. Surely there will be hard times in all denominations and between denominations. Taking pleasure in finding fault or pointing it out is what causes the bitterness. We should all have the same end in mind. The prize of salvation has nothing to do with any outside factors. Some of us find it easier to love the unchurched because we assume they don't know any better. We are called to love our *all* of our neighbors, even the ones who go to a different church.

Perspective

Therefore do not lose heart. Though outwardly we are wasting away, yet inwardly we are being renewed day by day. For our light and momentary troubles are achieving for us an eternal glory that far outweighs them all. So we fix our eyes not on what is seen but on what is unseen. For what is seen is temporary, but what is unseen is eternal. 2 Corinthians 4:16-18

Our light and momentary troubles? Is he serious? These troubles don't feel light or momentary to me. I have been going through this for years. Okay, so maybe it's not about me. Then look at my friend. She has suffered so much. Isn't this belittling her suffering to call it "light and momentary?"

Our light and momentary troubles. This world is not forever. This is passing away. The trouble I feel today will be my victory tomorrow. Look at my friend! Goodness, she's been through so much. Sometimes it seems as if she never gets any relief. Yet I know that victory is hers too. She knows it too. You can tell by the way she carries herself. She just lives the words, "God will make a way."

Which one of those is your reaction to the Scripture passage? In all honesty, I have reacted both ways, and I surely will again. I hope and pray for more and more of the latter, but I know the former will get me now and then.

The more I read these and other words of Paul's and consider where they were written, the more I can lean toward a positive response to adversity. Paul was most likely in prison when these words were written. Not the library, basketball court, here's your lawyer, three-hot-meals-a-day prison either. No, Paul was in a human filth up to your waist, chained to the wall, we-really-don't-care about-your-rights kind of prison. His "light and momentary troubles" consisted of facing death or worse daily. Most of the contact he had with friends was through writing, and there was no daily mail delivery.

My light and momentary troubles certainly pale in comparison, but they are my troubles, and to me some of them are pretty big. Still just like Paul I have to know that trouble is just training. Training to be the best I can be in Christ and to be ready to go home where it all makes sense.

Golden or Tarnished?

> But I tell you love your enemies. Do good to those who hate you, bless those who curse you, pray for those who persecute you. If someone strikes you on one cheek, turn to him the other also. If someone takes your cloak, do not stop him from taking your tunic. Give to everyone who asks you, and if anyone takes what belongs to you, do not demand it back. Do to others as you would have them do to you. Luke 6:27-31

As happens with so many things in the Bible, a piece of this passage is grabbed, watered down, and used by some to prove that they know right from wrong. Almost everyone is aware of the Golden Rule. That rule is borrowed from this Scripture. In the wrong hands this well-intentioned teaching goes terribly awry.

A friend of mine shared a story once of her teenaged daughter coming home very, very proud of herself because she had lived the Golden Rule that day. She told me that the girls recounted how a classmate had mistreated her, and when opportunity knocked, she responded in kind, mistreating the original offender. You may think that is crazy. I know I did. How could anyone beyond the age of six think that is what those words meant? On further consideration I realized it makes an odd kind of sense. She did to the other person exactly as had been done to her. What she didn't do was consider all the words that came before those few. It would be nice to think that young girl was alone in her thinking, but I guarantee you she was not.

We hear it all the time, people threatening to get even, get what is theirs. It is the "if they can do it to me, I can do it to them" line of thinking. It is in complete conflict to the Scripture teaching. In a very similar passage in Matthew 5:38-42, there is no admonition to do to others as we would have them do. There it is just clearly stated that for the sake of living for the Lord, we should not get into petty behavior. Our behavior should reflect the love of Christ not the need for fairness.

How many times have you heard someone say, "It's not fair?" Many, I'm sure. It isn't supposed to be fair, not while we live here. When we go home, there will be no need for fair or unfair. It will all be as God wills and therefore be perfect.

That teenaged girl had the wrong idea, but she came to it by living in this world. A world that neglects the difficulty of turning the other cheek or praying for someone of whom we are not terribly fond and embraces getting whatever you can grab regardless of who gets hurt. There is far more of the eye for an eye in our world than offering the other cheek. Let's remember to live and to teach the whole passage and not just the last few words.

Young Shoulders

He told this parable, "No one tears a patch from a new garment and sews it on an old one. If he does, he will have torn the new garment and the patch from the new will not match the old. And no one pours new wine into old wineskins. If he does the new wine will burst the skins, run out and the wineskins will be ruined." Luke 5:36-37

Among my gram's many proverbs was one that echoed this Scripture passage: "You can't put old heads on young shoulders." It wasn't a criticism. It was an explanation. Whenever one of her grandchildren would pull some dumb stunt, she would say, "You can't put old heads on young shoulders." When I was young, I thought it was just one of the "gramisms." Now I get it, I think. Youth meant lack of experience, and that meant that maybe we shouldn't be expected to make all the right choices.

You can't put new wine into old wineskins; the old skins aren't prepared for the effervescence of the new wine. Just like the young shoulders aren't prepared to support the experience and knowledge in an old head.

A few years ago, my daughter pulled away from our family in a rather dramatic and devastating way. A young friend of mine proved the truth of this Scripture. He said to me, "She can't be you at eighteen. It's got to be tough to be your daughter. She wants to do what you think is right, but she's eighteen, and what you know is right is not cool or fun." At first I thought he was wrong. His shoulders still being fairly young and all. Then I realized he was right. My daughter knew what was expected of her, and while she was willing to live it out someday she wasn't ready for it at eighteen. Now just a couple of years later, she walks much closer to God, and her still-young shoulders are aging nicely.

To God whether we are nine or ninety, our shoulders are still pretty young in terms of eternity. Much as we want our offspring to look to us for wisdom, our Father wants us to look to Him. Much as He doesn't expect us to be perfect, we cannot expect perfection from our fellow Christians, regardless of chronological age. You can't put a square peg in a round hole. You can't force a person to a level of behavior that for whatever reason they have not reached. God is patient beyond measure with us, and He expects us to mimic that patience with each other, never forcing someone into a role that will not fit them. God prepares our paths, and if we will follow His lead, we will all end up in the right place.

Seasons

> Daughters of Jerusalem, I charge you by the gazelles and by the does of the field; Do not arouse or awaken love until it so desires.
> Song of Songs 2:7

A few years ago I used the Song of Songs in a Bible study I was doing with high school girls. These words *"do not arouse or awaken love until it so desires"* are repeated several times. I *tried* to use them to make several points about purity to the girls. I'm fairly certain that particular point was not embraced. Thinking about that series of lessons, I realized these words can refer to many things besides love and sex. They are really more of the dreaded waiting words *"until it so desires"* or until the time is right.

Most of us are pretty good at encouraging the young people in our lives to move slowly, make right choices, and avoid disaster. Do we take our own advice? Isn't this more of the warning against the school of thought that demands everything now?

Of course we want young people to choose wisely, to save sex for marriage, but are we guilty of putting a different horse in front of a different cart? Does ambition win over devotion? Do the things of the world get top billing while Jesus gets a guest starring credit? Priorities can get messed up at any age, in any circumstance.

Song of Songs is about loving sexual expression. It is also a picture of God's love for His bride, the church. For those of us who are married, we need to make sure that physical and emotional expressions of love are freely given to our spouses. In the same way, we all need to fully love God. The book is full of loving words poured from lover to beloved and back again. We can learn so much about loving our spouses and loving our God in those few chapters. It is very clear that the expression of love is of absolute importance but has to be in the proper context. In Ecclesiastes it says there is a season for everything. We need to make sure that we are doing all things in the right season.

Building Projects

> Why do you call me 'Lord, Lord' and do not do what I say? I will show you what he is like who comes to me and hears my words and puts them into practice. He is like a man building a house, who dug down deep and laid the foundation on rock. When a flood came, the torrent struck the house but could not shake it, because it was well built. But the one who hears my words and does not put them into practice is like a man who built a house without a foundation. The moment the torrent struck that house, it collapsed and its destruction was complete. Luke 6:46-49

These words come right after the passage that explains about good and bad fruit. As I read about the man who digs deep to build his house, I realized that is the difference between seeing one piece of "good fruit" or a whole orchard. The man building a house without a foundation is still building. For a time, it may look like he is producing good fruit. After a while, it will be clear that his fruit is not as sweet as that which has been cultivated and nurtured. As his unfounded house of faith topples, the mediocre quality of his fruit will also show.

We all need to build on the firm foundation of Jesus Christ, but further we need to make sure that is a deep, wide foundation. Once that foundation is laid, all further building projects need to be based on that beginning. We need to make sure that any spiritual growth we do is based on the Scripture and the life of Christ. It is foolish to build that strong foundation, and then think we're finished. As each room is built, it must be made of the same high-quality material. There is never a time to stop learning or growing in knowledge and love of God.

Too often we feel secure in our circumstances and forget that they are blessings from God. Blessings we received because we built the strong foundation and gained grace from drawing close to the Master. Over and over in the Old Testament and the New, we are called on to lean on God's wisdom and not our own understanding. Everything we do must start with the knowledge that we are powerless to build anything on our own. With God's help, in Jesus we can build a beautiful mansions with room for everyone. On our own, we only build sandcastles wiped out by the first wave.

The Lord Speaks

"Can you raise your voice to he clouds and cover yourself with a flood of water? Do you send the lightning bolts on their way? Do they report to you? 'Here we are'? Who endowed the heart with wisdom? Who has the wisdom to count the clouds? Who can tip over the water jars of the heavens when the dust becomes hard and the clods of the earth stick together?" Job 34:38

The book of Job is in large part conversation. Bildad, Ziphar, Eliphaz, Elihu, and Job are all talking about what has happened to Job and why. Then in chapter the Lord speaks. He speaks for the next several chapters repairing all the damage the well-intentioned, ill-informed conversation has wrought. The power of the verses above and several that surround them amaze me. How do we miss it? How is it that sometimes we think we have some sort of control? We are literally at God's mercy.

We joke sometimes when our vehicles aren't working, or we are physically unable to drive that we are at the mercy of other people's schedules. That is fairly true, but it is also true that if we had to be somewhere, someone would get us there.

Day after day I see children who are truly at the mercy of their caretakers. They sit unable to speak or do for themselves. If the ladies in charge chose to ignore them all day long there would be precious little those poor angels could do about it. They are helpless. Thankfully all of the ladies who work with them are loving, caring individuals. The message to me, to all of us really, is in the children. They are at the mercy of the adults around them. They always have been and always will be. They look to the unknowing eye as if they were forgotten by God. Their plight seems cruel to some. To others, to those of us who know them and know God, the blessings are obvious. Those children may not understand much, but they are intimate with God.

Never do they try to take control from Him. They wait as patiently as Job did for God to come and speak to them. I have no doubt that He does. They wait for God's hand to restore them to what we see as wholeness. I have no doubt that He will.

The Lord speaks to Job and his pals, and He asks, "Can you speak to lightning?" They can't, and neither can we. They could speak to God, and we can too. These verses from Scripture help me begin to understand what my young "handicapped" friends already know. Everything I have is a gift of mercy from God. Anything that happens to me is within His scope of power. I don't need to understand. I don't need to be able to order clouds or lightning around. I just need to succumb to the almighty hand of God.

When Music Plays

Then the herald loudly proclaimed, "This is what you are commanded to do, O peoples, nations and men of every language; As soon as you hear the sound of the horn, flute zither, lyre, harp, pipes, and all kind of music, you must fall down and worship the image of gold that King Nebuchadnezzar has set up. Whoever does not fall down and worship will immediately be thrown into a blazing furnace."

Shadrach, Meshach and Abednego replied to the king, "O Nebuchadnezzar we do not need to defend ourselves before you in this matter. If we are thrown into the blazing furnace, the God we serve is able to save us from it, and he will rescue us from your hand, O king. But even if he does not, we want you to know, we will never serve your gods or worship the image of gold you have set up." Daniel 3:7, 16-18

> Call us all around
> Show us what you have made
> Command us all to fall
> When music starts to play.
> —Third Day, "Never Bow Down" Mac Powell

The story of Shadrach, Meshach, and Abednego has always intrigued me. It shows such a firm belief in God. Those boys stood on Romans 8 long before it was ever written. They were more than conquerors. They knew that God was for them, and nothing else could prevail. They knew nothing could separate them from the love of God. They would not bow.

I included the passage from the Third Day song because it references music as does the Scripture, and because I love that song. Music is one of my favorite things. It is a very strong motivator for me. When I feel discouraged, tired, happy, lost, or just too quiet, I put on my favorite praise songs or Christian CDs. I listen to music a lot. I cook to it, clean to it, and sometimes even write with it playing in the background. Anyone who knows me will tell you I drive with music blaring in my car.

In the days before Jesus rescued me from myself the music I chose was not at all uplifting. When I think of some of those lyrics now, I cringe. Not necessarily because of the content but because of what they could do to my mental state. I am very thankful to all the musicians who write and play faith-based songs. Music is not a problem in my faith life. Maybe it isn't in yours either.

In the passage from Daniel, the people were to bow to the idol when the music played. The Third Day song refers to that same music, but I ask this, "What is the 'music' in your life? What will cause you to bow down? Where will you ask God to take a backseat?"

We can all find ourselves in situations that are not of God. We look around and find that something or someone has become so important to us that we will put God aside. We are not alone. Paul says it in Romans 7:15-16. We do what we know is wrong because of our sinful nature. We can only pray to be as strong as those young men who faced the fiery furnace rather than bow to an idol. Let's listen to the "music" in our lives and make sure it keeps us mindful of whose we are.

Moses's MLM

"Take the staff and you and your brother Aaron gather the assembly together. Speak to that rock before their eyes and it will pour out its water."

Then Moses raised his arm and struck the rock twice with his staff. Water gushed out, and the community and their livestock drank.

But the Lord said to Moses and Aaron, "Because you did not trust in me enough to honor me as holy in the sight of the Israelites, you will not bring this community into the land I give them." Numbers 20:8, 11-12

My husband is the dearest man in the world. He works very hard and takes excellent care of me and our extended family. He is determined to always do what he sees as best for us. That has led him into some interesting situations. By interesting situations I mostly mean. Okay, let's be frank with all his great qualities, there has to be a flaw right? The poor man is a sucker for multilevel-marketing schemes—oops, systems—affectionately known as MLMs. It sounds so good to him that he has tried three different ones. What he fails to consider is that MLM is not in his makeup. He is not the type. He has been convinced twice after saying never again because he really wants to provide the best stuff for his family. He doesn't see that he already gives us his best. As he has been suckered—ooops again—encouraged by his friends to try these things, he was able to convince a couple of his friends to try them too. It is the pursuit of riches and fame or at least financial security without too much blood, sweat, and tears that is so attractive. MLMs are a small picture of how a lot of people live, chasing the brass ring. So many people spend life pursuing that one thing that will make them wealthy, happy, or thin. My hubby's quest is not unlike several of my friends who are chasing the latest diet craze. Most of us are fueled at least once or twice in life by the wrong ambition.

Why aren't we just as busy pursuing Jesus? In the story from Numbers, Moses was guilty of one offense against God, and it cost him the Promised Land. If he had known ahead of time, would he have done it? Maybe but most of the time Moses was pursuing God. He pursued Him all the time because the people were making him crazy. He pursued God because he felt unequal to the task at hand. We think if we'd been in Moses's shoes we would have acted differently. We are in Moses's shoes all the time. God says do it one way, and we do it another. It seems that some of that comes from the fact that we chase after the things of the world, money, power, prestige, size 2 jeans with the zeal of the truly committed; but we chase after God with way less passion, or worse we make Him chase after us.

I am happy to say that my husband has realized that he is not an MLM man, and fortunately he knows that he is God's man. I hope my sons are learning to pursue God first by watching their father. I hope we all learn that the only worthy pursuits will bring us to the throne of God and that once there we will be humble enough to do things God's way.

Full or Empty

The thief comes only to steal and kill and destroy; I have come that they may have life, and have it to the full. John 10:10

My adopted grandmother died recently. We called her Babci. She was ninety-two years old. Her death is tragically sad. Not in the way of a vital young person dying in a car wreck or a child dying from cancer but in a way that should make every family member take a good look at his/her own life. Babci died at ninety-two, but from what I know of her she never really lived.

She was blessed with a nearly blind, now fully blind daughter. I say blessed because my aunt Carol is an amazing woman. She is blind, fully blind but lives alone, does her own cooking and cleaning, and asks for very little help. She listens to TV and calls to tell my mom whenever there is a big news story or an interesting interview. She knows more about many things than a lot sighted people that I know. She loves the Lord, and best of all she is content. She's been kept in her whole life, and her life experiences are ridiculously limited, and yet she is content. Her mother on the other hand had all of her senses, was out and about in the world, had three great kids and a wonderful husband, and all I ever saw in her was sadness and self-pity.

Babci was blessed beyond measure, and she never knew it. Her life could have been full and fulfilling if she had embraced the gifts God gave her, but she did not. These words may sound hard and judgmental, but they aren't. I loved her exactly the way she was. Her slightly Polish accent made her speech colorful. She had a quirky little way about her that reminded me of gnomes or some other ethereal creatures. She could have been a lot of fun, and once in a while you could see a glimpse of humor in her. Most of the time, it was overshadowed by despondence.

I am sad that her life was not better, sad that she settled for second best. I hope all of us who knew her and now you who are reading about her will learn a valuable lesson from her life. We all need to appreciate what we have even if it is not what we think we want.

Minas Talents and Gifts

Then he said to those standing by, "Take his mina away from him and give it to the one who has ten minas."

"Sir," they said, "he already has ten!"

He replied, "I tell you that to everyone who has, more will be given, but as for the one who has nothing, even what he has will be taken away." Luke 19:24-26

"Take the talent from him and give it to the one who has the ten talents. For everyone who has will be given more, and he will have an abundance. Whoever does not have, even what he has will be taken from him. And throw that worthless servant outside, into the darkness, where there will be weeping and gnashing of teeth." Matthew 25:28-30

This parable is about money and is often taught from that perspective. I read it that way for years until one word started to really stand out to me, and I realized that it may be money, or as the word for money in Matthew's account suggests it may be talent or it may be a spiritual anointing. In any of those cases, the key word to me is gift. Money, talent, anointing all are gifts from God. That is what makes the last section of the passage the hardest to read.

Imagine giving someone a gift, a gift that could change their lives if invested correctly, and then some time later seeing that he/she tucked the gift away to return to you. It goes way beyond disappointment. Wouldn't you be offended that not only did they not appreciate it or do a single thing with it but also gave it back? It's insulting.

In both accounts, the master says that the talents/minas are given "until I come back." God has blessed us with gifts and talents to use until the day he calls us home or the day Jesus comes back. Everything we have is a gift to us, on loan from God. What are we doing with our talents? Are we using them? Are we blooming where we were planted or waiting for a better garden?

My son Jeffrey has great musical talent. He uses it but not for heavenly purposes. I believe that one day he will. He loves the Lord, and I believe that one day he will realize that the talent he uses is not truly his. One day he will see it for the gift that it is and want to honor the Giver. What if he doesn't? How will he answer for not making the best use of such a great gift? How will any of us answer that charge?

When our dear Lord takes account of our lives, we want to be able to answer as the first men in the passage that we did the best we could with what we had. Don't refuse to use the gifts God has given you. Don't save them for a rainy day and by all means do not believe the enemy's lies that the gifts really aren't gifts at all. Do not fall prey to the whispers that tell you that you don't actually have a gift at all. God has blessed all of us with some gift. Use whatever he has given you to the best of your ability. Make it easy for God to say, "Well done, good and faithful servant" (Mt. 25:21a).

Planting Seeds

Then he told this parable; "A man had a fig tree, planted in his vineyard, and he went to look for fruit on it but did not find any. So he said to the man who took care of the vineyard, 'For three years now I've been coming to look for fruit on this fig tree and haven't found any. Cut it down! Why should it use up the soil?'

"'Sir,' the man replied, 'leave it alone for one more year, and I'll dig around it and fertilize it. If it bears fruit next year fine! If not, then cut it down.'" Luke 13:6-9

My husband and I have four children, adult children now but ours in any case. As they grew, there were of course times when we had to correct their behavior and/or have conversations about boundaries and responsibilities. Too often we would see their eyes glaze over, and though their heads were nodding and they may even be offering slight verbal responses, they were not hearing us. On those occasions my husband would ask me, "Why do you bother?" My response was always the same, because some of it had to be sinking in somewhere, and maybe one day they would get it.

When my daughter was in junior high, she and some of her friends asked me to lead them in a Bible study, oh the stories I have from that! Many nights after the girls had left, I would go to the Lord and ask why I was doing it. There just didn't seem to be a point. When I would verbalize that frustration to my prayer partners, they would tell me I was planting seeds.

A young woman I am close to today was also in my life when she was a child. When I first knew her, she was full of talent and full of tension. When we were reunited, I saw the same exact girl although she was a few years older. I had prayed for her when she was young and began again in earnest when we were reacquainted. Once again I was planting seeds.

My husband and I still have four children; each one is on a different step of the path, and some of them have fairly sure footing. My Bible-study girls are in their twenties now. Most of them I no longer see and so have no idea where they are with God but two; my own daughter and her dearest friend are standing firm and really living their faith. My young friend is about to marry a pastor and has shown so much growth. The best part is she knows that like all of us, she still has miles to go.

The point of all of these stories is that sometimes the tree gives fruit, and sometimes it doesn't. Further, sometimes we get to see the fruit, and sometimes we just have to hope that the seeds we planted will come to fruition. The parable from Luke frustrates some of us because we like answers, nice tidy answers, and this parable is open-ended. I can't help but think this parable is in the Bible because so much of life is open-ended. Our precious Lord wants us to put our trust in Him, and if we do every now and then, we get to see the beautiful bloom of the seeds we so lovingly planted.

Abba

"Abba, Father," he said, "everything is possible for you. Take this cup from me. Yet not what I will, but what you will." Mark 14:36

For you did not receive a spirit that makes you a slave again to fear, but you received the Spirit of sonship. And by him we cry, "Abba, Father." Romans 8:15

Because you are sons, God sent the Spirit of his Son into our hearts, the Spirit who calls out, "Abba, Father." Galatians 4:6

The Old Testament has so very many terms for God. There are books written to explore the many names given to God and all of their meanings. When we get to the New Testament and Jesus arrives, to us God becomes God the Father. We begin to see the Trinity, Father, Son, and Holy Spirit. Jesus is God, and yet he speaks to God. We don't quite get that. We can't. The verses above may not help us understand how it is that Jesus, God in the flesh, is talking to God as in Yahweh, etc. They do help us understand why and why we need to speak to God as often as possible and with as much humility as possible. These verses outline so clearly the parent-child relationship we have with God.

*Recently our pastor talked about the word "abba" and how it literally means "daddy." That reminded me of my grandson who is just two and is learning about names and relationships. He loves to try out new things especially if they border on naughty. If I call to my husband, Joey loves to echo me. "Otto, Otto," he calls out and gives us all a big grin. The other day in the car he was talking to his father. We had just picked him up at day care, and he ran to my son with a huge smile yelling, "Hey, Daddy!" Then just minutes later in the car, he wanted Joe's attention and said, "Hey, Dad." We could tell by the look on his face that he wanted to see how we would react. Joe very calmly answered him. When we were talking about it later Joe pointed out that yes, Joey was testing the "dad" word, but when he is tired or wants something Joe is still "daddy."

As our pastor shared a very personal experience of his own, I remembered the day my father's mother died. I'd never seen them as being particularly close until she was hospitalized, and he drove an hour each way several times a week to feed her lunch. When the early-morning call came with the news that Grandma had died, I heard my father crying. That wasn't so strange; he'd just lost his mother. It was his words that grabbed my heart: "I want my mommy."

In times of sadness, pressure, or great joy, we all want our parents. Some parents are better than others and are much more "there" for their children. Some are neglectful or abusive, but most children still love their parents. For all of us, whether we were raised by the best or the worst, there is a parent who will never ever let us down. We have the distinct privilege of calling Him Abba. When we call, He will always answer, always care, and we can always depend on Him. Our own parents may let us down, but He never will. We grow and mature, Mommy and Daddy become Mom and Dad, but somewhere in all of us is that child who still wants his/her daddy. Call to Him, call Abba, Daddy. He's waiting to hear it.

Undesirables

Then Jesus said to his host, "When you give a luncheon or a dinner, do not invite your friends or relatives, or your rich neighbors; if you do, they may invite you back and so you will be repaid. But when you give a banquet invite the poor, the crippled, the lame, the blind and you will be blessed. Although they cannot repay you, you will be repaid at the resurrection of the righteous." Luke 14:12-14

I had a conversation with a young friend who has recently decided to develop a relationship with God. Although he was raised in a Christian household, this young man is not embracing the faith of his family. He has found his own path. Some of what he shared with me was great and made sense. Some was a little crazy. He told me that churches are for believers only and that nonbelievers have no place in church even as visitors. The very next day our pastor said, "There are no undesirables if we have God's heart." These verses from Luke back my pastor's words.

God loves all of us, not all of us Christians but *all* of us. He loves the people we see as horrible sinners and the people who see us as horrible sinners. He loves the people who struggle to live with what they think they are as well as the people who see themselves as above reproach. We don't always get that, but it doesn't matter. We don't have to understand it. We just have to imitate it.

God isn't asking us to go out and seek people we find repulsive for whatever reason and befriend them. He is asking us to befriend the people He puts in our paths regardless of their behavior. Sometimes we work with them, sometimes they are family members, and sometimes they even go to our church. We are the ones who want to sit in judgment over who gets to do what with God, and we base it all on what we think we are doing.

It all comes down to the same thing, God loves everyone, every single one, and He wants us to love everyone too. The good news is He's asking all of them to love, us so in the end it all comes out even.

Tunnels

Therefore do not lose heart. Though outwardly we are wasting away, yet inwardly we are being renewed day by day. For our light and momentary troubles are achieving for us an eternal glory that far outweighs them all. So we fix our eyes not on what is seen but on what is unseen. For what is seen is temporary, but what is unseen is eternal. 2 Corinthians 4:16-1

Years ago I heard a preacher on the radio talking about finding the words "now it came to pass" in the Scripture and how freeing that was for him. "It came to pass," he said, "means it didn't come to stay." What had previously given him great peace began to do the same for me. I didn't hear what translation he was using nor did he ever again mention the book of the Bible by name, but none of that matters. In fact, it may be helpful that I don't know. The important thing is that none of our circumstances are here to stay. They all came to pass.

Even better than the temporary condition of our lives is that there is always light at the end of the tunnel. We hear those clichés, and after a while it's just words, but some of them are true. It is darkest before the dawn. There is light at the end of the tunnel. There is hope no matter how hopeless something looks.

Light at the end of the tunnel may sound like a cliché, but the Bible makes the same promise in Titus 2:13: "While we wait for the blessed hope—the glorious appearing of our great God and Savior Jesus Christ." God will return to us. He will appear. This too shall pass, and surely there is light at the end of the tunnel.

While we are hurting, when we are terrified, it is hard to believe in the evanescence of the situation. It feels so unremitting; and we fear that there is nothing but tunnel, no light, no end, no hope. That fear, that belief is the work of the enemy. There is Light at the end of the tunnel, and the darkness can never overcome it.

A Great Chasm

> But Abraham replied, "Son, remember that in your lifetime you received your good things, while Lazarus received bad things, but now his is comforted here and you are in agony. And besides all this, between us a great chasm has been fixed, so that those who want to go from here to you cannot, nor can anyone cross over from there to us." Luke 16:25-26

Have you ever read this and wondered who would want to cross over to hell? I have. The passage says, "Those who want to go from here to you." This time as I read it I thought anyone who has a loved one on the dark side of that chasm, that's who would want to cross over. As I thought about it, I realized I would only want to cross over if I knew that I could cross back and bring them with me.

In this world what I want most of all for my children is to know that they are going to heaven. I want to know that they know and love their Father and want to be with Him for all eternity. If I knew that I were with Him and they were not, it would kill me, and that thought made me wonder about another aspect of the passage. Abraham sees both Lazarus and the rich man. It doesn't say that Lazarus can see the rich man. Earlier on it says the rich man can see Lazarus at Abraham's side (verse 23), but nowhere does it say that Lazarus can see him.

It also says that the rich man is in torment. Of course he is. He's in hell first of all, and it has to be worse because he can see someone to whom he felt so superior, seated beside Abraham. We have to know that he thought he could buy that seat. He couldn't, and no one else can either. Our places in heaven cannot be bought or earned. They must simply be accepted. Of course we have to accept the One who did earn that place for us, and that is where we lose people. Everyone may want to go to heaven, but not everyone wants to believe that Jesus's sacrifice is what is going to get them there.

I want so desperately to see all my children, original and by marriage, all my grandchildren, my siblings, my parents, and my friends fully devoted to

Christ. I pray for that every day. As much as I want to be in heaven, I want them to be there too. Each of us needs to pray for those we love to recognize the Truth and to pursue it. The rich man had no sight or hearing for the Lord, and he paid the price. It is a price I don't want anyone I love to pay.

A Child's Offering

As he looked up Jesus saw the rich putting their gifts into the temple treasury. He also saw a poor widow put in two very small copper coins. "I tell you the truth," he said, "this poor widow has put in more than all the others. All these people gave their gifts out of their wealth; but she out of her poverty put in all she had to live on." Luke 21:1-4

My grandson Joey loves our pastor. Whenever he hears the word "church" regardless of the context, he gets all excited. "See, Pastor Dave!" He also loves coins. I'm not sure how much he understands money, but he does grasp the fact that the coins are useful for some purpose.

My husband keeps a large jar of loose change in our bedroom. My oldest son does the same thing. Every weekend Joey finds either Pop-Pop's coins or Uncle Paul's and grabs a few for Pastor Dave. Whenever we tell him to put the coins back, he is quick to assure us that they are for Pastor Dave and Jesus. Somehow even his very young mind understands that it is a good thing to give his money to the pastor who will in turn somehow give it to Jesus.

The other day Joey came to me with twenty-seven cents. "For Pastor Dave and Jesus." When I told him we didn't have church that day, he looked a little sad. Then with a self-conscious look, he said, "Okay, for ice cream?" He gets money, sort of.

The money Joey gives is not all he has to live on. It is not even his money, but he has to have coins for church every week. In his child's mind, he is beginning to grasp the importance of giving. His father and I were talking about it the other day and agreed that it would be great if he could continue to see things this way. It's okay to use some coins for ice cream if you've already given some coins to Jesus.

Certainly Joey wants the connection to Pastor Dave. He wants David to pat him on the head and to be pleased with his offering, which usually hovers in thirty-forty-cent range. Joey glows whenever he is able to place that offering into David's hand. We can all learn from that. Tithing, giving in any sense, is hard sometimes. I think it becomes much easier if I can see my Father grinning at me the way David grins at Joey. We all see how touched David is by that sweet boy, and it is so wonderful to know that our Father sees us in an even better light.

What could be more precious than a two-year-old with a slight lisp handing his gift for Jesus to his pastor? To God, anyone of us doing anything, giving anything for His glory. My prayer is that Joey will continue to grow in his giving spirit. I also pray that all of us who see him will follow his example and give with a joyful heart.

Answer Carefully

As Simon Peter stood warming himself, he was asked, "You are not one of his disciples are you?"
He denied it saying, "No I am not."
One of the high priest's servants, a relative of the man whose ear Peter had cut off challenged, "Didn't I see you with him in the olive grove?" Again Peter denied it, and at that moment a rooster began to crow. John 18:25-27

There are so many powerful images in the story of the Crucifixion. In recent years we've had movies and videos to further enhance our understanding. Just in case we couldn't quite see and hear whips lashing and flesh tearing, movie/video makers have taken care of that for us. A bloodied, tortured Jesus is not just depicted in words. Now we have audiovisual images too. Still the idea of Jesus's best friend denying him cuts me very deeply.

You could argue that the questioner made it easy: "You aren't one of his disciples, are you?" It is a question that invokes a certain answer. No is the expected answer and no is what Peter says. The water is too hot; the situation too tense. Peter's reaction is one of "I love you but . . ." It is the answer none of us wants to hear from a good friend.

I am blessed with some really good friends. My friend Mary and I have been friends for forty years. It would kill me if she denied knowing me. Charlene and Karen are newer friends but have been with me in happy and hard times as I hope I have been for them. God is good to me when it comes to friends. Recently He has restored for me a friendship I considered ruined beyond repair. Those gifts, those precious women that our Father has placed in my life, confirm for me that relationships, friendships are important to God. So imagine His heartbreak to hear Peter say of Jesus, "I don't know him." If it hurts when someone rejects me; it hurts twice as much if they do it to my kids. You would think then that I would go out of my way not to betray my friends, and I do except when it comes to Jesus.

I fear that when I hear His name being trashed and do nothing that I am just like Peter. I know that when I choose to sin, not fall into sin unwittingly, but choose it decisively I am Peter. I love Peter and relate to many of his foibles. I would love to have a fraction of his strength and determination, but I do not want to imitate him in that courtyard. I am reminded of that every Holy Week and every time I read this account. When I am asked with words or otherwise, I want to say, "Yes, I know Jesus. I love him, and I'm proud to be called his friend."

Watchful Eyes

"How do you know me?" Nathanael asked.

Jesus answered, "I saw you while you were still under the fig tree before Philip called you."

Then Nathanael declared, "Rabbi, you are the Son of God; you are the King of Israel."

Jesus said, "You believe because I told you I saw you under the fig tree. You shall see greater things than that." John 1:48-50

Nathanael was in awe because Jesus had seen him without his knowledge of anyone being near or watching him. He was awed enough to change his whole life. God sees us all day, every day, and has since before we were born. When we know someone is watching us, we sometimes change the way we do things.

The last time my mom was here to visit, she and my daughter were watching me make dinner. They told me that they wanted to see how I prepared a certain roast and its marinade. So I prepared it as I always do. When I was finished, they were both laughing. When I asked why, they both said the same thing, "We wanted you to show us how to do it. You didn't show us anything." I was stumped. I did the same steps I always do, and they saw me do them. In that case, I didn't change my behavior, but I guess I should have changed it. They wanted a step-by-step verbal instruction. How often is the opposite true?

We are more cautious in what we do because we know someone is observing. His/her eyes on us make us more aware of each step we are taking.

Now think about Jesus watching Nathanael or God watching us. If we were truly aware of God's eyes on us all the time, would we sin? Could we if we truly felt God's presence? It is because we forget or ignore the fact that God is always present that we are able to sin.

Jesus's response to Nathanael's awe is to tell him that he will see far greater miracles. He is more than ready to get on board for that. His heart is so touched by knowing that Jesus saw him and wanted him that he is drawn to whatever Jesus is about to do. Nathanael's heart is now tuned to Jesus's heart. Jesus calls us every day. He sees what we are doing. Sometimes the rush and worry of this world crowds Him out. We need to slow down and just feel His presence. He is calling us just like He called Nathanael. I want to answer the same way. How about you?

Whose Will Be Done?

He released the man who had been thrown into prison for insurrection and murder, the one they asked for, and surrendered Jesus to their will. Luke 23:25

Jesus was surrendered to the will of an angry mob incited by jealous, vicious phonies who only wanted to protect their own status quo. We read those words, study the events, and we are appalled. We cannot imagine how they could have chosen to take part in crucifying Jesus. Then we do it ourselves.

The key word in the passage is "will." Jesus was surrendered to the will of the people. Will is such a sticky thing. It is always a problem. We find ourselves in deep dirty water and ask, "Why God?" The answer is always the same, free will. God would love for us to live lives free of sin. He gave us that option, and we blew it. From Adam and Eve on down, we are incapable of living sin-free lives, but most of us really want to live that way.

We study the Word, and we pray. We gather with other believers for encouragement and guidance, and we pray. We seek, we question, and we pray because we truly want to live in a way that pleases God. Sometimes we find words or ways that help us resist temptation. I find this passage from Luke very helpful.

If I can see my sin as my will taking over instead of God's will, I have to make the connection that I am part of the Crucifixion. Jesus died once for all. *All*, not all of that era but a-l-l, all as in all of us. I do not want to see my face in that angry crowd, but when I sin, it is there. I do not want to choose the murderer instead of the Savior, but when I choose my will instead of his, it is the same thing. Most sin is about our will. Maybe if we can see what that means in terms of Jesus's sacrifice, we will choose His will over our own.

Get Behind Me

Peter took him aside and began to rebuke him, "Never, Lord!" he said. "This is shall never happen to you!"
Jesus turned to him and said to Peter, "Get behind me, Satan! You are a stumbling block to me; you do not have in mind the things of God, but the things of men." Matthew 16:22-23

When Jesus tells his disciples what is coming, Peter's first reaction is to put a stop to it. We understand that. None of us wants to see a friend go through trying times. The difference here is that Jesus knows he has to face that trial. He understands that a greater good will come from his temporary, albeit horrendous, pain.

Most of understand Peter, but we don't quite get Jesus. We can all relate to wanting suffering, our own or that of someone close to us, to end. It is so hard for us to think that there is a purpose to all of the anguish and trials. It is especially hard when we feel that the one suffering is not the one who needs the lesson. Living sacrificially sometimes means we suffer for another person's benefit. That is truly knowing Jesus in His suffering.

We work hard for our paychecks. Some days that paycheck is the only motivator that gets us to work. What if we had to then hand it over to someone else? What if we had to hand it over to someone who felt no remorse when they mistreated us or said horrible things about us? That is what Jesus is talking about here. His suffering on the Cross was for all of us, not just for the ones who would eventually be grateful. He suffered and died for the fools who are trying to remove His name and the Father's name from any and every activity and/or surface.

We understand Peter wanting to prevent Jesus's suffering. We're not nearly as clear on why someone would offer so much, suffer to such a degree for people who don't even recognize His name. Learning to accept suffering as a learning or growing tool makes us that much for useful to Jesus. Are you being asked to get out of the way? Is Jesus asking you to support His plan? When we look at it that way it doesn't seem as impossible because we know that God will make a way where there seems to be none.

Everywhere You Look

In the beginning God created the heavens and the earth. Now the earth was formless and empty, darkness was over the surface of the deep, and the Spirit of God was hovering over the water. Genesis 1:1-2

He who testifies to these things says, "Yes I am coming soon."
Amen. Come Lord Jesus.
The grace of the Lord Jesus be with God's people. Amen.
Revelation 22:20-21

It seems that people are only too happy to talk about the evil they see in the world. Listen to conversations going on around you. There is a lot of "poor me," "life is so hard," "the world is going to hell in a handbasket" talk everywhere you turn. It would seem that the greatest influence in the world is that of our enemy. Take another look and listen with a different ear. Nothing in this world came from anywhere besides God. People have certainly made huge ugly messes of God's work and His plan, but it all originates with God's ideas.

Often in our church our pastor will show a movie clip. I'm not talking about *The Ten Commandments* or *The Passion of the Christ*. I'm talking about *Braveheart, Star Wars,* and *Gladiator*. He sees the message of the Master wherever he turns. I do too, and I hear it.

In my car I have several CDs, lots of praise and worship music, tons of Third Day, and one Tom Petty. It's a long and not-very-interesting story as to why Tom Petty is there, but there he is. It's a greatest-hits CD which includes the song "I Won't Back Down." Is that an original idea do you think? Or does it sound a lot like Shadrach, Meschach, and Abednego?

How about the Beatles telling us all you need is love? Is that their very own thought? It sounds a lot like "and the greatest of these is love." Or even "love the Lord your God and love your neighbor."

What about all the movies, comic books, TV shows, and video games with a superhero? Good triumphs over evil in the end; the good guy always wins. Is that one original? I don't think so. It sounds like the Good Friday/Easter Sunday theme to me.

People argue that there is no God. Others reply, "Look at the trees, flowers, birds of the air, and people around you. Of course there is a God." Look around, there isn't an idea for a book, movie, painting, or song that didn't come from something God created. All ideas have their origin in God's work. Many of them get twisted for evil; there is no doubt about that, but even if the story ends with the bad guy winning, there was a good guy involved. The struggle between good and evil is a biblical one.

Try it. Look around, watch a movie, read a book, listen to a song. God's ideas may be very distorted, but obvious or subtle, I bet you'll find them pretty much everywhere you look.

Someone Else's Plans

"For I know the plans I have for you," declares the Lord, "plans to prosper you and not to harm you, plans to give you hope and a future." Jeremiah 29:11

"Plans," that word elicits so many emotions. For some it's excitement if they have big plans. For others it's dread. They would just like to relax today, but, no, they have plans. We all talk about God's plan. We'd love to know what it is and where we fit in.

My husband and I take turns one day each month making plans. We set aside one day, usually a Saturday, and one of us is in charge of planning something fun and/or relaxing for us to do together. I love when it's Otto's turn. It doesn't matter what he plans. It's just fun to anticipate what we might do. Besides, the person responsible plans the whole day, start to finish. When it's Otto's turn, I don't have to worry about errands, chores, or planning dinner. I'm his for the day, and because I trust him and know that he loves me, I know it will be a good day.

"For I know the plans I have for you," declares the Lord, "plans to prosper you and not to harm you, plans to give you hope and a future" Jeremiah 29:11. These words, along with the ones from Hebrews, came from God. He has plans for us. Just the other day I got up, and I did not want to do anything. I wasn't sad or depressed; I was just blah. As I considered the day that was stretched out before me, I did not see any possibility of enjoyment or blessing. I saw the same old things, and I didn't want to do any of it. I realized how negative and defeating my thoughts were and began to pray. Praying to be in God's will, I suddenly realized God had plans for me that day as He does every day. Just like one day every other month Otto has plans for me. Why then was I not eagerly anticipating the day in front of me? Because I knew what the day would hold? Sure, I was going to walk through the same activities as many other days in my life but what about God's plan?

I trust Otto's plan because I know he loves me and wants me to be happy. Otto doesn't love me nearly as much as God does. He has far less knowledge of what is best for me or will ultimately make me happy. God knows everything and wants me to have joy and peace. When I looked at it that way, the day looked so much better. The same routine still waited there, but in God's hands I had no idea what could happen.

I am writing this on a regular weekday. Today will involve work, household, responsibilities, and Bible study. I've done every one of the things I expect to do today hundreds of times. Still I wonder what God is going to do with me today. I can't wait to see what He has planned.

True Love Words

In the beginning was the Word, and the Word was with God, and the Word was God. He was with God in the beginning.

Through him all things were made; without him nothing was made that has been made. In him was life, and that life was the light of men. The light shines in the darkness but the darkness has not understood it. John 1:1-5

Your attitude should be the same as that of Christ Jesus. Who being in very nature God did not consider equality with God something to be grasped,

> But made himself nothing,
> taking the very nature of a servant,
> being made in human likeness.
> And being found in appearance as a man,
> he humbled himself
> and became obedient to death—
> Even death on a cross!
> Therefore God exalted him to the highest place
> and gave him the name that is above every name,
> that at the name of Jesus every knee should bow,
> in heaven and on earth and under the earth,
> and every tongue confess that Jesus Christ is
> Lord, to the glory of the Father.
> Philippians 2:5-11

Do you remember your first kiss? How about the first time you held your newborn child? The words from John and from Philippians always make me feel that same type of thrill but bigger. It is the feeling I cannot accurately describe or explain. It is simply a rush of joy that seems to have no bounds. I would never pretend to be able to unequivocally explain these Scriptures. It isn't that either of them have ever been a direct answer to a particular prayer. It is simply the reading of them, the sight of them on a page.

Think of how you feel when you have been away from someone you love, and suddenly there he/she is. It takes your breath away for a moment, and then you feel that warmth, that thing I can't describe. That is what these words do for me. To look them up and purposely read them is great, but coming on them while reading something else is even better. There they are my dearest friends, words that are true love to me.

Whenever I doubt that I truly love God, when I know that I have made Him take a back seat, I can turn to these two passages, and it all comes together. Why? I have no idea. Nor am I saying that these two passages should do the same thing for you. There is something in the Bible that will, though. There is something in those hundreds of thousands of words that will catch your heart, stop your breath, and make you realize that God is the one thing you cannot live without.

As you read the Bible, try to find your true love words or better yet, like I did, let them find you.

Deals, Deals, Deals

> For the Son of man came to seek and to save what is lost.
> Luke 19:10

> Here I am! I stand at the door and knock, if anyone hears my voice and opens the door, I will come in and eat with him and he with me.
> Revelation 3:20

This is a once-in-a-lifetime opportunity. If a salesman is speaking those words to you, run. That is a sales pitch and one that has been and will continue to be pretty successful. Of course the words are not usually that clear. There are many variations on the theme. The offer is only good for a few hours. You can only get that deal while the manager is out of the office, in a really great mood. The list is quite long, but the idea remains: you have one shot at this prize, and that's it.

As with so many things the way God works is exactly the opposite of the way the world works. God promises to stand and knock (Rev. 3:20). He promises that He will never leave us (Joshua 1:5b).

I grew up with a salesman for a father. He taught me not to nod my head yes along with the salesman because that is a very short step from saying yes. He taught me that the offer is never only good for an hour and that in fact the next hour's offer might be better. He taught me that if something sounds too good to be true, it probably is too good to be true. That last adage is another great example of how differently God works.

The plan of salvation absolutely sounds too good and too simple to be true. I only have to believe that Jesus died for me, and I'm saved. That surely can't be right. There must be a flaming hoop somewhere for me to jump through. To be fair there is a flaming hoop; it's called free will, and it can derail me at any moment. The truth is the gift of eternal life, and of life here lived with the incredible support of the Holy Spirit is ours for the taking.

Nod your head with the preacher. Sign up today even though that offer will be available until you draw your last breath. The offer is as good as it sounds. There are no strings attached, no hidden agendas, no loopholes. We only have to accept the fantastic offer that is good forever, open to everyone and comes with an eternal lifetime guarantee.

God loves you. He is standing at your door knocking. He will stand there tomorrow and every day after that until the ultimate choice is made. This is an offer far too good to refuse.

Cactus of the Mind

> Brothers I do not consider myself yet to have taken hold of it. But one thing I do; Forgetting what is behind and straining toward what is ahead. I press on toward the goal to win the prize for which God has called me heavenward in Christ Jesus. Philippians 3:13-14

I've just been through a huge battle. I'm not sure yet if I've allowed God to have victory in this with me. I hope that is the case because I do not want to go through the same battle again. This wasn't the first time I've fought this fight although it was possibly the most draining. It was also a less-than-brilliant move on my part. I let the past get a really good grip on the present. As I said, this wasn't the first time, but this time I did respond a little differently.

It is my nature to internalize those dark and ugly things the past can hold. It is also my natural inclination to believe everything Satan thinks of me and not much of what God thinks of me. Normally I keep it all to myself and fight it out, not to victory but to a place of compromise, and there is no room for compromise with the enemy. God may allow us a little wiggle room, a little comfort zone now and then, but the enemy when given the slightest opportunity will take over and destroy. Leaving any area open allows the enemy free reign.

There is a song by Ben Glover called "Dancin' with Cactus." It has great imagery and talks about temptation, in particular the sting of giving into temptation and then enjoying the bad choice. It has always taken me aback to a particularly bad choice I made earlier in life. The memory of it brings some guilt but also some pleasure. The song talks about romance and the inability to resist it. It used to make me think of just that, the romance I should have resisted. The road to hell as the song says is "paved with good temptation." I've always seen that road as calling us to pleasant sins, something self-serving but fun. This past battle cast a new light on that song for me.

My particular temptation is to believe the enemy and allow him to thwart any good I might do for my family, my friends, my church, my God, or myself. If Satan can keep me on that same road, in that same thought pattern, I am useless. That makes me perfect in his sight, but I want to be perfect in Jesus's sight. This last time I desperately wanted to crawl into my own space and lock the door with several big locks. I was pretty willing to believe any and all negative thoughts about my life that came my way. The worse I felt the easier it was to believe that anything that looked positive in my life was a façade.

The key I found this time was to share it. Just to talk to one or two close Christian friends and admit to what was happening. It is best to first take our struggles to God, but sometimes I am so blinded by my sin that I cannot. I avoid God because I know what He will say, and I don't want to hear it. I don't think I'm alone in that feeling. The problem is sometimes we are so wrapped up in the sin that we just cannot or will not go to God. The next best thing is to talk to strong Christian friends. Mine not only pointed me in the right direction, but they didn't run from me as I was somewhat sure they would. They assured me that I was not alone, that the enemy was in fact lying, and that God does love me and has a plan for my life. Did I already know that? In my head, yes, but in that battle my heart was not so sure.

When the enemy wants to send you back to some dark place from which you have already escaped, fight with all you've got. Don't dance with that cactus. It hurts not just you, but everyone around you. Picturing Satan as the cactus and God as a nice, comfy pillow might help. Friends will probably help, and God will certainly help. We may lose a battle or two, but in the end because we belong to the Victor: we will win the war.

"And God's People Said"

While we wait for the blessed hope—the glorious appearing of our great God and Savior Jesus Christ, who gave himself for us to redeem us from all wickedness and to purify for himself a people that are his very own, eager to do what is good. Titus 2:13-14

Many times in my life I have heard a pastor say, "And God's people said," and the response is of course, "Amen." The other day during our church service as we all answered together, I thought about those words: "And God's people said." God's people. Oh yeah, there's Jorie, Tonya, and Dwayne. Oh, and over there, Kaye, Betsy, and that sweet girl whose name I don't know. Oh, and that guy that I don't like. There's Jen, Leann, and George and across from them that new woman who looks so snooty. Woah, woah, woah, wait a minute. That guy whom I don't like? The snooty woman? Is there room for that here? No, there is not. God's people, these people are God's people. The guy I don't like and the snooty woman are as much God's people as Jorie, George, or Kaye. I don't have to like them, but I do have to love them. I may not want to be best friends with them, and that is okay, but God said, "Love your neighbor."

There's my neighbor over there. She's so sweet. I don't really know her, but she seems friendly and sweet enough. What if God asked me, "Would you like to know what she's thinking?"

"Yes, I would, Lord."

"Okay, here it is. 'There's Sandy and Jay. They are so good. There's Joe, Laura, and Mike. Oh, and there's that Tricia. Ooh I can't stand her.' That is what your neighbor is thinking."

"Me, Lord? I'm the one of your people that she can't stand?"

Ouch! It hurts then, doesn't it? We need to know that it hurts God every time we look at one of His people and think ugly thoughts. Paul said we are many parts of one body. Granted I prefer my eyes to my nose, but I realize that my nose is rather necessary.

"God's people said." And God loved the sound of each and every voice. God said, "Love your neighbor." It isn't something the pastor thought would be good PR? "We are the church of people who love their neighbors." It is a directive from God. Your neighbor may not be in too much of a hurry to love you either, but there is no wiggle room in that commandment. Maybe if we truly loved God and gave Him top priority all the time, it would be easier to love His people, our neighbors. After all, we want Him and them to love us.

Out of the Depths

> Out of the depths I cry to you,
> O Lord hear my voice.
> Let your ears be attentive
> to my cry for mercy.
>
> O Israel, put your hope in the Lord,
> For with the Lord is unfailing love
> And with him is full redemption.
> He himself will redeem Israel
> from all their sins.
> Psalms 130:1-2, 7-8

O Lord hear my voice. Have you ever cried out to the Lord begging Him to just hear you? Sometimes we all feel so defeated, pushed on all sides, maybe a little useless, or hopeless. Like Israel we need to put our hope in the Lord. Nothing is too big for him. His love is unfailing.

Recently I was just sick over a situation concerning a friend. After a long night of praying, dozing, and dreaming of her and her dilemma only to wake and pray again, over and over for hours, I read this psalm. When I saw it in my Bible, I also saw that where it says that Israel I had penciled in Tricia and where it says their sins I had penciled in her sins.

Sadly my friend is not in a place where I can suggest this to her. I know I feel better when I pray this psalm, "O Tricia put your hope in the Lord." It reminds me that He will answer my cries for mercy and peace.

The Bible was written years and years ago certainly, but it was just as certainly written for you and me. We can put our own names in where there is a promise as long as we put our faith in the Lord who inspired all of those precious words. Try it. Put your own name in this psalm or anywhere a promise is given. Those promises are for you and in them and the One who made them; there is great hope.

Impressions

"What things?" he asked.
"About Jesus of Nazareth," they replied. "He was a prophet, powerful in word and deed before God and all the people."
Luke 24:19

Recently someone described a friend of mine to a person standing beside me. The speaker had no idea that the woman she described was one of my good friends. I was astonished at her view of my friend. It was so far-off and based on very surface information. The worst part was that it was the second time I had this experience. Another person had spoken to me about not wanting to associate with another of my friends based again on observations, not knowledge. That made me wonder what people see when they see me.

In this passage Jesus is walking with two men who obviously cared for him before Good Friday and are now in grief. He is hearing high opinions of himself. This talk comes after the events that sparked disappointment in the followers of Jesus, but still they are describing him in glowing terms. Jesus could only be described in glowing terms. He's Jesus.

If we were to hear a conversation about ourselves, it might not be flattering, but it would still be useful. It's great to hear someone saying how wonderful we are or how highly they think of us, but all we get from that is "the big head" as my gram used to say. If we hear someone describe us in less-than-glowing terms, that gives us the opportunity to assess and possibly correct our behavior. Of course it is always best to pray about what we hear. As already stated some observations are just not true.

If something negative is said about you or pointed out to you that you realize is true, give it to God. He can fix it. It is also wise to withhold forming an opinion until you have gained a little more knowledge. Most of the time, my first impressions are fairly accurate. Every now and then I am surprised. Even when we know someone well an action of theirs may take us by surprise, just as the Crucifixion took Jesus's followers by surprise. It is then that we have to weigh the circumstances and again wait for a little more of the picture to come clear. Like those old Polaroid snapshots that looked so distorted until they dried completely life sometimes needs a little drying time.

In all things and people God knows the truth. If you're unsure, ask Dad.

Love You Forever

For God so loved the world that gave his one and only Son that whoever believes in him shall not perish but have everlasting life. For God did not send his Son into the world to condemn the world, but to save the world through him. John 3:16-17

Yesterday I heard a young man reading the book *Love You Forever* to his daughter. I heard him explain with great patience why the mommy was doing whatever she was doing on that particular page. He was very kind and sweet with his daughter, but the most amazing thing to me was that he was able to read the whole book without a single tear. I commented on that to a friend and then to his mom. Both ladies agreed that they couldn't read that book without tears.

The words that get me every time aren't even the ones spoken by the mommy. I have four children, and I love them dearly. Most of the time when I read the book, it is the idea that they all grew up so fast that sends my heart to my throat. Every time it is the man saying to his mother, "As long as I'm living, my mommy you'll be." That I cannot get past. Three out of four of my children are boys, and one of them, the twenty-three-year-old still calls me mommy every now and then. He is a mama's boy and proud of it. He wants his son to be a mama's boy because he wants Joey and Kayla to have what he and I have to this day, a bond that can't be broken. My relationship to each child is unique. I love them equally but not the same.

That sweet book and the four distinct bonds I have formed with my own children helps me begin to understand how our Father in heaven feels about us. He loves us forever, and in Him we will be alive forever. It also reminds me that to Him we are so precious that the thought of holding us close swells His heart.

Our Father was willing to give His only Son to bring us home to Him. He sacrificed what was dearest to Him to make us His own, and if that isn't forever love, I don't know what is.

Cross to Bear

As they were going out, they met a man from Cyrene named Simon, and they forced him to carry the cross. They came to a place called Golgotha (which means The Place of the Skull). Mt. 27:32-33

Carry each other's burdens, and in this way you will fulfill the law of Christ. Galatians 6:2

The words from Matthew say that Simon was forced to carry the cross with Jesus. I remember as a child being taught that Simon stepped up to help. That doesn't match the Scripture, and it doesn't make any sense to me. Jesus, a seemingly harmless, actually quite likeable guy has been tortured and is now on his way to his death, how many people are likely to jump out of the angry crowd and ally themselves with him? No, the picture of someone being reluctantly forced into service makes more sense. It is more plausible, and it certainly teaches us a greater lesson.

I've never seen a crucifixion, thank God, but I have been asked to help someone carry his or her cross. The cross has become the symbol for all the things we feel are weighing us down, hurting us body and soul. My gram was fond of saying, "Accept your cross, and it will fly away." I hated that saying. She meant I had to accept the circumstances, bloom where I was planted, give in to an authority other than my own, and none of that was very comfortable. As I got older, it got worse. I realized that I not only had to accept my cross, but in order to serve God I would most likely be called upon to bear another's burden as well.

At first that just seemed like too much. It was enough just to try and keep myself straight. I really didn't have time to worry about anyone else. As time progressed, disciplines improved and my knowledge of God grew I began to understand that I would never be forced into service as Simon was, but if I were lucky, I would be asked.

It is not a burden to help bear someone's load it is an honor. If our Lord thinks enough of me to entrust to me one of His own children, I should be more than willing to accept. Simon had no idea what kind of blessing was involved in carrying the cross with Jesus but we do. We fully understand how bountiful God's blessings are for those who are in His will. It is hard to be a part of another person's suffering, but it is also beautiful. Need, fear, and heartache break down barriers and allow us to bond with each other in ways that the good times cannot. I bet Simon was covered in Jesus's blood by the time that cross reached its destination. That same blood covers us, and that covering protects us from anything that would attempt to separate us from God. Covered in that blood we are more than able to bear our own burdens and those of the people God sends our way.

Presents

When they found him on the other side of the lake, they asked him, "Rabbi, when did you get here?"

Jesus answered, "I tell you the truth, you are looking for me, not because you saw miraculous signs but because you ate the loaves and had your fill. Don not work for food that spoils, but for food that endures to eternal life, which the Son of Man will give you. On him God the Father has placed his seal of approval."

Then they asked him, "What must we do to do the works God requires?"

Jesus answered, "The work of God is this to believe in the one he has sent." John 6:25-29

Jesus tells the people that they are interested in him because he fed them. He wants them to understand how much more he has to give than bread. He wants us to understand that too. Too many people see Jesus as a means to an end. In a sense he is the means and the end. Jesus is our way to the Father. He gave his life so that we could live forever. Certainly eternal life is the end but knowing Jesus should be our focus while we are in this world.

Too often we are all guilty of wanting to pray or be close to the Lord because of what he can do, not because of who he is. Perhaps we see the people in the Scripture passage as greedy, but we aren't any different. Whether it's healing, finances, or our own daily bread, we plead with Jesus to fill our needs; and he is happy to do it. Jesus wants what is best for us. He wants us to want the will of our Father.

We are more than well provided for; we have perfect provision in Jesus. Scripture repeats the assurance that God will supply all of our needs. We read of God's bountiful blessings, His mercy, and love. It's okay to want those things. It's okay to pray for healing, financial help, our daily bread, and anything else we want as long as we understand that none of it has any worth when compared to salvation.

It is hard to learn that your only value to another person was what you had to give them. We like to think that our family and friends love us for who we are, not for what we have. Apply that then to our love for Jesus. We should love him because he is the Son of God who came to save the world and not just because he could cure that cold or pay that bill.

We need to be more interested in God's presence than in his presents.

It's Not Fair

Love is patient, love is kind. It does not envy, it does not boast, it is not proud. It is not rude, is not easily angered, *it keeps no record of wrongs*. Love does not delight in evil but rejoices with the truth. It always protects, always trusts, always hopes, always perseveres.
1 Corinthians 13:4-7 (italics mine)

It is so hard to "keep no record of wrong." It is our human nature to respond in kind. About a week ago my feelings were pretty badly hurt by someone very close to me. The worst of it was that this particular offense almost seems to be cyclical. It's one of those I should be used to it, but it still breaks my heart things. Then just a few days later that same person expected a response from me that I did not want to give. When I was put in the position of having to respond all I could think about was my own hurt feelings. In that moment those words from Paul's letter to the Corinthians were literally bouncing around in my head. *"Love keeps no record of wrong."*

Without the recent hurt feelings, I would have been happy to do just what was expected of me, but the hurt I had felt was such a high hurdle. I had two choices. I could hold onto my hurt and disappoint and cause a further breach in the relationship, or I could respond in love, keeping no record of the wrong. I chose the latter. Wait, don't be too proud of me yet. I spent the rest of the day going over it, trying to find a loophole in the Scripture. There isn't one.

I wanted it to be fair. I wanted the other person to realize that I had been hurt, and in responding in love and kindness I was unable to use the tit for tat that would point out the initial wrong. It's not fair! Friends, think of how we respond when we hear a child say that to us.

There is not a single word in Paul's description of love that says that it is fair or that it will always be equitable. The truth of it is that my loved one has most likely thrown a charge or two out the window. I'm sure there have been times when my wrongs have not been recorded.

My life is not devoid of record keepers. I've had offenses thrown in my face, and I don't like it. I've been treated poorly because the other party saw that as only fair. The words Paul wrote about love are not his own. He learned about love from God. God keeps no record of our wrongs and we offend Him on a daily basis. I'm glad I made the choice not to hold my dear one accountable. Maybe next time I'll do it in an actual loving manner not looking for a loophole. I would rather protect, trust, hope, and persevere than be *fair*.

Delightful

**Delight in the Lord and He will give you the desires of your heart.
Psalm 37:4**

Just the other day, I saw all four of my children throughout the course of the day. This may not seem unusual, but none of my children live at home. From midafternoon until early evening they arrived, visited for a bit, and left. I was also able to spend some time that day chatting with my husband. None of these events were terribly special. No one had any thing of great importance to share. Still at the end of the day I felt so blessed. I could physically feel the love I have for each of them, even the one who is quite a challenge these days. As I was thinking over the day, I realized it had been an exceptionally good day spiritually as well. I had become aware of some things that really brought me closer to God. In the earliest part of the day I had delighted in the Lord, and for the rest of the day He blessed me.

Some days I get up feeling so tired or unprepared. Some days include things I just don't want to face. On those days I tend to petition the Lord rather than delighting in Him. Every once in a while, I remember that it will go much easier if I start out just being happy to be in His presence. The circumstances may not change. I may still feel tired, but somehow the day does go better. Perhaps it is simply because I am willing to take the focus off of me and put it on Him.

Delight in the Lord and He will give you the desires of your heart. Does that mean that everything we want will come our way if we just praise God? No, because some of the things we want aren't good for us and Father truly does know best. What it means is that our hearts will be light, and yes some of our wants will be fulfilled. It also means that by focusing on God we may well stop wanting what isn't good for us. The desires of our hearts can change when we get closer and closer to God. Things that were of great importance suddenly seem insignificant. We are joyful just because He loves us. Every day our Father delights in us. We should return the favor and delight in Him. It will make everything we do look different.

Body Parts

> For we were all baptized by one Spirit into one body—whether Jew or Greek or slave or free—and we were all given the one Spirit to drink. 1 Corinthians 12:13

Once a week I am privileged to sit with a group of women with whom I work and pray. Each one there has made the effort to get to work early so that we can begin our workweek with prayer. It makes Monday morning a lot easier knowing that they will be there. The prayer time sets the tone for the week. It is a wonderful blessing, and because it happens on Monday, one or more of us often references something from our church. Maybe we've heard a special message, have a prayer request, or saw a new person there.

Last week as I wrote the different prayer requests and heard about a member of one friend's church, it occurred to me that no two of us belong to the same church. I was sitting with eight other women, and not one of the nine of us shares a church. There we were nine women all coming together to honor and to petition the same God where the day before we were all in different buildings with slightly different slants on how to "do" church. There was no Jew, Greek, Baptist, Catholic, Anglican, or Assembly of God; there were just nine women wanting to praise one God.

We've all seen and/or read the news stories about various denominations. We all know that even within a denomination there can be strife. There are churches whose label is Nondenominational, but even that label can't protect them from power struggles. I do not claim to know exactly what form God had planned for His church. Of course I think my own church does a great job of getting it as right as humanly possible, but I bet the other eight ladies who prayed with me last Monday think that about their churches too. What I do know is that in those moments on Monday morning when we come together with Christ at the center, as the focus, with no Baptist/Catholic/Anglican/Assembly agenda, we are getting it right.

If there is an opportunity for you to get with a group of believers and pray, take it. We are many parts of the same body (1 Corinthians 12:12-31). Guess what nose, you need that foot as much as that foot needs you. Say a prayer with a group of friends and enjoy a warming drink of the Spirit of God.

Running Away

Simon Peter answered him, "Lord to whom shall we go? You have the words of everlasting life. We believe and know that you re the Holy One of God." John 6:68

I said to the Lord, "You are my Lord apart form you I have no good thing." Psalm 16:2

Have you ever had a day/week/month when you felt that you just weren't growing spiritually? Have you ever been angry with God or felt so distant from Him that you decided to just give up? We all go through tough times. Everyone has at least a day or two when they wonder why they are getting up so early or staying up so late to pray or read Scripture. We all have times when we feel it isn't making a difference. In those times there is a temptation to stop pursuing God. We choose something else to fill up the time we were giving to the Lord. I don't know about you, but that has never worked for me.

Simon Peter had the answer: "Lord to whom shall we go?" In the times that I have been angry or disappointed to the point of ignoring God I have found that, like Peter, I have nowhere else to go. I may take my troubles or fears to my friends and family, but in the end I have always gone back to my Father. The truth of it is I can't do it without Him.

I am blessed to have had the same best friend for forty years. Whenever something great happens I call Mary. Whenever something tragic happens, I call Mary. When we were children, we would argue on occasion, and when we did, of course we didn't call each other for a few days. That was awful. I would think, "Oh, I have to tell Mary," only to remember that we were mad at each other. That is a small picture of what walking away from God is like. There is a need or desire to pray, but, no, I've given up on that. A feeling of loneliness accompanies that lack that no person or thing can replace.

To whom would we go? After all, the psalmist said it best, apart from Him we have no good thing.

Make and Model

As for those who seemed to be important—whatever they were makes no difference to me; God does not judge by external appearances. Galatians 2:6a

A car passed me yesterday, and I noticed the pretty color. I'm not much of a car person and never know the make or model of a vehicle. I don't even recognize my family member's vehicles. As the pretty-colored car passed me by, I thought of it as just another minivan. The only thing special about it to me was the paint. Then I saw the make. It was, I'm sure, a very expensive minivan. The name of the company suggests a high-price tag. The thing is even after I knew this was no ordinary run-of-the-mill minivan to car connoisseurs, to me it was still just an ordinary vehicle. I just happened to like the color. I do realize though that other people would most likely be impressed by the make of it.

That whole train of thought took a turn to the way we view each other. Too many people judge others by what they wear, what they own, and where they live rather than on what is inside. What if we had to wear labels that listed our value to God? By what criteria would you label yourself? How you treat others? How much you tithe? How often you pray? What label would you give yourself? Would you be an ordinary run of the mill vehicle or a high priced fancy model?

The truth is it does not matter to God. He sees us all as precious. He looks at our hearts and sees what is there, and what is lacking. If we are souped-up, high-performance Christians He loves us. If we are little beaters barely making it from here to there without breaking down and sometimes with a break down or two, He loves us.

They may be invisible, but we all wear labels lovingly given to us by our Father. Like the make and model on the vehicles on the road we have been stamped at the factory and our labels read:

Precious
Mine

Translation Please

"Why is my language not clear to you? Because you are unable to hear what I say." John 8:43

My days are filled with children who are difficult to understand. The speech impediments are varied in severity and in type. There are four adults in our classroom, and often we look to each other for translation. These words Jesus spoke to the Jews reminded me so much of my days at work. I hear myself constantly translating, especially outside our classroom. One of our children loves to chat with any and everyone, but he is somewhat difficult to understand. As he is speaking the listener's eyes turn to me for the translation, and it is as natural as breathing to give it. Once they understand him, they will of course respond to him, not to me. What if I could translate for God? What if I understood Him so well that when other people were confused I could translate?

A couple of years ago our pastor ended a midweek message with this challenge, "Fill in the blanks: 'What do I believe is impossible in my _____? But if it could be done would fundamentally change _____.'" If I could truly understand God as well as I understand my little people, I could translate for Him and that would surely change not just my life but the lives around me. I can't of course, and it is pure arrogance to think that I could. We will never fully understand God while we are here in this place. Still I think I could come closer.

The reason I understand the children as well as I do is because in addition to having four of my own, I have fifteen nieces and nephews, and have worked with children since I was sixteen years old. I know kids. Is that the key? I do all forms of "kidspeak" very well because I am so familiar with it. I will never be able to fully explain God or speak for Him, but I can know Him so well that I can make a pretty educated guess. I could certainly spend enough time with Him and His Word to be able to imitate Him to the best of my human limitations.

As with anything else, we get out of Scripture what we put into it. I did not develop an ear for kidspeak by listening for a few minutes one day a week to the same child. I won't develop an understanding of God by listening to one pastor a few minutes a week either. To be able to understand God, we need to hear, truly hear what He has to say. Reading and listening to His word will make us more familiar with it. Maybe we can become familiar enough to be able, once in a while, to translate it for ourselves or someone else. I want to be able to hear God and understand Him better than I hear and understand anyone else. As it does with the children, it will just take the investment of time.

Satisfaction

And I—in righteousness I will see your face; when I awake, I will be satisfied with seeing your likeness. Psalm 17:15

Everyone has those nights when we toss and turn or worse have nightmares. Our daytime stresses manage to invade our sleep. With our resistance down we are unable to shove them away, and there they are nipping at the peace we so desire. Then we wake up, and if we are smart, we immediately turn to God. A prayer, regardless of how long or short, how eloquent or faulty, will bring us our Father's attention; and if we are willing to lean on Him, calm can be restored.

This can be seen in a larger sense too. Sometimes we can fall into a dark place in our lives. We struggle with our own recurrent sin, and we feel so awful, but when we "wake up" and realize that we have drifted off the path, swerved right out of God's will we can make it better by seeking His face.

Troubles are going to come. We live in a fallen world that is daily becoming more comfortable with sin than righteousness. We are not going to be able to glide along toward home without encountering a pothole or two or two hundred. It is then that we need to be satisfied with seeing God's likeness. If we are in His will, then we can know without doubt that He will work everything to good for us. Even when the circumstances seem so bleak, so overwhelming, we have to remember that God sent us His son Jesus and that precious light still shines no matter how much the darkness tries to extinguish it.

Seek His face every day and be satisfied.

Careful Listening

How sweet are your words to my taste, sweeter than honey to my mouth!

Your word is a lamp to my feet and a light for my path.
Psalm 119:103, 105

I overheard a conversation the other day between two close friends of mine. To be more accurate I heard one side of the conversation. Oddly enough they were talking about something that would involve me. Hearing only the one side, I was pretty sure I knew what was up. I was pleased with what I thought was going to occur. The next day while talking with one of them, I learned what had transpired on the other end. While the result was still positive and both friends had my best interest at heart, it was not at all what I thought it was going to be. The moral of the story? A little information in the wrong hands can go very far awry.

The Bible is a wonderful tool for us. We can read it and "hear" conversations between the Father and the Son, the Father and his people, and the Son and his friends. We get to read both sides of most of the conversations in the Bible. Still there is so much room for misunderstanding. A verse pulled out of context and/or paired with another can cause all kinds of conclusions to be drawn, not all of them accurate.

Just as in this life, we can become excited or get our feelings hurt for the wrong reason; we can become confused or doubtful if we aren't careful with Scripture. We aren't supposed to play Bible roulette, opening pages and grabbing the verse that suits us that day. We are supposed to prayerfully study the Word of God and learn as much as we can from and about it.

Have a conversation with God today. Read His conversations with others. But always make sure you are hearing both sides before you react.

Near Death

> The cords of death entangled me;
> the torrents of destruction overwhelmed me.
> The cords of the grave coiled around me;
> the snares of death confronted me.
> In my distress I cried to the Lord for help.
> From his temple he heard my voice,
> my cry came before him, into his ears.
> **Psalm 18:4-6**

I don't know many people who have truly had a near-death experience. In fact, at the moment I can only think of one friend, but then he's had enough for several of us. Still there are those moments in life that feel like death. I remember when my oldest son was just five days old, and I was told that he might not live. It seems surreal now, but at the time it was all too real. Death was coming for a life I had tried so hard to start well. In my distress, I cried to the Lord with exactly those thoughts. I took the vitamins, got extra rest, and basically did everything the doctor said to do. How had this happened to my child?

"From his temple he heard my voice." One by one God sent people to me to pray for Paul, to bless him, and to ask for God's mercy. God started with me. By day two my prayer had changed from "why God" to "your will" albeit with some restrictions. I wanted God's will if God's will were for Paul to live. Again in His mercy God answered that prayer. I was told Paul would live, but that the quality of his life was still in question. At that point, I truly did pray for God's will, and peace flooded my whole being.

It wasn't until nearly two years later that I began to realize the extent of God's mercy. He could have answered my prayers as I prayed them. He could have called in the marker of my willingness to accept any shortcoming just to have a living child. He didn't. He heard the prayer of my heart and returned to me a very bright and capable little boy who has grown over the years to be a wonderful, accomplished young man.

At each milestone of Paul's life I am reminded that God is always here for me. He granted me peace in my time of terror. He granted me mercy then and every day before and since. If I doubt that for a minute I have a six-plus-foot reminder that God's mercy and love are boundless. The torrents of destruction may try to overwhelm me but they cannot win. God is for me so who would dare be against me? (Romans 8:31b)

No Secrets

Almighty God to whom all hearts are open, all desires are known and from whom no secrets are hidden, cleanse the thoughts of our hearts by the inspiration of your Holy Spirit that we may perfectly love you and worthily magnify your holy Name.

The sacrifices of God are a broken spirit; a broken and a contrite heart O God you will not despise. Psalm 51:17

In the Anglican Church, we say the collect for purity which includes the words "from whom no secrets are hidden." No secrets are hidden from God. He sees and knows all. He knew before we did that we would behave in lovely and/or loathsome ways. Our Father has intimate knowledge of how our hearts work. He knows what weighs heavily on our hearts and hears our cries before we even think to send them.

The enemy, on the other hand, operates much more like a fortune-teller. He has knowledge of human nature in general and knows only what we tell him about our mind-set. Think of the horoscopes in the newspapers written with huge all-encompassing, broad strokes. If we want to badly enough, we can prove that our day went exactly as Madame Z said it would.

Have you ever known anyone who has had his or her fortune told? Can you imagine it? The fortune-teller looks the client over, sizes up the situation, and makes a fairly general statement. The listener gasps. "Ah." The fortune teller thinks, "I'm onto something now."

Our enemy operates the same way. We flinch, and he jumps on that fear with both feet stirring us up to full-blown panic. The secrets we're so pointlessly trying to keep from God have now been revealed to the enemy. We moan and complain about our weakness and failings while our enemy sits by happily taking notes.

On the other side of the room, God sits quietly encouraging us to lift our hands in praise or fall on our knees in supplication. The enemy will get a very different picture if we obey. He will see a person devoted to God, seeking God, imploring the Father for help or thanking Him for blessings.

In that moment he has no power. Our secret is revealed then too, but it is one of victory not defeat.

Picture the fortune-teller revealing the next big event in a life only to have the listener laugh in her face. Wrong road try again and again and continue to get it wrong because no one knows our future except God.

The enemy stalks us in our weakness attempting to learn our secrets. Our Father knows our secrets and loves us in our brokenness. Which one do you prefer?

Treasured Words

and all who had heard it were amazed at what the shepherds said to them. But Mary treasured up all these things and pondered them in her heart. Luke 2:18-19

Be kind and compassionate to one another, forgiving each other, just as in Christ God forgave you. Ephesians 4:32

Do not store up for yourselves treasures on earth, where moth and rust destroy, and where thieves break in and steal. But store up for yourselves treasures in heaven, where moth and rust do not destroy and thieves do not break in. For where your treasure is there your heart will be also. Matthew 6:19-21

A few months ago at the end of a Bible study, we were asked to collect several items that represented various kinds of grace. I was blessed to be in a group with my husband and my daughter. Many of their items really touched my heart. In general, I could feel the Lord using that time to heal some wounds between my daughter and I as well as to give me an insight I hadn't had with her and with my husband. The most precious moment came when we got to the grace that forgives.

As it came to my husband's turn, I had stood up to grab an item I had forgotten to add to my collection. "Trish," he said, "would you sit down." Embarrassed at first because I thought he was chastising me, I quickly realized he was asking me to sit on the table where we were placing our items. "What?" I replied, trying to recover some dignity. "Please sit on the table," he continued, "because you are the best example I have of grace that forgives."

Now my husband is pretty good about compliments. I can count on less than one hand the number of meals I have cooked that he hasn't complimented. He tells me he loves me all the time. The man is not stingy with kind words, but that particular incident was a treasure to me, and it reminded me of that verse about Mary treasuring things in her heart.

It also reminded me of the verse about storing up treasures for heaven. Forgiveness can get tough sometimes. We don't want to forgive for various reasons even when we know that we should. For the most part, I think those words are a treasure to me because my husband is such a good man and rarely offends me in any significant way, and yet he relies on my forgiveness and sees me as the type of person who easily forgives.

It is rare to be offered a treasure of any kind, and when we receive one, we should store them in our hearts for those days when we feel sad or defeated. The treasures we receive here are just a glimpse of what is waiting. My heart swelled when I realized what my husband was saying about me. I can only imagine how I will feel when my Father tells me that He saw forgiveness or kindness in me. That after all is the greatest treasure.

Feed My Lambs

When they had finished eating, Jesus said to Simon Peter, "Simon son of John do you love me more than these?"
"Yes Lord," he said, "you now that I love you."
Jesus said, "Feed my lambs."
Again Jesus said, "Simon, son of John, do you truly love me?'
He answered, "Yes Lord, you know that I love you."
Jesus said, "Take care of my sheep."
The third time he said to him, "Simon son of John, do you love me?"
Peter was hurt because Jesus asked him the third time, "Dou you love me?" He said," Lord you know all things, you know I love you."
Jesus said, "Feed my sheep." John 21:15-17

I've had a children's Bible song stuck in my head for days. It's about feeding the lambs, and it isn't one of those cool kid songs. It is singsongy and annoying. The message is great, but the music is not. When my children were little, we listened to it daily. In other words, I know it really well. It got stuck in my head the other day as I prepared food to go to several different places including my own table. It seemed very appropriate, and I was grateful to God for putting it in my mind even though it is rather aggravating. As the words went through my head, I became aware that cutting up chicken, glazing a ham, dicing potatoes all can be God's work. Another day I may have felt stress at getting it all done and delivered, but all of it felt like a blessing to me. I felt the joy of doing even that simple task for God's glory.

Just a few days later a friend asked for some advice, some guidance, and as I was searching for just the right Scripture to share with her, I found that song once again in my head.

Several months ago I was part of a group that created a quilt for a friend with cancer. I teased that I had no sewing ability but would be happy to supply cookies for the crew. I'm a feeder. I've never seen that as having any real significance as far as Kingdom purposes are concerned.

I have prayed for years to be of more and more use to God. In my mind I had to be doing something big or noteworthy for it to really count. In the past few weeks, God has used me to open doors for people with arms full of stuff, give rides to people without transportation, feed the sick and the well, welcome a group into my home to study His word, advise a friend whose faith is shaky, wipe a nose, and celebrate a couple of milestone events. All of those things are great service to God.

It is a gift to be able to literally feed His lambs. It is a gift to be able to create a quilt or lend a sympathetic ear. My friends, you all have gifts. God is calling you to feed His lambs. He has given you the ability to do it. God feeds us with spiritual food, and we are called to share that with everyone around us. Feed a lamb today and tomorrow. Be faithful to do the small things, and before you know it, you'll be feeding a flock and loving every minute of it.

New Sight

He replied, "Whether he is a sinner of not, I don't know. One thing I do know, I was blind and now I see!" John 9: 25

Some Pharisees who were with him heard him say this and asked, "What? Are we blind too?"

Jesus said, "If you were blind, you would not be guilty of sin; but now that you claim you can see, your guilt remains." John 9:40-41

A blind man meets Jesus and can see. He is thrilled. The Pharisees talk to Jesus, and he tells them they are not blind. They don't seem as happy. There seems to be a lot of vision issues in this story and some questions about sin. Thankfully we can shake our heads and be grateful that we didn't live in that time. Wait a minute, that doesn't sound right. Times may change, but God never changes.

I am blessed to have a couple of new or renewed believers in my life right now. They were *blind,* but now they see, and as newly sighted persons, they want to describe the things they see to everyone. It's exciting to be around. Conversely I am also in pretty close contact with a couple of Pharisees. They see too, but their vision seems terribly skewed. The purity of the newly sighted is gone. They have forgotten that God is good all the time. They don't seem to realize that "mercy triumphs over judgment" (James 2:13b) or that it (mercy) is required of us (Micah 6:8b). They see God and somehow see themselves as very much like him although "false humility" is often the word of the day.

The newly sighted are much more fun to be around. There is a whole "did you see that!" quality to them. They are truly discovering God's grace, mercy, and fullness. The greatest desire of their hearts is to share that sight with everyone around them, and in their zeal they can sometimes step on toes.

It is easier for me to forgive the newbie's toe crunching because somewhere in that zest they inspire me. It is hard for me to even converse with the Pharisicital types because the injustice, the harshness of their "faith" is grating.

Where is your sight today? Can you see or do your spiritual glasses need a little cleaning? Are you beating people up with Scripture or loving them with great mercy? God calls us to see something new every day. Sometimes we forget to look because we think we've already seen it. Clean your spiritual glasses or sit with a person with new vision. The view hasn't changed, but maybe the perspective can.

Light Speed

And God said, "Let there be light," and there was light. God saw that the light was good and he separated the light from the darkness. Genesis 1:3

"When God commanded light to come it came at 186, 000 miles per hour." I heard someone make that statement and it really stuck with me. The message centered on light, walking in the light, being lighthearted, things of that nature. It was a good message, but what stayed with me the most was that one sentence about the speed at which light came. God said come, and it came faster than I can begin to imagine.

I'm originally a New Yorker. They do things faster there, much faster, than we do here in the South. The last time we went to visit, among all the joking about the pace of things, my daughter quite seriously asked me if they were about to run out of something in the grocery store. It isn't just the speed of movement either; it's an attitude of hurry. Having been away for so many years, as I observed it, I had to wonder what they were all hurrying toward. The answer is nothing in particular. It is simply the style there to move fast.

How different speed for speed's sake is from speed with a purpose. Aimless rushing around just causes high blood pressure and angry feelings. There is certainly something, many things, to be said for a slower pace in life. Yet there are times when a quick response is the best response. When we dial 911, we don't want them to take their time. When labor begins, the about to be mommy isn't interested in a long drawn-out process. When God calls, I want to answer with great alacrity. I would like to be in the day when I wouldn't hesitate, making sure that it is God calling or counting the cost of the response.

Years ago a friend of mine told me a story about teaching swimming at a summer camp. She said, "If those kids never see water again, I know one thing will always stay with them, OWA, obedience with alacrity." I remember thinking then how much better my pre-k class would run if I could get my angels to understand OBA. A few years later, I thought about that conversation again in terms of my response to God. Now I've heard that fact about light.

Think of where we would be if light had tarried. It wouldn't be nearly as pretty an existence. A little hesitation when God calls can change the whole picture. When God calls me to come, I want to exhibit obedience not only with alacrity but also at the speed of light. I want to be sure when things get separated that I am on the light side.

Cost of Worship

Now there were some present at that time who told Jesus about the Galileans whose blood Pilate had mixed with their sacrifices. Luke 13:1

In order to worship at the temple, the Galileans risked death. Pilate as the emissary of the Roman government could and would order raids on the groups of worshipers for real or imaginary infractions. They were literally taking their lives in their hands to worship God. In many places that has not changed. All around the world people are suffering for their Christian beliefs. Here in America, we are free to worship our God when and where we please, for now.

There is a movement here in America to remove God from schools, the Pledge of Allegiance, and money. On the surface, it would seem that the school battle has been won. There is no organized prayer in public schools, and as employees of any school board we aren't supposed to impose our beliefs on anyone else. We may praise our Lord as long as no one can see or hear us. Whatever! I've heard enough misinformation about the division of church and state to last me several lifetimes. It isn't that I don't know about it or that I don't understand it. I do understand it better than some who would "warn" me. I just do not care.

No one is going to spill my blood, that I know of today, but that day could come. In the meantime I am free to endure the dirty looks, whispered conversations, and pointed remarks. As people tell me why I can't do or say what I am doing or saying in a public school, I smile and nod. I'm always amused by the remark "you can't say that" after something has already been said. I can, I did, and I will again because right up there with that division of church and state thing is the amendment that says I have a right to say whatever I want, and you can't kill me for it. Above all of that is a God who says that He is for me, and therefore no one else dare be against me.

The worst I have ever endured for my faith is nothing when compared to what the Galileans were facing every day. It is not even a distant cousin to the terror of people living in countries where there is no freedom, religious, or otherwise. Here in America, we are allowed to praise our God as long as it doesn't offend anyone. I long to push the envelope, rock some boats, and make heard the name of God. I pray to have the courage to do all of that even if my life, not my job, or reputation, but my life were on the line.

Blessings

"I will give you the keys of the kingdom of heaven; whatever you bind on earth will be bound in heaven and whatever you loose on earth will be loosed in heaven." Matthew 16:19
We love because he first loved us. 1 John 4:19

Some weeks are busier than others. I was in the middle of a particularly hectic week rushing home from work to make a dessert for a small group that was meeting in my home that evening when I got a phone call. It was from a member of the group just letting me know that she would be bringing some goodies for the meeting. "Oh, bless you!" I said as I drove. As I finished the phone call, I thought how truly I meant those words. If I were literally in the business of bestowing blessings, she would absolutely have been a recipient at that moment. She had just taken a task off of my hands that I didn't quite have time to accomplish. It was a blessing to me, and I wanted to return the favor.

I thought about it for quite a while as I drove home, prepared dinner for my husband and got the house ready for the group. If we can bind and loose, then can we bless? Further it brought me to the whole idea of how God treats us. God does not need a single thing from me. He is all, owns all, and can do all. No phone call from me is going to lift a burden from His heart. Nothing I do is going to relieve stress from a being that is devoid of stress.

We love God because he first loved us. A friend of mine told me a story of her little boy's answer when asked why he loved his mommy. He said, "Because she loves me." In among the kindergarten answers of "she buys me stuff", "she's pretty," and "she cooks good," how precious it was to that mom to hear, "because she loves me."

I really don't think God *needs* our help. I think He allows us to help because He loves us. It is more evidence of His mercy that He allows us to serve and to feel useful. By blessing my day, my friend made God's heart happy. We are all able to please God when we bless His people. We are privileged to be His hands, feet, eyes, etc., in this world.

I hope my friend was blessed in at least the same measure that she blessed me. I'm pretty sure she was or will be. God is never outdone in generosity.

A Humble Woman

"Therefore I tell you, her many sins have been forgiven—for she loved much. But he who has been forgiven little loves little."
Then Jesus said to her, "Your sins are forgiven." Luke 7:47-48

I love the story in which this verse sits. Jesus has come into the home of a woman who literally throws herself at his feet. She has washed his feet with her tears, dried them with her hair, and anointed him with expensive perfume. She is in awe. Once upon a time she was a naughty girl. This was the girl who has not allowed to play with the nice girls. She had a reputation, but she wanted a new life. She wanted to feel clean, so she offered what she had to the One who could change her situation, and he did. Do you think she would soon forget that moment? Do you think that in the next day or so she was back to her old ways? I don't. I think she was profoundly changed by her encounter with Jesus. Of course because she remained human she most likely made other mistakes, but I believe that her life radically changed after she put herself at Jesus's feet.

She loved much, so her many sins were forgiven. There isn't a verse where the woman offers big flowery words to Jesus to obtain forgiveness. No, she lets her actions speak. Perhaps she was too remorseful too even look up at Jesus let alone talk to him. She asked his forgiveness with her actions. Just like her, we too have to humble ourselves before the Lord of Lords. We must lay prostrate at his feet and allow him to see our remorse. He will change us if we let him. Jesus stands with his arms wide open, waiting and wanting to set us free from our sins.

What happens when we don't confess our sin? What happens when we carry it around with us out of pride or shame? It festers. If we hang on out of pride, too foolish to admit we were wrong, we are likely to commit the same sin over and over. If we allow shame to cripple us, it will do exactly that. We will be no good to ourselves, to our family and friends, or to God. We will be useless, and eventually we may become bitter or even ill. We need to ask for forgiveness. We also need to be prepared to forgive.

I realized just a few hours ago that I was still harboring resentment over an event that happened four months ago. Just the thought of it made me anxious. I want to remind the person who injured me. I do not want to forgive her. I do however want to be forgiven. Nothing we do is too large or too small to be forgiven by God. Who are we to withhold forgiveness from another?

We all need to let go of our sins and let the love of Jesus flood our lives. As forgiveness flows into us, so then let it flow out from us. The woman in this Scripture is a beautiful example of how we should approach Jesus. Let us all strive to follow her example.

Loving Gestures

Husbands in the same way be considerate as you live with your wives, and treat them with respect as the weaker partner and as heirs with you of the gracious gift of life, so that nothing will hinder your prayers. 1 Peter 3:7

Wives submit to your husbands as to the Lord. For the husband is the head of the wife as Christ is the head of the church, his body, of which he is the Savior. Ephesians 5:22-23

It's all about love. Sometimes that is so hard. We may be standing on each other's last nerve or maybe one or the other is just carrying some hard feelings. Still sometimes it is so hard to feel love, and yet we are called to act and to respond in loving ways. It is just nice to remember a special event that demonstrates how precious love can be and how far one will go for love's sake.

Friends of ours shared a story from their courtship that touched my heart. When they were courting the young man was in school 150 miles from the young lady. One very snowy evening, he drove that 150 miles just to kiss her good night. Then he turned around and truly risking life and limb drove back to school again. For them that evening it was all about love.

My own dear husband often stays up later than I. He knows that I don't particularly like that, but really can I make him comply to my schedule? Every now and then he will come into our room as I am preparing for bed. He waits for me to get ready, and then he tucks me in. He leaves again and returns sometimes much later, but that doesn't matter. The important detail is that he stops whatever he is doing and comes to minister to me. He shows me tenderness.

In both stories the men see and answer their ladies need to be loved, to feel lovely, and to know that we matter. In those instances, each of us was treated the way Christ treats the church with tenderness and with caring.

It doesn't always take the grand gesture of a three-hundred-mile round trip. A loving gesture can be as simple or dramatic as you care to make it.

When our friends share their story, which is in the neighborhood of fifty years old, the wife's eyes light up as if it were yesterday, and the man looks just a tad proud of himself. It is a very sweet thing to see. When I think of my dear one coming in to make sure I'm all cozy, it makes my heart swell with love for him. It also makes me want to return the gesture. Our Lord will never be outdone in loving gestures, but we can certainly imitate him to the best of our ability.

The Right Food

Jesus said to them, "I am the bread of life. He who comes to me will never go hungry, and he who believes in me will never be thirsty." John 6:35

"We buy new clothes to hide our hungry souls." Are you who people think you are? At the core of your being, are you the person you present to the world? Are you pleased with your life as it is? Most importantly who (or what) sits on the throne in your life?

"We buy new clothes to hide our hungry souls." I heard this statement last weekend from a young priest in a Greek Orthodox church. It was part of a sermon that spoke to our need as followers of Christ to seek him first and share him with others. I knew when I heard it that I would have to borrow it, and meeting Father Kevin later I asked his permission to do so fully expecting to use it as my own. When it came time to write it, I had to give him credit. It is in fact *his* profound thought, not mine. It is a bold statement that cannot be watered down or easily forgotten. I applaud this young priest for making it. I have thought about it, repeated it, and lived with it for the past week. Here is what it says to me.

We live, even those of us with great faith, with one eye and one ear tuned to what the world thinks. We hide or at least minimize our love of Christ in certain situations to avoid being seen as religious fanatics. We are happy to wear the latest fashion and quick to follow the trends in accessories, but what do we look like underneath?

I'm not a shopper, so in some ways it's surprising that this quote has spoken so deeply to me. I buy clothes because I have to and find more aggravation than pleasure in shopping. On the other hand, I love chocolate. Hurt my feelings and that will give me a perfect excuse to eat something made with cocoa. It used to be the other way around; the more I hurt, the less I ate, but that wasn't any healthier a response. The point is when we are hurting, we look for any way out. We reach for things—food, alcohol, drugs, activities, clothes—to fill a void that only Jesus can fill. "We buy new clothes to hide a hungry soul."

There is so much wisdom in that simple statement. Over the past several days as I've sat with it and it with me, images of unhappy but busy, beautiful people have crossed my mind. There is the idea that someone who looks that good just has to be all right. Combine that with the idea of an emptiness that has to be filled and off to the stores we go for the latest thing.

Two women repeatedly came to mind for me. One dresses well all the time. She never ever lets her guard down. She owns no denim but lots of silk and linen and lots of jewelry. She always looks lovely—on the outside. Get closer, and you'll see nothing but pain and insecurity on the inside.

The other is younger and falls more into the-devil-may-care dress area, but she cares very deeply. Underneath the funky, chunky outfits is a little girl crying for acceptance. She owns plenty of denim in various colors and stages of disrepair. Her clothes cry "look at me/no, don't look at me" with equal intensity.

One is elegant to the naked eye. The other is just this side of dirty. Both are a tragic mess. Style, statements, and status are vying to fill a void created for the spiritual. Hungry souls may buy new clothes, but somehow the hurt shines through.

There is only one outfit that is going to fit well on those two women, on you and on me. That is the garment of love provided by the sacrifice of the blood of Jesus. We sing it. We pray it, and we hope for it. If we will let him, Jesus will come and clothe us with his love. We are upheld by his truth, washed clean by his willingness to become filthy, and saved by the shedding of his blood for our sins. Jesus lived his entire life to bless and save us. He cares for us beyond what we can ask or imagine. He is our food, clothing, and shelter all in one. There is no need for our souls to go hungry if only we would reach for the right food.

Trust

I will put my trust in him. Hebrews 2:13

Worry is the antithesis of trust. If we truly trust God, we know that all we have to do is pray and obey. Sometimes He asks us to leave things in His hands. To the world that looks as if we are doing nothing. It seems that we don't care. So instead of obeying we take other actions, taking us farther and farther away from His plan. The farther we get from Him, the messier things get, and we worry.

The result is that the worrying consumes our time and our thoughts. God takes a backseat. We may be talking to Him or more to the point giving him directions, but the minute we let worry take over, we've said in essence, "I don't trust you to take care of this." There are so many places in both the Old and New Testaments that advise us not to worry, but when trouble comes, it is the natural response. That is when we need to step away from our own nature and do our best to take on the nature of Christ.

You may have people exhorting you to do something but don't listen. Don't do a single thing unless God directs you to it. Remember Abraham and Sarah. They took things into their own hands with less-than-positive results.

Shock the world and stand firm. Put yourself in God's hands. Trust in the One who never changes and demonstrate His saving power.

Thief

Why are you downcast, O my soul?
Why are you so disturbed within me?
Put your hope in God,
for I will yet praise him,
my Savior and my God.
Psalm 43:5

There has been a thief at my door recently. No bell rings or knocker knocks, but I know he's there, skulking around, oozing into my thoughts. It's a little frightening when I first wake up to have him there waiting in those first moments when I am still a little groggy. At that time my resistance is somewhat compromised. That is his best chance, and he knows it, so every morning for the past few weeks he has waited. Every morning by God's grace, I have sent him packing. Prayer and praise will accomplish that, but still I wanted to know why. What is he doing here? Prayer will answer that too, and prayer is a large part of the answer.

Many people have come to me with their concerns lately, and in the same time I have faced a couple of challenges of my own. In those times it is easy to lose sight of God's plan. It is easier still for doubt to creep in for the lies to take hold. We do not have to be fearful when this happens to us. We do not have to believe the lies. No matter how things look or what the future seems to hold, we know that God is in control. We know He is good all the time, and that He loves us beyond reason.

Why is that thief so persistently at my door? He is there because all the concerns of my heart, and the requests of my friends bring me to my Father's side. He doesn't want me there. He wants me in despair, terrified, depressed. In that state I am completely useless.

When praise and adoration are my response even in the hard or confusing times, our Father honors my faith. I am blessed in ways I never saw coming. The thief continues to try to sneak in and take over, but he has no chance. In this case, my dad really is bigger. He stands there every morning too. He invites me to bring those concerns, real and imagined, to His throne. If I bring praise and honor with my fear knowing who is in charge, I feel His power wash over me.

> **For you did not receive a spirit that makes you a slave again to fear, but you received the Spirit of sonship. And by him we cry, "*Abba,* Father" Romans 8:15.**

> **What shall we say then in response to all of this? If God is for us who can be against us? He who did not spare his own Son but gave him up for us all—how will he not also, along with him, graciously give us all things? Romans 8: 31-32**

If God is for us . . . . I believe that God absolutely is for me. Many things may try to steal my peace and joy, but in the end, God wins.

Praise Him Still

I will extol that Lord at all times; his praise will always be on my lips. My soul will boast in the Lord. Let the afflicted hear and rejoice. Glorify the Lord with me; let us exalt his name forever. Psalm 34:1-3

We sing a song in our church called "I Will Praise Him Still." It is a beautiful song, very easy to sing along with great music. Watch out for the words because hidden in that pretty melody is a challenge to live radically opposed to the norm.

A few years ago a family in our church suffered the loss of their older daughter. It wasn't something they were prepared for as in a long illness. The younger sister went to visit the older sister at college and found her dead—with no warning at all just the sudden death of a supposedly healthy nineteen-year-old girl. I cannot begin to imagine the pain they must have felt. This all happened on a weekend, and ten days later at a Wednesday-night service, there they were as usual and we sang "I Will Praise Him Still."

There is a point in that song that says, "When the dark trials come and my heart is filled with the weight of death, I will praise Him still." Never had those words carried the impact of that Wednesday night. I watched as three people stood just in front of me, hands raised to heaven singing praise. Ordinary if you aren't the parents and sister of the girl who just died, extraordinary if you are.

How did they do it? The song answers that question. "He gave us life in His perfect will, and by His good grace I will praise Him still." We are able to praise in the midst of heartbreak, failure, and devastation because He enables us to by His grace.

To this day I have not suffered a loss that even begins to compare, but I am learning to praise God when the dark trials come. There was a time not too long ago when one of my children in a fit of rebellion went off for two weeks with no word to any family member. We had no idea if she were alive or dead. Two things got me through that time, amazing support from my prayer partners and the ability to still praise God.

God is good all the time. His will is perfect and best. We mess up. Our blind eyes can't see His purpose, but our Lord never changes. His faithfulness is far beyond our understanding.

When dark trials come and the weight of death, loss, failure, or shame fills your heart, praise Him still. He is strong to save, and thankfully He is willing to save.

Praise God with your words, actions, and thoughts. That sacrifice will not return empty.

Jude Doxology

**To him who is able to keep you from falling and to present you before his glorious presence without fault and with great joy—to the only God our Savior be glory majesty, power and authority, through Jesus Christ our Lord, before all ages now and forevermore! Amen.
Jude 24-25**

To him who is able to keep you . . . We sing a hymn in our church called the "Jude Doxology." It is basically the above verses. When something is set to music it is much easier for me to memorize it and to keep it in my head. Often I find myself walking along with these words humming through my mind. "To him who is able to keep you, who is able to keep you from stumbling."

There it is the promise of support and ultimate protection from the God of the Universe. He is able to keep me from stumbling. Yet I stumble. I'm sure you are way ahead of me here and know that the stumbles are a result of my taking matters into my own hands. God *could* keep me standing firm but I'll give Him a break. I've got this one—oops, maybe not.

Then the verses go on to say that Jesus wants to present us without fault and with great joy. He paid the price so that we could be presented without fault. Do you feel the joy of that? I know sometimes it's hard to feel it in the midst of trials, but it is still there. The joy of knowing that our days are numbered and our steps can be without peril if we place ourselves completely in His hands.

It is such a comfort to me to know that when circumstances beyond my control knock my emotional or physical legs out from under me, all I have to do is lean back. There I will find the arms of God our Savior who is able to keep me from falling. I need not have any reserve of strength on which to call. I just need to stand on the Rock.

J-O-Y

I have told you this so that my joy may be in you and that your joy may be complete. My command is this; Love each other as I have loved you. John 15:11-12

Joy, we all want it, don't we? I hope most of us also want to bring it to others. Do you know how to have joy? Do you know how to share it? Sometimes I do, and other times I do not. The surest way for the enemy to get a hold on our lives is by stealing our joy. It's very easy for him to do. He just gets us to look inside. As soon as most of our thoughts are self-centered, joy takes a walk.

The acronym is J-esus O-thers Y-ou. When we live that way, joy is abundant. Times may still be hard. Life may still hold a lot of pain and problems, but when our focus is on Jesus, then others then ourselves joy still reigns.

Recently I have had a great opportunity to be of service. It has been a golden moment of giving but full of challenges. There is a part of me that feels absolutely fulfilled in this. I am doing what I was created to do and loving it. On the other side, there is this voice calling to me to look over here at this disappointment, look at that failure. It calls to me to focus on every hurtful word that is spoken to me or about me. It invites me to dwell on every slight, every incident of being left out. The enemy really wants me to see myself as the last child chosen to play the game and worse. Even as I am serving God through serving His children and doing things I love to do, there are moments when I am so overwhelmingly sad. Why? The answer is simple. That sadness focuses me on me and keeps me from being truly effective.

As we are serving, doing something God has called us to, something that we have prayed to be allowed to do grace abounds. That grace will strengthen and enable us to then do even greater things with God's help. If I take my eyes off Jesus and others and put them on me, everything shifts. Suddenly, I'm not receiving enough thanks or recognition. All at once no one cares, or at least they don't care enough. In that same moment, I see that my hand has a withering touch that nothing grows under my care but fails terribly. Oh gee, poor me!

It is then my choice to stay there and wallow in the mire of self-pity or to stand up and say, so what? It is time then to turn things around and focus correctly, Jesus, others and then me. With my eyes on Jesus all things are beautiful. I will not become a doormat because the Holy Spirit will not only direct my movements but also fill me up never allowing me to become empty. I have forgotten this too many times in my life.

We've all heard that attitude is everything, and I believe that. I also believe that our attitude comes from our focus, and our focus has to be on Jesus. I love the movie *Remember the Titans*. There is a line in it that says, "Attitude reflects leadership." What better leadership to reflect than that of Jesus Christ?

Prayer

Dear Lord,
Thank you for today, for all it has held so far and all it will hold before it ends.
Where I have failed you forgive me, please. Where I have obeyed and been
a blessing to another, thank you for using me.
I know there are times when I stumble, and you help me up.
I know there are times when I ignore, and yet you always
welcome me home with open arms.
Help me to live to serve you and bless those you put in my path.
In Jesus name I humbly pray.
Amen.